VICTORY
PRINCIPLES

VICTORY
PRINCIPLES

Leadership Lessons from D-Day

Col. Leonard Kloeber, Jr.

New York

Victory Principles
Leadership Lessons from D-Day

Hardcover ISBN 978-1-60037-592-7
Softcover ISBN 978-1-60037-591-0

Library of Congress Control Number: 2009922066

MORGAN · JAMES
THE ENTREPRENEURIAL PUBLISHER

Morgan James Publishing, LLC
1225 Franklin Ave., STE 325
Garden City, NY 11530-1693
Toll Free 800-485-4943
www.MorganJamesPublishing.com

In an effort to support local communities, raise awareness and funds, Morgan James Publishing donates one percent of all book sales for the life of each book to Habitat for Humanity. Get involved today, visit **www.HelpHabitatForHumanity.org**.

SPECIAL DEDICATION

To my father, Cpl. Leonard Kloeber, Sr., who served in a US Army Air Corps special ground reconnaissance unit in North Africa and Burma; and to my father-in-law, 1 Lt. John D. Garvik, who served with the Fifth Rangers and landed on Omaha Beach on D-Day with the US 29th Infantry Division, 115th Infantry Regiment. He was killed in action on June 12, 1944 in Normandy, France. Their service in World War II is a personal inspiration for this book.

Dedication
This book is dedicated to the Soldiers, Sailors, and Airmen who took part in what General Eisenhower called the "Great Crusade." Their story of personal courage, sacrifice, and ultimate victory has forever earned them an honored place in history. A special dedication is made to those, both military and civilian, who paid the ultimate sacrifice as a part of the tragedy that is war. May their souls forever rest in peace.

CONTENTS

INTRODUCTION

On June 6, 1944, the English Channel was churning with six-foot swells and whitecaps despite a break in the stormy weather of the previous day. Based on limited information, the Supreme Commander Allied Forces Europe, General Dwight D. Eisenhower, had just made the difficult decision to proceed with the invasion despite the unfavorable weather conditions. The breaking dawn revealed the largest armada ever assembled, over five thousand warships, transports, and assault vessels. The D-Day invasion of the Normandy coast of France was underway. It officially began just after midnight, with airborne infantry dropping behind the beaches to secure key terrain, disrupt the German defense, and cause general confusion around the landing areas. At about 0630 hours, the first waves of Allied assault troops waded onto the beaches after intense air and naval bombardments. It was a pivotal moment in history and a high-risk venture to secure an Allied foothold on the European continent. The mission of the Allied forces was to open up the Western Front against the German Third Reich, liberate occupied France, and defeat the Nazi Army.

Amphibious assaults are always high-risk ventures because the invaders are extremely vulnerable while they secure a beachhead and get adequate forces and supplies onshore. Until this is accomplished, they are highly exposed to a counterattack that can drive them back into the sea. That was the plan of the German commander, Field Marshal Erwin Rommel. Fortunately for the Allies, he was away from France at the time of the attack and the Germans were slow to react. Nevertheless, the assault was still an extremely arduous undertaking, and the German forces in France fought fiercely to defend their turf. Overcoming numerous obstacles and significant casualties, the Allies successfully accomplished their objectives and thus began the campaign to drive on to Germany and bring World War II in Europe to an end.

The epic story of D-Day has been well chronicled over the years since the war ended. The first accounts were recorded by unit "after action reports," official Army historians, and journalists at the time. Later historians have written numerous books and articles on every aspect of the Normandy battles. Hundreds of movies and documentaries have since portrayed the events. Some of these accounts focus on specific aspects of the battle or various unit actions. Other accounts focus on the overall campaign or the larger-than-life personalities of the generals. Many of these are well-researched versions of the story supported by actual eyewitness reports and archived official documents.

So why do we need yet another book on D-Day? What more can be told about these events that has not already been told? What else can be researched and discovered that has not already been uncovered by the diligent historians whose studies have lasted longer than the events themselves? These are logical questions one might ask when one goes to a bookstore or library and discovers the rows of books on the subject already in print.

The answer is easy. This is not just another book that simply retells the story. This book is written as a "Staff Ride." Staff Rides are a way of studying historical accounts and drawing lessons for the present. The Staff Ride technique was first developed by the Prussian Army as a way to train general staff officers. Count Helmuth von Moltke, the nineteenth-century Prussian general and military theorist, used the Staff Ride concept to develop his staff officers by visiting actual European battle sites to discuss what happened and learn lessons for the future. It was later adopted by the U.S. Army.

In the early 1900s, the U.S. Army used the Staff Ride technique to study the engagements of the American Civil War. Students from the Command and General Staff Officer School visited the sites of Gettysburg, Sherman's March to the Sea, and First Bull Run after studying about these events in the classroom. The study phase that preceded the actual site visits was preparation to understand what the commanders intended and what actually took place. The critical objective was to understand how lessons learned could be applied to future battles. Much of the focus centered on leadership lessons so that aspiring officers could learn how to lead soldiers in the stressful and chaotic context of battle. A wise old army dictum says that "no plan survives the first contact with the enemy."

Successful leaders need to understand how to apply lessons from history to future events. When leaders find themselves in circumstances that require decisions based on limited information or in the "fog of war," it helps to know how other leaders made decisions in similar circumstances. When decisions are time constrained, as they usually are, it helps to know what other leaders did to achieve success. The Staff Ride is an attempt to draw out these lessons learned through study, reflection, and discussion. It is an attempt to understand how general principles can be applied in the future, even under different circumstances.

Thus, *VICTORY Principles* is not simply another version of the events that took place in 1944. Although it begins with an overview of what happened, it is about why things happened as they did and, most important, what can be learned from what happened. It is not simply a detailed chronological telling of the events, although some of the story needs to be told in order to provide context for the readers. The story of Operation Overlord, the code name for the Allied invasion of Europe, is recounted with enough detail to highlight significant lessons learned. Numerous other books have been written to tell the tale of this epic event in much greater detail. This Staff Ride points to those pertinent parts of the story that contain leadership lessons. These lessons are forged in the context of a military campaign but are relevant for all students of the art of leadership.

This Staff Ride is also more than just a study of military history for professional military officers. It is intended for leaders or would-be leaders from all walks of life. As you read about the story of D-Day, ask yourself some of these questions:

- How do these events of over sixty years ago have any relevance today?

- Can leadership lessons from these events transcend armed conflict and be applied to business or other endeavors?
- Can we use this story as a metaphor for other challenges in life?
- What general principles can be learned and applied in future circumstances?

I believe that as a participant on this Staff Ride, you will discover leadership lessons that were learned many years ago under the almost unimaginable circumstances of desperate life and death combat. I also believe that these leadership lessons are not just for the military, but are universal and can be applied to all leadership endeavors. It is sometimes said that "what is past is prologue." It is also our best teacher.

My personal journey in the study of military history began even before I entered the U.S. Military Academy. As a high school student, I was intrigued by the writings of Caesar as he described his campaigns in Gaul during the time of the Roman Republic. And although we studied "Military Art," as the history classes were called at West Point, it was not until I entered the army as an officer that I developed a deep interest in the study of military history as part of my professional development. It was only after I became a senior officer and then an executive at a large corporation that I really appreciated the lessons learned and began to apply them with varying degrees of success.

The lessons that I have chosen are simply a collection of those that appeared for me based on my experiences as an officer, executive, and leader. I use the acronym VICTORY to help make the lessons easier to remember. Although some of the lessons are related to military leadership, they are not intended to make you an expert in the art of war. Some people may question whether these lessons have wider application; you can decide for yourself whether they will enhance your capabilities as a leader.

After each chapter, I have included questions for a Staff Ride Notebook. One lesson that I have learned over the years is the benefit of keeping a personal leadership journal. I have used it to capture my thoughts and reflections on leadership from my own experiences. I would recommend that you complete your answers to these questions in such a notebook.

Readers who are familiar with the story of D-Day may identify different lessons from those that I have selected when they reflect on these events. The stories and lessons from June 1944 are as varied as the thousands of D-Day participants, and this Staff Ride could not possibly cover all of them. I hope that reading *VICTORY Principles* may spark your interest in the study of history. You might choose to read more about some aspect of this story by selecting one of the references in the bibliography. If I can simply frame the discussion for learning, then my mission has been accomplished.

Finally, I apologize in advance for any factual errors. In some cases, various authorities differ on what really happened. This would be an expected outcome in the "fog of war." Where discrepancies exist, I have made an effort to point them out. Although I have attempted to make sure that the facts for the discussion are accurate and supported by references, any errors in details are mine alone. I trust that these errors, if any, will not detract from the overarching lessons themselves that supersede the finer details of the specific events.

I have always been intrigued by the events of World War II and, in particular, those of D-Day. The sheer scope and size of the invasion along with the personal courage of the participants makes this a truly amazing story. After many rewarding years of personal study and reflection, I offer you the opportunity to learn along with me from history.

Leonard Kloeber, Jr.
Colonel, U.S. Army Reserve (Ret.)
Prior Lake, Minnesota

PART ONE
THE GREATEST INVASION IN HISTORY

SUPREME   HEADQUARTERS
ALLIED   EXPEDITIONARY   FORCE

Soldiers, Sailors and Airmen of the Allied Expeditionary Force!

You are about to embark upon the Great Crusade, toward which we have striven these many months.   The eyes of the world are upon you. The hopes and prayers of liberty-loving people everywhere march with you. In company with our brave Allies and brothers-in-arms on other Fronts, you will bring about the destruction of the German war machine, the elimination of Nazi tyranny over the oppressed peoples of Europe, and security for ourselves in a free world.

Your task will not be an easy one.   Your enemy is well trained, well equipped and battle-hardened.   He will fight savagely.

But this is the year 1944 ! Much has happened since the Nazi triumphs of 1940-41. The United Nations have inflicted upon the Germans great defeats, in open battle, man-to-man.   Our air offensive has seriously reduced their strength in the air and their capacity to wage war on the ground.   Our Home Fronts have given us an overwhelming superiority in weapons and munitions of war, and placed at our disposal great reserves of trained fighting men.   The tide has turned ! The free men of the world are marching together to Victory !

I have full confidence in your courage, devotion to duty and skill in battle.   We will accept nothing less than full Victory !

Good Luck !   And let us all beseech the blessing of Almighty God upon this great and noble undertaking.

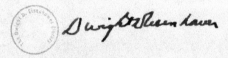

Supreme Commander's Order of the Day (US National Archives)

The "Big Three" Allied Leaders: Churchill, Roosevelt, and Stalin.
Photo U.S. National Archives

CHAPTER ONE
PRELUDE: THE WORLD AT WAR

Context, early war years

When the Germans invaded Poland in September of 1939, the war in Europe turned into a shooting war. After staging what appeared to be an unprovoked attack by Poland, the Germans retaliated with an army of over a quarter of a million soldiers and airmen crossing the Polish border. Efforts by the European Allies to deter Adolph Hitler from invading his neighbors did not work. He had continued his quest to expand the German Reich and restore national pride following their ignominious defeat in World War I. The British Prime Minister, Neville Chamberlain, had led an effort to contain Germany through negotiations in Munich the previous year, but under Hitler's leadership Germany annexed Austria, the Sudetenland, and Alsace Loraine. Britain and France pledged to draw the line in Poland. So when the German Army crossed the Polish border, the time had come for Britain and France to take their stand. The Allies were officially at war with Germany. The Polish Army was no match for the Nazi juggernaut. Eventually, the Germans had poured over 1.5 million men into the effort.[1] In a matter of weeks, the German Army quickly consolidated their position by overrunning Poland and negotiating a nonaggression pact with the Soviet Union. As winter approached, the "hot war" cooled down for awhile. There was a short period over the winter months when no actual fighting took place. This was to change in the spring of 1940.

In April the German Army occupied Denmark. Simultaneously, the German Navy moved against Norway by attacking multiple ports and landing troops to march on the Norwegian capital, Oslo. The Norwegians resisted, but they were not prepared to defend against the powerful German war machine. The Germans subsequently claimed that they were moving into Norway and Denmark to prevent a British expansion of the war into those territories.[2] This was their version of preemptive warfare.

With the eastern border secured by his pact with Russia, Hitler ordered the German Army to assemble on the western front. On May 10, 1940, he launched what would be known as the blitzkrieg against the combined French and British Armies. The Allies had not anticipated that the Germans would strike through the Ardennes Forest in Belgium or the Low Countries. By doing so, they bypassed the French fortifications of the Maginot Line that were built along the German border to protect France against an attack from the east. The German attack was launched using airborne forces to assault key fortifications and secure bridges needed by the advancing armored formations. The concept of airborne assaults was an untested concept developed during the interwar years by the German Air Force, also known as the Luftwaffe. Specially trained volunteers were parachuted into battle ahead of the main assault. They used the element of surprise to overcome the defenses of key installations. It worked very well, and the paratroops were quickly followed by the main assault force. The German blitzkrieg was now unleashed against Western Europe. In less than a week, the Dutch had capitulated and the Germans were moving through Belgium and on to France.

The Germans also pioneered the tactics of a combined arms team led by armor (panzer) forces that were supported by mechanized infantry, artillery, and air forces. Their speed and shock action quickly threw the Allied defenders off balance as they tried to consolidate a defense.

Many of the French Army units were swiftly overrun. The remaining French forces and their British Allies were forced to retreat to the port of Dunkirk on the English Channel to make a stand. By May 26, the new British Prime Minister, Winston Churchill, realized that the Germans had succeeded in achieving their objectives and that the soldiers in the Dunkirk pocket would be wiped out if they continued to fight. While France negotiated a separate peace, he ordered the evacuation of the British Army and surviving Allies so that they could live to fight another day.

A makeshift fleet of civilian and military ships was quickly organized under the leadership of Admiral Bertram Ramsey. When the evacuation commenced, the British only expected to recover 20,000 to 30,000 troops, but miraculously, the Royal Navy was able evacuate over 338,000 soldiers back to England.[3] About two-thirds of the evacuees were British, and the balance of the survivors was a mix of Dutch, Belgium, Polish, and French troops. The evacuation had been possible not only because of the skill of the British Navy but also because Hitler had surprisingly halted the German army before they could deliver the final death blow to the surrounded Allied force. Instead, he directed the Luftwaffe to finish the job while the army completed the conquest of France, but weather prevented the Luftwaffe from operating for several days. Hitler's direct intervention would set a precedent for his personal influence in future operations with similar unfavorable results for the Germans. As what was left of the Allied armies evacuated the European continent for England, they either destroyed or abandoned their equipment. Now the British Empire stood virtually alone against the German war machine, but they had to lick their wounds before they could continue the fight.

The next phase of the war would be the Battle of Britain, a desperate fight to the death for air superiority in anticipation of a German invasion of the British Isles. Although the Germans had been bombing England in June and July, the Luftwaffe commander, Field Marshal Herman Goering, ordered the full onslaught of his attacks to begin in

August. The German Air Force outnumbered the British four to one. As the attacks increased on English ports, cities, and airfields, the Fighter Command of the Royal Air Force valiantly resisted. They skillfully used emerging radar technology to respond to the incoming attacks and shepherd their resources. With advance warning, the anti-aircraft batteries and fighter squadrons scrambled to meet the aggressors or to avoid being hit on the ground. The Nazi attacks grew in intensity over the coming months. During September they concentrated their bombing runs on London, but the German losses continued to mount as the attacks proceeded. Although many casualties were inflicted on the British population and facilities, the Germans eventually recognized that they were not going to succeed in destroying the Royal Air Force. By October 1940, the Battle of Britain ended and the air raids were less frequent. The Royal Air Force had prevailed.

After losing the Battle of Britain, the German invasion of England, called Operation Sea Lion, was no longer viable. So once again, Hitler personally intervened to cancel the operation. The Germans then tried to isolate the British Isles using submarine warfare. Groups of submarines known as U-boats operated in the North Atlantic as "wolf packs" to interdict the convoys carrying troops and war materials from America to Britain. The Germans operated over one hundred submarines from ports along the Continent. Until the Allies were able to develop countermeasures with surface ship escorts, sonar, and evasive maneuvers, they sustained significant losses from torpedo attacks on the shipping lanes. Eventually, this threat, too, was contained as the Allies learned through experimentation how to counter the U-boats.

Hitler next turned his attention again to the East. In June of 1941, he broke the nonaggression pact with Soviet Russia and launched Operation Barbarossa. Another blitzkrieg of panzer-led forces made quick progress toward Moscow. Three massive German armies of over three million men stretched across a front from the Baltic states to the Crimea and the Black Sea. As this powerful force smashed everything in its path, the Russians skillfully delayed the advance in a series of bloody battles while they scorched the earth as they retreated. By December, the Germans would eventually fight their way to within several miles of Moscow, but then the Russian winter assisted the Soviet Army in halting their advance. Moscow was saved.

Meanwhile, Germany's partner, Italy, had moved into North Africa. The Italian dictator, Benito Mussolini, had visions of reinventing the Roman Empire's domination of the Mediterranean. At the same time as they were coming off their defeat at Dunkirk, the British appealed to their colonial empire for support. The British Eighth Army in Egypt was joined by Australians, New Zealanders, South Africans, and Indians to blunt the Italians in the desert. Hitler and his generals were concerned that the Italians would be overrun. Fearing the worst, Germany sent additional forces to support their ally, along with one of their best commanders. General Erwin Rommel would now lead the combined German–Italian Africa Corps against the British.

Then, on December 7, 1941, the Japanese Combined Fleet made a preemptive attack on the U.S. Naval Base at Pearl Harbor, Hawaii. Until this time, U.S. President Franklin D. Roosevelt had tried to maintain the appearances of neutrality; however, he had been discreetly providing some material support to Britain and Russia through a program known as Lend–Lease. Now with the preemptive Japanese attack on Pearl Harbor, the President asked the U.S. Congress for a declaration of war on Japan, which was quickly approved. Two days later Germany declared war on the United States. When Japan quickly joined the Axis alliance with Germany and Italy, the Tripartite military alliance was formed. A pact was signed on December 27, 1941, in Berlin to make it official. The United States was now in the shooting war but was not militarily prepared to strike back.

In the fall of 1939, the strength of the United States Army was only 190,000 men. This included the First Cavalry division and its six thousand horses.[4] Raising and training a modern army capable of fighting the war would require skillful leadership and mobilization of the entire nation in the months and years ahead.

General Marshall and the American Army

The task of quickly building the American Army fell to General George Marshall, the Army Chief of Staff. The meager American force would eventually grow to seven million soldiers in eighty-nine combat divisions at its peak. General Marshall was the right man in the right job at the right time. He had attended the Virginia Military Institute and was commissioned in the U.S. Army in 1902 as an infantry officer. His first assignment was in the Philippines, but in 1906 he was sent to the Army Staff College at Ft. Leavenworth, where he graduated first in his class. After an assignment as an instructor at the school, he completed a series of command and staff assignments in a variety of infantry units. This gave him a broad range of experiences and he gained a reputation as an outstanding officer.

When the United States entered the First World War in 1917, Marshall was posted to France with the American Expeditionary Force (AEF). He eventually worked directly for the AEF commander, General John J. "Black Jack" Pershing, as an aide-de-camp, where he put all his experience to work. It was this experience that showed him how difficult it was to conduct coalition warfare with other Allied nations. After the war, Marshall was promoted through a series of jobs, including instructor at the Army War College and assistant commandant at the Infantry School, where he was able to observe many junior officers as they studied to enhance their professional education. In other assignments, he was an advisor to the National Guard and helped to organize the Civilian Conservation Corps. All of these jobs would provide valuable experience for him, including understanding the citizen soldiers and gaining organization skills that would be needed to win the war.

Throughout his career, General Marshall developed the habit of keeping notes on officers with whom he had served or who worked for him in a variety of capacities. Many of the officers who would be advanced to general officer rank had languished in the peacetime army with promotions coming slowly and only after many years of service.

General Marshall knew many of them. He had a keen sense of who was the most promising among them, and this was a critical factor in his ability to quickly identify capable officers and promote them immediately into key assignments. His philosophy was to give them responsibility and guidance for a task and then get out of their way. He placed many of them in critical assignments to organize and train the forces necessary for the upcoming campaigns. In fact, one of the qualities that he prized most among his subordinates was their willingness to take charge and make decisions without always checking back with higher commands. One such officer who exhibited this skill was a Lt. Colonel, Dwight D. Eisenhower, known to his friends as Ike.

Eisenhower graduated from the U.S. Military Academy at West Point in the Class of 1915. He was commissioned as an infantry officer but also had experience with the fledging tank corps after World War I. American tanks had made their debut in France under the leadership of another future general, George Patton. During the interwar years, Patton and Eisenhower were stationed together. They teamed up to develop and promote new tactics for the employment of tanks. Although their suggestions were not readily accepted by most of the Army hierarchy, they were favorably received by General Fox Conner, who was a leading military thinker at the time. When Conner was commander of the forces guarding the Panama Canal Zone, Eisenhower accepted a request from Conner to serve as his deputy. Conner mentored his protégé on tactics and how the Army worked. After that assignment Eisenhower attended the Army Staff College at Ft. Leavenworth, where, like Marshall, he graduated first in his class.

Just before the outbreak of the war in the Pacific, Eisenhower had been serving in the Philippines as an assistant to General Douglas MacArthur. Eisenhower had previously been MacArthur's assistant when MacArthur was the Chief of Staff of the Army in the 1930s. This gave him an opportunity to observe the workings of the War Department at the highest levels. After MacArthur retired from active duty to accept a job from the Philippine president to build and train the Philippine

Army, he insisted that Eisenhower accompany him. Although Eisenhower respected MacArthur as a soldier, their relationship became more contentious over time. Eisenhower was eventually reassigned back to stateside units, where he served as a regimental executive officer and later as the Chief of Staff for the Third Army. It was at the Third Army where he showed his expertise for strategy and planning during war games known as the Louisiana Maneuvers. This was one of the large scale maneuver exercises that the Army conducted to train and evaluate units in preparation for overseas deployments. His skill caught the attention of General Marshall who was now Army Chief of Staff and always scouting for talented officers.

After the hostilities with Japan broke out, General Marshall brought Eisenhower to work at the War Department in Washington, D.C. Eisenhower was assigned to the Army Staff in the War Plans Division (WPD). He once again quickly proved his abilities as a strategist and planner. General Marshall relied on his expertise to organize the war effort by writing strategy papers and plans on how to win the war. He was eventually promoted to head up an expanded War Plans Division that was renamed the Operations Planning Division (OPD). Here Ike directly assisted Marshall in defining the American global war plan that was approved by President Roosevelt. In the process, he established his reputation with Marshall and Roosevelt as a visionary. As noted by historian Mark Perry, "for Marshall that was an essential quality for any officer aspiring to high command."[5] Eisenhower would become the Supreme Allied Commander for the D-Day invasion of Europe, but it was in the War Department assignment that he established his credentials with senior leaders.

Eisenhower genuinely regretted that he had not seen combat experience during the First World War. He was always disappointed when he saw his peers being promoted to command assignments. More than any other assignment he desired a troop command. Although he proved to be an extremely capable administrator, his most important skill was an ability to navigate the politics of the institutions of government.

The rivalry between the War Department and the Navy Department was intense and very competitive for resources. Also contentious were the relations with the American and British Chiefs of Staff, otherwise known as the Combined Chiefs of Staff. Eisenhower proved to be adept at dealing with the strong personalities of the senior officers who filled these positions. It was this skill and his talent as a visionary that led Marshall to believe that Eisenhower had the talent needed for a high-level command.

In late December 1941, Prime Minister Winston Churchill and his military staff traveled to Washington, D.C. to conference with the Americans about the path forward. Known as the Arcadia Conference, this was the first opportunity for the Americans and British to jointly plan strategy. Since the British had been fighting the Germans for over a year and the Americans were just organizing their forces, the British military leaders naturally felt that they had more experience. However, they also knew that the Americans would soon be making a major contribution to the effort, and this was their chance to influence the strategy for the conduct of the war before the Americans became the dominant partner.

There was considerable tension as they each tried to posture for control. The one thing that they all agreed on was the strategy that became known as "Germany first." This concept meant that the Allies would put their primary efforts toward defeating Nazi Germany while making any effort against Japan a secondary priority. This would have far-reaching implications for the allocation of fighting forces and material resources. It pitted the American Navy and General MacArthur's Southwest Pacific Command against the army in Europe that would soon be led by Eisenhower for troops and war material. The availability of critical resources would be the determining factor in deciding when and where operations could be mounted, including the invasion of continental Europe.

Although the Combined Chiefs agreed on the overall "Germany first" strategy, they could not agree on how best to accomplish it. The

British had suffered a major defeat at Dunkirk and also had sustained tremendous losses during the trench warfare of the First World War. They were inclined to fight on what Marshall considered to be the periphery of the occupied territories and not make a direct assault on the continent of Europe. Prime Minister Churchill favored offensive action in the Mediterranean and an attack on what he called the "soft underbelly" of Europe. Largely because of the staggering British losses from the First World War, he was extremely reluctant to consider a cross-channel attack into France as the most direct way to defeat Germany. He was not anxious to repeat the trench warfare experience, where artillery barrages and frontal assaults against machine gun positions claimed hundreds of thousands of casualties. He also had bitter memories of the unsuccessful amphibious landings by the British Empire troops at Gallipoli in the eastern Mediterranean when he was First Lord of the Admiralty. He and his senior staff who had experienced this carnage firsthand were committed to avoiding a repeat of the tactics that had cost their country so dearly.

Conversely, the Americans favored the more direct approach, but at the time they were not in a strong position to press their case. Marshall proposed an invasion of the European continent—if not in 1942, then for sure not later than 1943. His view, which was shared by Eisenhower and his other senior advisors, was that operations around the periphery of Europe were a distraction from the main task of defeating the German Army. These periphery operations would also have the effect of squandering precious combat resources without the possibility of inflicting a decisive blow. Among Marshall's other concerns was support for their other ally, the USSR, otherwise known as Russia or the Soviets. The Soviets had an uneasy truce with the Germans after they both invaded Poland. Marshall believed that the Germans would defeat the Russians before the Americans and British could implement their plans. His concern with Russia was well-founded. Since June of 1941 the German Armies were advancing across the two-thousand-mile front in violation of their nonaggression pact. The Russian Army was quickly overwhelmed and was retreating in the face of another German blitzkrieg.

The prime minister worked hard to make his case to President Roosevelt that any near-term offensive action should not be a direct invasion of Europe. He based his arguments primarily on the fact that the Allies were simply not prepared to undertake the operation in sufficient strength to succeed. The British staff officers also were convinced that the Americans were novices who needed to gain combat experience. Remarks along these lines caused tension and resentment among the Allies while they continued to make their respective arguments. After much political wrangling, the British convinced Roosevelt that the first effort in the war should be directed at North Africa. Although Marshall and Eisenhower were not happy with the decision, once it was made they went about the business of planning the operation as the professional soldiers they were. In retrospect, the British were correct. This operation would provide the American Army much needed combat experience before the undertaking of a major assault into France.

Yet, the truth was that they *all* needed experience, just *different* experience. Clearly the American Army, overwhelmingly comprised of draftees, needed to taste the harsh realities of actual combat. However, the entire Allied military structure needed experience in working together. In addition to the rivalries between the British and the Americans, there were also inter-service rivalries among the army, navy, and air forces within each country. They needed to learn how to operate as a joint force, which meant having the different services working together. They also needed to work together as Allies, a combined force from different nations under a unified command. This required strong leadership and mutual confidence, which could only be gained by actual experience working together. Without the crucible of a successful campaign, they would be allies in name only.

The invasion of North Africa was code named Operation Torch, but it still needed an overall commander who could navigate the politics of coalition warfare while building a cohesive team. Once Roosevelt had conceded to forgo the invasion on the continent in favor of the North African operation, Churchill then agreed to appoint an American as the overall commander-in-chief. Marshall recommended Eisenhower because of his demonstrated political acumen and organizational skills, and President Roosevelt quickly approved. Now the relatively junior general would assume the difficult task of commanding the combined American and British invasion force. Eisenhower had received his first combat command.

Joint and Combined Operations: North Africa and Sicily

Operation Torch was launched in November 1942 with three task forces landing on the northwest African coast. Major General Patton would lead the American forces of the Western Task Force that landed in Casablanca, Morocco. Another American, Major General Lloyd Friedendahl, would command the Central Task Force that landed in Oran. British General Kenneth Anderson led the British army into Algiers. All three reported to Eisenhower, commander-in-chief of all Allied forces in the theater. The western part of North Africa was defended by French Vichy forces. When the French capitulated and made peace with Germany in 1941, a new pro-Nazi government was set up in Vichy, France, under the French Marshal Philippe Petain to govern unoccupied southern France and its colonial territories. The French troops in North Africa were under the nominal control of Petain's government and were considered hostile to the Allies. In advance of the landings, the Allies sent American Major General Mark Clark on a covert mission to seek an accommodation with the Vichy commanders. The Allies' attempt to negotiate a French capitulation before landing did not succeed. As they came ashore, they met considerable resistance, particularly in the western zone where the Americans landed. Altogether sixty-five thousand Allied troops landed in the initial operations. After several days of fighting, the French conceded. Admiral Jean Louis Darlan, who was deputy to Marshal Petain and who just happened to be in the area, came over to the Allied side in exchange for his recognition as the French High Commissioner in North Africa. The Allies had negotiated a cease-fire with the Vichy troops. They moved quickly to consolidate their positions while advancing further east toward Tunis.

Yet the battle for North Africa was far from over. The British Eighth Army under General Montgomery advanced westward from Egypt, where they had been fighting a seesaw campaign against the German and Italian Africa Corps. Led by Field Marshal Erwin Rommel, the German Army now pivoted to meet the Americans and British in the west. The Germans met the Americans in a series of engagements that included the Battle of Kasserne Pass. It was at Kasserne that the American Army experienced its first significant combat that resulted in a defeat. They sustained two thousand casualties and a loss of confidence. The loss at Kasserne Pass reaffirmed the British argument that the Americans needed combat experience.

As a result of this setback, General Eisenhower quickly relieved the American II Corps commander, Major General Lloyd Fredendall, and replaced him with Major General Patton. Patton quickly asserted himself as the commander of the II Corps. He immediately set about to instill discipline and a fighting spirit among the troops. Since the American intelligence had also been caught off guard, Eisenhower concurrently replaced his chief intelligence officer with General Kenneth Strong. With these personnel changes, Eisenhower demonstrated that he would not tolerate failure and that he had the determination to provide the leadership necessary for success.

Kasserene Pass was the one and only major American defeat in World War II in the European Theater. From that point forward, the Americans quickly learned how to adapt and became a formidable fighting force. By May 3, only six months after the Allies had landed, they had defeated the combined German and Italian forces in North Africa. Although the Allies had sustained seventy thousand casualties in the process, over a quarter of a million German and Italians were taken prisoner and another sixty thousand were either killed or wounded. By the end of the campaign, the Allies controlled all of North Africa from Morocco to the Suez Canal in Egypt.[6]

The Allied leaders then met in Casablanca and determined that the next major operation for the European theater would be the invasion of Sicily, known as Operation Husky. The Italian island of Sicily was selected for several reasons. First, it offered a strategic location where the Allies could establish a forward operating base to launch an attack on the Italian mainland. Sicily was located about ninety miles north of Allied-controlled North Africa, and the port of Messina on the north side of the island was only a few miles from the mainland. Secondly, with Sicily secured, it would protect the Allied shipping lanes in the Mediterranean and also provide forward airbases to attack Italian and German industrial areas. Finally, it would provide further experience for the Allies in launching an amphibious assault and working together as a combined force.

The ten thousand square mile island was defended by a combined German–Italian force under an Italian commander, Field Marshall Guzzoni. The preponderance of the force was Italian with approximately 250,000 soldiers. Most of these were poorly trained, and many units lacked sufficient equipment and munitions. However, they were supported by approximately thirty thousand Germans who were much better trained and equipped. As the battle unfolded, it would be the German units, including the 15th Panzer Grenadier and Herman Goring Divisions supported by tanks, that offered stiff resistance. They would skillfully utilize the mountainous terrain as a natural defensive barrier to effectively keep the Allies at bay.

The Sicily invasion would be spearheaded by the American Seventh Army on the Allied left flank under the leadership of Lt. General George Patton with Major General Omar Bradley as his deputy-in-command of the U.S. II Corps. On the Allied right flank, the British Eight Army would be led by General Bernard L. Montgomery. The overall Allied commander was again General Eisenhower with British General Alexander as his deputy and commander of the Allied land forces. The landings took place on July 10, 1943. Although the Sicilian campaign was an overall success for the Allies, it came at a higher than expected price. The campaign would also uncover many problems associated with coordinating joint and combined operations.

The beach landings were preceded by an airborne assault in both sectors. In the American sector, elements of the 82nd Airborne Division under Colonel James Gavin were tasked to parachute behind the beaches. Their mission was to secure key road junctions and to prevent a German counterattack on the landing sites. However, during the day preceding the assault, the weather had turned for the worse with high winds. Additionally, neither the parachute units nor the air corps transports had trained for night missions. This was a difficult mission because it required navigation over water at night with several dogleg turns in the approach pattern. When the planes left from their bases in North Africa, some of the pilots missed their navigational guides. With the combination of the high winds and night flying conditions, they missed the planned drop zones. The result was that only one battalion landed as a unit near their intended target. The rest of the units, including Colonel Gavin and his small group, were scattered over twenty-five miles all along the southern coast of Sicily and even into the British zone. Since the British were not familiar with the American paratrooper's distinctive uniforms, some were mistaken for enemy troops and were taken under fire causing friendly casualties. Others were severely injured on the jump due to the windy conditions. Nevertheless, small groups of paratroopers fought with tenacity wherever they landed. Although the Americans were disorganized, they also confused the Germans and Italians, too.

Similar to the American airborne assault, the British attempted to land glider troops in their zone with the same mission of disrupting counterattacks. Again, due to the high winds and lack of training with the transports they fared no better than the American parachutists. Gliders crash-landed because the pilots were poorly trained and the soldiers on board sustained severe injuries. Out of 144 gliders, only

12 landed on target, and 69 actually landed in the sea.[7] Both of these attempts to deliver an airborne force, whether by parachute or glider, would cause some senior leaders to question the wisdom of using airborne techniques ever again. The casualties sustained even before they engaged the enemy were significant. However, some valuable lessons for the future had also been learned in the process.

The American force landed on three beaches on the southern coast of Sicily in the Gulf of Gela. Their mission was to support the British, who would make the main effort up the eastern side of the island to seize the port city of Messina. The American First Infantry Division landed at Gela in the center of the zone. They began to experience problems from the very start of the amphibious operations. Some landing craft in the initial waves hit sandbars as they approached under the cover of darkness. Thinking they were close to the shore and not realizing that they had hit a sandbar, they lowered their ramps and the soldiers stepped off into deep water. Burdened with over eighty pounds of equipment many of them drowned before even reaching the beaches. Overloading the assault troops with nonessential items should have been a lesson learned for future amphibious operations. Some soldiers who made it to the beach moved inland only to walk into minefields, where they quickly became casualties. One of the new vehicles being tested were the DUKW, amphibious trucks that could "swim" to shore. Although these worked well in calm waters, they were not seaworthy in rough waters. Since they also could not go fast, they were easy targets until they reached the shore. Once on shore they were also susceptible to land mines. The mines not only destroyed the vehicles but also killed or wounded the troops and damaged the cargo onboard. Those vehicles that were disabled on the beach became obstacles to the reinforcements who were landing in successive waves. Despite these problems, the First Division, which was supported by a Ranger force, overcame the immediate resistance from the Italian defenders. The Italians counterattacked with their tanks, but support from accurate naval gunfire disrupted the assault. By mid morning American troops were moving inland.

Farther to the east of Gela, the U.S. 45th Infantry Division landed at Scoglitti on the American right flank. The 45th was a National Guard unit whose soldiers were mainly from Texas and Oklahoma. Although they were led by a very able commander, Major General Troy Middleton, the naval unit that provided their landing craft was manned by sailors who had been insufficiently trained in amphibious operations. The twelve-foot sea swells lingering from the stormy weather the day before caused some boats to land at the wrong beaches. Others crashed into each other in the surf. Two hundred boats eventually were stranded on the beaches or on sandbars just offshore.[8] In the confusion, supplies were misplaced and operations were slowed down. Eventually some of the beaches were deliberately closed, and oncoming waves of reinforcements were redirected to other beaches.

After several days, Patton decided to reinforce the beachhead with another regiment of the 82nd Airborne. The 504th parachute infantry was tasked to jump in to reinforce the First Infantry, but the assault was not coordinated. The fleet, as well as the 45th Division onshore had not been advised, and as the transport planes came over their area, they were mistaken for Germans. The Luftwaffe occasionally had been attacking the fleet and in the course of the campaign had sunk twelve ships. Unaware that these were American planes, the ships and soldiers on the ground engaged them with antiaircraft fire. As the transport planes approached, twenty-three were shot down and another thirty-seven were damaged. Battle casualty reports estimated that 410 paratroopers were killed by friendly fire.[9] The British suffered a similar tragedy when they tried to use an airborne assault to break the stalemate south of Catania with a British airborne assault to capture a bridge. Both of these actions were the result of poor planning and a lack of training and coordination.

While the 45th Division struggled to get ashore at Scoglitti, Major General Lucian Truscott led the assault by the U.S. Third Infantry Division fifteen miles to the west of Gela at Licata on the American far left flank. Here they did not encounter as many problems. Truscott also had a Ranger force to reinforce his division. Ten battalions of the Third Division and the Rangers were able to quickly move inland because the beach defenses were less formidable in their sector. Many of the Italian defenders surrendered to the Americans, and by noon the Americans had secured the town. Truscott was one of the American Army's experts on amphibious operations. He had also been one of the senior officers who sponsored the organization of the Rangers at the beginning of the war. The Rangers were all volunteers who were highly trained in infantry assault tactics. It was Truscott who coordinated initial Ranger training with the British Commandos and worked with the original Ranger commander, LTC William Darby. Now the Rangers were supporting Truscott's Third Division. With additional tank support from the Second Armored Division, and after they secured the town of Licata, Truscott ordered a reconnaissance force farther west toward the port city of Palermo.

As the Americans landed in the Gulf of Gela, the British were landing thirty-five miles farther east on the tip of Sicily at Syracuse in the Gulf of Noto. Despite their prior combat experience, they were having the same problems as the Americans. Their problems began in the hours of darkness when their large transport ships anchored about twelve miles offshore. This was the first of their misfortunes because they had planned to launch their landing craft from only seven miles offshore. They were fortunate that on this side of the island the seas were not as rough. The sailors who were initially disoriented by landing farther out to sea regained their bearings and proceeded to the beaches. The landings were initially a success, but they soon came upon determined resistance by the Germans. The Germans effectively used the terrain to their advantage as they would do later when the campaign shifted to the Italian mainland. The British attack stalled as they moved up the east coast near Catania around July 16. Even the airborne assault did not succeed in changing the momentum back to the British.

Montgomery then decided to divide his army into two separate wings. He attempted to advance on an alternate axis further to the west on Highway 124. With his primary attack stalled on the coast, he felt this was necessary because of the limited routes available in the mountainous terrain. In order to make his two-pronged assault, the American 45th Division was required to halt its advance because Highway 124 was in their sector. Although Montgomery got agreement from his superior, General Alexander, this decision upset the Americans, especially Patton. Patton did not want to be in a support role while the British seized the main objective, Messina. After a vigorous protest by Patton, Alexander allowed him to continue his push to the west and northwest of the island. With tacit approval for continuing what was originally a reconnaissance in force, Patton now made it his main thrust. He shifted his focus toward the port of Palermo on the western side of the island.

The same day that the British attack stalled in front of Catania, Patton's troops were in Agrigento advancing west onto Palermo. By July 22, Truscott's Third Infantry reached their objective, Palermo. Patton had also directed the II Corps to move up through the mountains in the center of the island to compliment Montgomery's move up Highway 124. By this time, the Germans had prepared formidable defensive lines in the rugged terrain. They also reinforced the island with two more divisions, the 29th Panzer Grenadier and the First Parachute. The Germans were learning their skills at mountain warfare in Sicily. With the additional German reinforcements dug into defensive positions, the Allied advance slowed. The mountainous terrain restricted movement and canalized convoys so that they were vulnerable to attacks by artillery.

The Americans continued to move farther west and advanced to the north side of the island. The campaign then became a contest between the British and the Americans to seize the port of Messina on the north end of the island. Montgomery continued to slowly slug it out with the Germans on the eastern side of the island while Patton did the same in the center and the west. For several weeks, the German force of about fifty thousand effectively defended their ground against an Allied force almost ten times their size. A testament to the fierce fighting was the long list of battle casualties: Americans lost over 11,000 killed and wounded and the British suffered another 15,500; their adversaries lost close to 30,000 dead and wounded with another 140,000 taken as prisoners of war. By August 17 Messina was under Allied control, but the Axis troops were gone. Near the end of the campaign, the Germans were able to conduct a strategic withdrawal of over one hundred thousand troops and ten thousand vehicles to fight another day. They would meet again on the Italian mainland.

It was also in Sicily where Patton was involved in several infamous incidents where he slapped soldiers while on routine hospital visits. The medical facilities were insufficient to handle the casualties. Most senior commanders made an effort to inspect the facilities as part of their overall command responsibilities. Such inspections not only ensured that the evacuation and medical systems were functioning properly but also conveyed the sense of care for the soldiers that would be expected from the best commanders. On such occasions commanders also awarded military decorations and were able to check on the morale of the troops. On two different inspections, Patton encountered soldiers who were evacuated for "shell shock." Otherwise known as combat fatigue, it was a condition where soldiers were mentally unfit due to the extreme stress of constant combat. When Patton found these soldiers who otherwise had no physical wounds, he immediately went into a rage and began slapping them in front of the hospital staff and other wounded soldiers. He ordered doctors to remove them from the same wards with the other soldiers who had been shot or physically wounded.

Patton later explained that he was trying to "shame" them into doing their duty; nevertheless, the hospital staff and later reporters were deeply offended by his conduct. Patton would later be ordered by Eisenhower to apologize to the soldiers whom he had slapped as well as to the doctors and nurses. He would also be required by Eisenhower to apologize to all the units under his command. Whereas many viewed this as a minor incident in view of all the other carnage of war, it was a sensitive issue for public relations back home. There was the specter of Congressional inquiries and public outcry on the home front. Neither General Marshall nor President Roosevelt needed this kind of attention as they continued to seek the additional resources needed to continue the war effort. At the end of the campaign, Eisenhower removed Patton from command, even though they were long-time personal friends, and promoted General Bradley to replace him. Ike did it to avoid being forced to take a more drastic reprimand against his most aggressive senior leader. He knew that he would likely need to call upon Patton's combat leadership skills in the future. As well, he showed that he would not hesitate to make tough personnel decisions when required for the benefit of the entire command.

The Sicilian operation was yet another opportunity for the Americans and the British to gain experience in working together while conducting an amphibious assault on a defended beach. For both Allies, hard lessons were learned. This is especially true of the airborne, Ranger, and Commando units who had spearheaded the attack. General Eisenhower also gained additional experience as a senior commander controlling the combined Allied forces with strong-willed commanders such as Patton and Montgomery. As they squabbled between themselves even while they fought the Axis, Eisenhower realized that their attack plan was not closely coordinated. Partly to blame was British General Alexander who was the ground forces commander and superior for both Patton and Montgomery although as overall commander, Eisenhower bore the ultimate repsonsiblity. The Allies also learned hard lessons about inter-service coordination among the army, navy and army air corps. Eisenhower proved that he was capable of dealing with these inter-service problems, too.

The Sicilian campaign ended when the Americans and British forces met in Messina. Although the Allies had enjoyed air and naval superiority, they allowed the Axis forces to retreat across the Straits of Messina to the Italian mainland. Eisenhower soon regretted that he had not been more aggressive in cutting off the German evacuation route from Messina. General Marshall rarely criticized Eisenhower because he realized the myriad of command problems in holding together an effective coalition. However, he expressed his disappointment over what he perceived as the lack of creativity in formulating a battle plan, especially because they had local air and naval superiority. He also felt that Eisenhower should have been more forceful with his deputies, especially Alexander, who certainly could have been more effective in directing the campaign. Nevertheless, the Allies had won another significant victory under Eisenhower's leadership.

Meanwhile, the Italian Dictator, Mussolini, had been overthrown. His successor, Marshal Pietro Badoglio was inclined to surrender to the Allies but feared a German backlash. Eisenhower sent an emissary, Major General Maxwell Taylor, to get the Italians to switch sides. As the Allies invaded mainland Italy in early September, the new Italian leader eventually gave an order for his troops to stand down but only after some delay. The overall German commander in Italy was Field Marshal Albert Kesselring, and he had anticipated this possibility. It was Kesselring who had reinforced the German Army in Sicily, and now he moved quickly to reinforce his army in southern Italy. Again, the Germans dug in for a series of very effective defensive battles utilizing the natural defenses offered by the mountains and rivers. They applied the lessons learned from their Sicilian experience fighting the Allies in mountainous terrain. The slugfest on the Italian mainland would cost the Allies many more casualties and drain significant resources, specifically the available landing craft. Several attempts to flank the Germans with amphibious landings at Salerno and Anzio almost ended in disaster. Ironically, it would take them until June 4 to reach Rome, just a day before the Normandy invasion was scheduled to commence.

Meanwhile, the Russians were clamoring for the Americans and British to open a second front on the European continent. Prime Minister Churchill, who had pushed hard for the invasion of Italy, still preferred to launch an effort against the "soft underbelly" of Europe.

The Americans were determined to strike across the English Channel. Despite their growing pains, the American Army had now gained much-needed confidence from the victories in North Africa and Sicily. American industry was providing ever more war materials to the Allies, not only to western Europe but also to Russia in the east. Additionally both the Navy in the mid Pacific as well as General MacArthur's Allied forces in the southwest Pacific were succeeding against the Japanese. Their "island hopping" strategies were resulting in victories in spite of being a lower priority for men and supplies due to the "Germany first" policy. Since the Americans were gaining stride in both combat experience and overall contribution to the effort, they gained more leverage over the British in dictating the way forward. General Marshall could now effectively make his case for the cross-channel attack.

The Allied leaders—Churchill, Stalin, and Roosevelt—met next in Tehran, Iran, in December 1943 to discuss the upcoming phases of the war. Stalin desperately wanted to open a second front in Europe to help take pressure off the Russian front and to further stretch the German war machine. His Red Army had been fighting three German armies, three million strong for over two years. On the way to Tehran Churchill and Roosevelt met in Cairo to discuss U.S. and British joint strategy going into the conference with Stalin. The Americans were quickly becoming the senior partner in the Alliance by virtue of their contribution of forces and logistics. Roosevelt and Churchill both knew that they would need to open the second front now favored by the Russians. This would mean an invasion across the English Channel into France, which was favored by the Americans.

The decision for the second front was made at the Tehran Conference with significant urging from Stalin. The Russian leader needed a second front to relieve the pressure on his own army that had been locked in a brutal struggle with Hitler's legions since June 1941. When they got to Tehran, Stalin quickly pressured Churchill and Roosevelt to commit to the invasion of northern Europe. He insisted on the appointment of an overall commander, which would be a sign that the

British and the Americans were serious and that the invasion would really take place. In return, the Americans and British wanted Russian cooperation to launch a major summer offensive to tie down German forces in the east. Such an attack would provide a diversion until their troops could get a foothold on the continent. Although Churchill was still lobbying to focus operations in the Mediterranean, Roosevelt assured Stalin that they would decide within a few days and subsequently convey to him their decision on naming the commander. With the Americans and Russians in agreement on the need to open the second front in Europe, Churchill knew that he would have to concur. Reluctantly, Churchill agreed not only to the invasion of France but also to an American officer as the supreme commander.

Appointment of the Supreme Commander and Staff

Roosevelt originally thought that General Marshall would be his first choice to command the invasion. Marshall had wanted a field command and Roosevelt wanted to reward him for his achievements in organizing the war effort. He was the prime mover in rebuilding the American Army and managing the relationship with the British Chiefs of Staff. However, many of Roosevelt's key advisors were very concerned that they could not afford to loose General Marshall's leadership as Army Chief of Staff and on the Joint Chiefs of Staff. Marshall, who accompanied the President on the trip to the Tehran Conference, was asked by Roosevelt what he would like to do. Marshall, who epitomized the value of selfless service, replied that he would do whatever the President wanted him to do that he deemed in the best interests of the country. It became clear to the President that Marshall was still critical to the overall worldwide war effort. He told Marshal that he wouldn't sleep well if Marshall was out of Washington.[10] Marshall then realized that he would not be leading the invasion.

Marshall then recommended his protégé, General Eisenhower. Roosevelt approved Eisenhower to fill the position of Supreme Allied

Commander. He realized there was no other American officer who had the respect of the British and who could effectively lead this difficult coalition. Furthermore, Eisenhower had been working successfully with the British since the invasion of North Africa. After some initial problems, he had begun to instill a spirit of cooperation between the various factions. Additionally, Eisenhower had made it known that he did not want to return to Washington to a staff position. He would have preferred instead to be a subordinate army commander in Europe. Roosevelt thus instructed Marshall to send a message to Stalin that General Eisenhower would lead the invasion of Europe as the supreme commander. Marshall later gave Ike a copy of the handwritten note from Roosevelt confirming the appointment as supreme commander. Marshall was aware of the historical significance of the moment and wanted his friend to have it.

Following Eisenhower's appointment, the next key decisions involved the selection of principal subordinates, including deputies for army, air, and naval forces as well as primary staff officers. To provide balance for the command and Allied unity, as well as leveraging the experience gained by fighting since 1940, mostly British officers were considered for the key subordinates, with a few exceptions. One exception was the position of chief of staff (COS). General Marshall had recommended Major General Walter Bedell Smith to Eisenhower for his chief of staff when the North African invasion was beginning to take shape under Operation Torch. Marshall's keen eye for talent was on target once again, and Smith was a great choice to fill this role. He had been secretary to the general staff in Washington, so Marshall had observed him in action and was very impressed. Having worked with Eisenhower from the beginning of the North African campaign, Smith was now selected for this important role in the Supreme Headquarters Allied Expeditionary Force, or SHAEF as the command would be known.

The chief of staff would represent the commander at many meetings where critical decisions were made with senior officers from all branches of service and all Allied nations. Additionally, he ran the headquarters and all the staff sections that were responsible for the critical functions that supported the operations. This included the primary staff sections of G-1 (personnel), G-2 (intelligence), G-3 (operations), and G-4 (logistics).

Smith was a no-nonsense soldier who took charge and got things done. He had a skill for looking after the details. The supreme commander needed someone on the inside to take care of all the details while he focused on the big picture. Additionally, Smith could be firm when he needed to be and effectively dealt with the many strong personalities of subordinate commanders and staff officers. Having had the prior experience of working together, they were comfortable playing their respective roles. Eisenhower could not have had a better right-hand man for the job.

The deputy commander slot went to the British. Air Chief Marshal Arthur Tedder was selected for this role. He had been the air forces commander in the Mediterranean and developed a close working relationship with Eisenhower from the time they first met in December 1942. Tedder also proved to be a good choice for several reasons. First, like Eisenhower, Tedder was a strong proponent of the use of air power in support of the invasion. As an airman, he was a perfect advocate for this strategy and was effective at countering the arguments of other senior air commanders who strongly favored the strategic bombing of Germany over the tactical employment of airpower in support of the ground operations. Second, there were heated arguments over command relationships with the air forces of both Allies. These airmen were looking for independence as a separate service because airpower was a relatively new branch of service. They resisted being subordinated to SHAEF and supporting a land invasion. After heated arguments with the Combined Chiefs of Staff about who would control the air forces, Eisenhower eventually prevailed over the airmen. Tedder, as his deputy, was a key player in directing the airpower resources. Like Eisenhower, Tedder was also very much a team player. He went out of his way to minimize rivalries and made every effort to ensure that the British and Americans worked together as a unified team.

There was considerable debate over who would command the ground forces. The plan called for a unified ground commander for the initial phase of the operation. This responsibility would fall to whoever was selected as the commander for the 21st Army Group, British Army. He would have a dual role as the overall ground commander in addition to commanding British and Canadian forces directly. Although this largely a British decision, it also made the decision more complex because they needed to select not only the best ground commander but also someone who could lead a coalition. Eisenhower preferred General Harold Alexander, but the British Chief of Staff, General Alan Brooke, supported General Montgomery. Brooke viewed Montgomery as a more aggressive commander. After setbacks with previous commanders, it was General Montgomery, "Monty," who successfully led the British Eighth Army across North Africa in pursuit of Field Marshal Erwin Rommel's Africa Corps. He was considered by many as Britain's most capable field general. However, Eisenhower's experience with Montgomery was difficult and strained. Montgomery had a strong personality with an enormous ego, and he resisted taking direction from above. At times he verged on being insubordinate. Although Eisenhower preferred Alexander, Alexander had not been effective in settling the disputes among the Allied commanders in Sicily. So the British appointment went to Montgomery, who Eisenhower would have to work as the land forces commander. Even as the supreme commander, Eisenhower was hard-pressed to refuse Britain's most successful general.

On the American side, General Omar Bradley was quickly selected as the American forces commander, and he would command the First U.S. Army. Bradley was Eisenhower's West Point classmate, and they had a long working relationship. He had proven his effectiveness as a leader in both North Africa and Sicily. Unlike either Montgomery or Patton, Bradley's personality was low-key, yet he was extremely competent as a field commander. Most importantly for Eisenhower, they had a long personal relationship, and the supreme commander knew he could always trust Bradley implicitly.

As the deputy for naval forces, the British selected Admiral Bertram H. Ramsey, who had orchestrated the successful evacuation of the British Army from imminent destruction at Dunkirk. In addition, Admiral Ramsey was a skilled planner and experienced commander. He had planned the naval operations for the invasion of North Africa and commanded the naval forces for the invasion of Sicily. Now he would be tasked with planning and leading the greatest naval armada in history. His planning skills would be tested not only by the complexity of the operation but also by the need to plan for the delivery of massive reinforcements and supplies in the weeks following the landing. This needed to be accomplished without the benefit of a major port facility during the initial phases of the operation. As he had been creative in the Dunkirk evacuation, he would again be creative with novel approaches such as constructing artificial harbors to solve the problem of bringing supplies onto the beachhead.

Finally, British Air Chief Marshall Trafford Leigh-Mallory was appointed as the air forces commander. His background was the commander of the British Fighter Command. Since fighter protection for the beaches was a critical success factor, the British Chiefs of Staff selected him for this role. However, his responsibilities were limited to the tactical air support and did not include the responsibility for Bomber Command. This task would go to Tedder, the deputy supreme commander, to mollify the other strategic air commanders. Leigh-Mallory had a difficult personality, and he was viewed by the strategic airmen of the bomber commands as mainly a tactical fighter commander. Nevertheless, Leigh-Mallory strongly advocated the use of the bomber force to support the invasion by isolating the battlefield in what became known as the Transportation Plan. He also ensured that the Allies would have air superiority on D-Day. As these appointments were made, the planning for the invasion commenced in earnest.

Staff Ride Notebook

Q1. A key to effective leadership is establishing core values. For example, both General Marshall and General Eisenhower valued Allied unity. What are the core values of your organization?

Q2. General Marshall exhibited the Army value of selfless service to the nation. What core values do you exhibit as a leader or are exhibited by leaders whom you admire?

Q3. General Marshall and General Alan Brooke considered one of their primary roles the identification of key subordinates. How does your organization identify future leaders and assess talent?

Q4. When assessing talent, how do you distinguish between an individual's potential and performance? How do you measure potential? How do you measure performance? How are they related?

Q5. On what basis are promotions made within your organization? Are the criteria clearly set forth? Do people know where they stand in relationship to the criteria and their peer group?

Q6. Faced with unsatisfactory performance, Eisenhower made tough personnel changes with key commanders and staff. How is nonperformance dealt with in your organization? How is unethical behavior dealt with in your organization?

Q7. Despite their senior rank, both General Montgomery and General Patton argued and provided minimal mutual support to each other during Operation Husky in Sicily. How would you deal with squabbling subordinates who are in key positions within your organization?

Q8. Competition among the Allied commanders and the inter-service rivalries risked a suboptimal performance in the overall war effort. How does your organization deal with competition for resources between various teams or business units?

Supreme Commander, General Dwight D. Eisenhower
Photo U.S. National Archives

CHAPTER TWO
OPERATION OVERLORD:
PLANNING AND PREPARATION

Preplanning the Invasion

The planning for the Allied invasion of the Continent actually began before the Allied supreme commander and key senior staff officers were designated. Following the Casablanca Conference in January 1943, the Combined Chiefs of Staff from Britain and the United States had appointed a planning staff under the leadership of Lt. General Fredrick Morgan of the British Army. This was both a joint and combined staff because it included representatives of the different branches of service and also the various Allied nations. Their intention was to develop an integrated plan that reflected the best of both British and American military thinking and doctrine. But, as often is the case, taking the best from each part does not necessarily optimize the whole organization.

Doctrine was the framework or philosophy on how to wage war. Since the staff was led by a British General and located in wartime London, the planning reflected more of the British way of war, but in many respects it was a mix of American and British doctrine that did not optimize the capabilities of either force. The result would be operational problems that potentially risked the overall success of the operation. Nevertheless, the combined staff of American and British planners did their best to develop the initial plan for the invasion until the key leaders were appointed. After grappling with many of the critical decisions for the better part of a year, they were able to get the initial concepts in place.

When the planning began in earnest in April 1943, there were mostly unknown answers to an endless list of questions. The list included:

- Which and how many friendly forces would be available for the task?
- What forces would the Germans use to defend against the invasion?
- Who would command the invasion force?
- What would be the commander's intent and what would be the concept of the operation?
- How would the services, Army, Navy, and Air Forces, from different countries be integrated into a single plan that maximized their combat power?
- Where would be the best place for the invasion?

To get answers to these and a myriad of other questions, the staff began to gather information. They used a variety of sources—official and unofficial—to get answers and information. One of the more creative solutions included canvassing the British public for photographs of the coastline from vacations to the Continent before the war began. They supplemented this with aerial photographs, reports from the French resistance, and small reconnaissance raids.

Since the invasion commander had not yet been appointed, the British and American Combined Chiefs of Staff provided General Morgan with some directives and assumptions for planning. Normally, a commander would provide the staff with his intent and concept of the operation in the initial part of the planning sequence. Clearly understanding a commander's concept of the operation allows a staff to conduct more detailed planning focused around the intent of the operation. Without a commander in place, this role was met by the

Combined Chiefs of Staff. Their planning guidance and considerations included the following:

- Gaining and maintaining naval and air superiority in the invasion area
- Selecting a landing site within range of English-based air cover
- Port facilities that could support a force of up to thirty divisions with three to five divisions offloading per day during the initial phases
- Sufficient maneuver area for buildup of the forces
- Beaches that could support the landing craft and armored forces
- Proximity to good road and rail networks
- A weakly defended area where the initial assault could quickly breach the beach defenses[11]

Thus, one of the initial tasks was to choose an invasion site. The shortest distance from England to the Continent was to cross over to the Pas de Calais in France from Dover, England. This was a distance of about twenty miles. It was also the most logical invasion site not only because it was the shortest distance but also because it offered high-quality port facilities to offload men and material once the invasion commenced. Further, it was a shorter distance from Calais to the German border than from anywhere farther down the coast.

The Germans also recognized these advantages. Consequently, they fortified the area in the vicinity of Calais with concrete reinforced fighting positions, minefields, and obstacles. It became one of the best fortified zones along Hitler's Atlantic Wall, which stretched from Norway to southern France. Calais was also the location where they positioned some of their best armored troops—panzer divisions—who could quickly react to any assault with a mobile tank and infantry counterattack. The German high command was convinced that this was where the main Allied assault would be made, and they were determined to be ready to defend against it.

Alternatively to the Pas de Calais, the Allies could land farther to the west. Two possibilities existed: Normandy and Cherbourg. Both options were at a farther distance of about seventy miles from England. This would require more ships because they could not make the round trip as quickly as to the Pas de Calais. Furthermore, the longer distance would make the fleet more vulnerable and subject to attack by the German Navy or Luftwaffe. Normandy, which was the less likely invasion site, offered some good beach areas, although parts of the coast were not suitable due to cliffs that came down to the water's edge. A significant disadvantage of Cherbourg was that it was located at the end of the Cotentin Peninsula. This location made it less favorable because it also offered the Germans the possibility of sealing off the invasion on the peninsula while they brought forward their reinforcements. After considering the advantages and disadvantages of each of these courses of action, the planners decided to choose Normandy, where they could hopefully gain tactical surprise. Achieving strategic surprise would be difficult since it would be hard to conceal an invasion force of this magnitude, but Allied intelligence had also indicated that this was the weakest area of the German defenses. So their plan would be based on the principles of tactical surprise, attacking the enemy's weaknesses, and speed.[12]

In deciding on the Normandy area, the planners knew that it did not have port facilities to bring in the follow-on forces and support the logistical buildup. Accomplishing these tasks would require some novel ideas, and the planners sought to improvise a solution. They planned to construct several artificial ports by sinking large concrete platforms. These would be constructed in England and floated across the Channel. One artificial port would be constructed off Omaha Beach in the American sector and another in the British sector off Gold Beach at Arromanches. Known as Mulberries, these would provide temporary port facilities until a deep water port, Cherbourg, could be captured.

The planners also intended to innovate in other ways as well. To supplement the Mulberries, they planned to lay a pipe across the English Channel to transport petroleum, which was code named Pluto. Finally, they would also overcome the limited port facilities by using amphibious vehicles that could be driven from ships offshore across the beaches without first being off-loaded at a port. Amphibious vehicles had been first used in Sicily and were known as "ducks," with an official nomenclature of DUKW. Additionally, there were specially modified tanks called DD tanks, "duplex drives." These featured canvas skirts to make the tanks float and special drive mechanisms to power them in the water. Although they were not very seaworthy, a limited number of these could provide significant firepower on the beaches until field artillery units would be available when they got farther inland. The plan called for DD tanks to land with the initial infantry assault forces so that they could engage fortified pillboxes and gun emplacements with their heavier weapons to breach the initial beach defenses.

Another key decision for the planners was the size and composition of the initial assault force. After considering the available troops, landing craft, and naval support ships, they planned for an initial invasion of three divisions plus several armor brigades. This force would comprise battle tested divisions, two British/Canadian divisions and one American division. The size of the assault force was primarily based on the availability of landing craft for the operation. Availability of landing craft was an issue because of other operational requirements in the Mediterranean and in the Pacific. Given the size of the force, they planned to use three beaches—one beach for each division. Additionally, they planned for one airborne division to be dropped behind the beaches as well as some smaller special forces units that would capture some key installations and communications networks.

Just as the size of the beach assault was limited by the number of available landing craft, the limiting factor for the airborne units was the number of transport airplanes available to carry the troops.[13] The entire force would be supported by naval and air forces. They would commence the invasion with an initial bombardment of the coast defenses. After destroying beach defenses, the air support would shift to destroy key bridges, roads, and rail facilities that the Germans could use to bring in available reinforcements for an anticipated counterattack. The Germans had perfected the counterattack fighting the Russians on the eastern front as a means to blunt an attacking force by using their armored and mechanized infantry. Although this was a small force (Operation Husky in Sicily had been larger), the planners nevertheless anticipated that it would be sufficient to breach the beach defenses and capture inland objectives by the end of D-Day.

German Defenses

While the Allied planners were busy developing their assault plans, Hitler had tasked Field Marshall Erwin Rommel to inspect the Atlantic Wall and take appropriate actions to make sure that the defenses would be adequate. Rommel, the famed panzer commander of the German Africa Corps, had escaped being captured in North Africa when the Allies defeated the combined German/Italian army in 1942. When he arrived in France and inspected the defenses toward the end of 1943, he found them to be lacking and immediately set in place an aggressive construction campaign. He ordered mines and obstacles emplaced on beaches and at likely airborne and glider landing sites. Millions of mines were buried just behind the beaches and on the beach obstacles themselves. He strengthened likely beach exits with fortifications and reinforced pillboxes. These gun emplacements could provide grazing and indirect fire across likely beach approaches. Widerstandsnests, resistance nests, were constructed to defend these areas and provide hardened concrete positions for the defenders. If the Allies were to succeed, he would make them pay a heavy price.

Rommel also sought to gain operation control of the panzer reserve forces that were located in the Pas de Calais area. As the Army Group B commander, he envisioned an aggressive counterattack response by the Germans to push the initial assault forces back into the sea on D-Day. This concept of the defense was not fully shared by the rest of the

German high command, including Field Marshal von Rundstedt who was the overall commander in France. Along with other generals, he thought that the counterattack should come at a time and place of the Germans' choosing once the allies had penetrated the beach defenses and the invasion site could be confirmed. In this way, he concluded that they could better utilize the principle of war that called for massed armor formations at the decisive point where the invasion was taking place. Although Rommel was one of the most respected German commanders, Hitler refused to give him control of the reserve panzer forces. In fact, he refused to give control even to his overall commander in the West, von Rundstedt, and personally retained control unto himself. Without control over the panzer reserves, Rommel focused his efforts on strengthening the beach defenses hoping to stop the Allied invasion at the water's edge.

The Crux of the Plan, Expanding the Assault

When Field Marshal Montgomery was selected to be the commander of the 21st Army Group and the overall ground forces commander, Eisenhower gave him a copy of the initial plan to review along with his guidance for the operation. After an initial meeting with Eisenhower, he immediately went about reviewing the plans that General Morgan and his staff had made prior to Eisenhower's appointment. Montgomery concluded as Eisenhower had also that the plans were inadequate. Together, they thought that Morgan had planned for an insufficient force, that the assault area was too narrow, and that more airborne units needed to be added to the mix. Basically they wanted to expand the plan to include multiple landing sites across a broader front to avoid being pinned down by the Germans. Montgomery also envisioned a preliminary phase of air and naval operations. Air operations would be conducted to isolate the battle area and gain air superiority. Meanwhile the Navy would assemble the troop-carrying ships and train the landing forces necessary to make the assault. Montgomery intended to move quickly inland from the beachhead. He planned to capture as soon as possible the City of Caen in the east and the port of Cherbourg in the west. The port was important so that the buildup of forces could continue unimpeded once the initial assault had succeeded.

After Monty's assessment and proposed revisions, Eisenhower held a meeting on January 21, 1944, with his senior leaders so that the new approach could be briefed. Eisenhower opened the meeting with some initial comments but quickly turned the meeting over to Montgomery to brief the new plan. Montgomery outlined the operation and asked each of the senior leaders for the other services to comment on their part of the plan, describe how it would be executed, and explain the required resources. The staff then got to work on planning the details for the operation and passed orders on to the subordinate commands so that they could commence their planning too.

Eisenhower also worried about a planned supporting invasion of southern France, code named Anvil, which was to take place simultaneously with the invasion of Normandy. The intended purpose was to draw enemy forces away from the Normandy coast while creating a second front that could eventually link with the allied forces entering France from the north. The British did not support this course of action for a variety of reasons, which included the fact that they did not want to draw Allied forces from the Italian campaign for the purpose of Anvil. Additionally they did not feel that there were sufficient landing craft to conduct both assaults. General Marshall was a strong advocate for Anvil, and he worked hard to press the case for the supporting operation. He was particularly interested in capturing port facilities in Marseilles to supply the Allied armies in France. As the Anvil planning proceeded, it became clear that there were not enough resources to conduct both assaults simultaneously. There was simply a critical shortage of available landing craft. So the supporting operation was postponed until September.

The invasion for Normandy, originally planned for May, was now set for early June when the combination of tides and moonlight would meet the requirements for the plan. The airborne units required moon-light to optimize their parachute assault. The navy preferred to come in at low tide to avoid the beach obstacles that would otherwise be under-water and damage the incoming assault boats. The expanded Opera-tion Overlord plan now called for an assault on five beaches over a fifty-mile front. The beaches were code named Utah, Omaha, Gold, Juno, and Sword from west to east along the Normandy coast. The American First Army commanded by General Omar Bradley would land at Utah and Omaha beaches while the British Second Army, which included the Canadians and was commanded by General Miles Dempsey, would land at the three beaches located farther to the east. The assault forces were arrayed so that the Americans would capture the port of Cher-bourg located farther to the west. This would allow supply ships com-ing directly from the United States to sail directly to the port without interfering with the forces farther up the coast. Furthermore, the troop dispositions in England dictated that the Americans sail directly across the Channel from their staging areas in southwest England while the British could do the same from the southeast.

While the Americans seized Cherbourg, the British and Canadian forces were expected to capture the key terrain around the city of Caen and block the expected German reinforcements coming from Pas de Calais. Beyond Caen the terrain was conducive to armor operations and from there it would be possible to threaten an armored thrust onto Paris. Such a move would threaten the German rear areas and take the pressure off of the Americans in the western zone. Just south of the Canadian landing sites were critical airfields that, if captured, would provide the Allies with operational airfields on the continent to avoid flying missions from England.

The beach assaults were scheduled to begin just after daylight fol-lowing an air and naval bombardment to destroy the beach defenses. The navy commanders also wanted to commence their bombardment in daylight so that they could identify the targets. Experience from the American amphibious operations in the Pacific would have also dictated a longer and more intensive naval bombardment, but this advice went unheeded. Many of the assault division commanders preferred to use the cover of darkness to get their troops ashore while the Germans would have limited visibility. This was an example of conflicting doctrine between the army and the navy. The attempted compromise provided for neither the cover of darkness nor an extended naval bombardment to destroy the fortifications.

It was decided that the fleet would begin their bombardment at first light with the objective of destroying German artillery. They then would shift their fires to the beach defenses approximately twenty minutes before the troops were scheduled to land. As the naval bombardment took place, the army air force bombers would conduct a mass-area bombing of the beach area. When the landings commenced, the Navy would then shift their fires back again to inland targets. They would also be available to engage "on call" targets of opportunity for the assault forces. The planned bombardment, although short in duration, was designed to neutralize and destroy any German beach defenses so that the assault forces could quickly conduct their assault and move on to inland objectives. It was also intended to gain the element of tactical surprise by not foreshadowing the specific landing locations with an extensive bombardment.

The revised Operation Overlord plan also called for two American airborne divisions, the 82nd and 101st, to land behind the American beaches. Their job would be to seize the key exits from the beach areas while neutralizing any German counterattack. Additionally, a U.S. Army Ranger force would assault the cliffs between Utah and Omaha beaches at Point du Hoc, where intelligence had reported a battery of 155-mm howitzers emplaced to defend both beaches. This was a key target because it could not only cause havoc in the landing areas, but potentially would also engage the ships off the coast. Meanwhile the British Sixth Airborne was tasked to seize key bridges and targets in the British sector. Among their key objectives were the Pegasus Bridge over the Orne River leading to Caen and the Merville Battery where another coastal artillery unit was emplaced. Just as the guns at Point du Hoc could threaten the American sector, the Merville Battery could cause significant damage to the landing forces in the British zone. The airborne assaults were planned to commence just after midnight, whereas the Ranger assault would be conducted simultaneously with the beach landings.

The Chain of Command—Air Forces

One of the many challenges of command for Eisenhower was the control of both the American and British Air Forces. Both General Marshall and General Eisenhower had insisted on a unified command structure for the operation that included all ground, naval, and air forces under one supreme commander. They both felt so strongly about the principle of unity of command for the Allied effort that they would risk their careers on this one issue. Coalition warfare was difficult to wage when the Allied nations and their separate services did not always agree on the strategies and tactics. Without a unified command effort, the Allies risked not being able to maximize their combat power against a formidable foe. Both generals understood this essential issue of command very well.

During the run up to the planned invasion, the Allied air forces were conducting a strategic bombing campaign on key industrial targets in Germany. Air commanders were generally of the belief that an intensive strategic bombing campaign could successfully defeat the Germans without the need for an invasion. The Combined Chiefs of Staff had authorized them to conduct this strategic campaign against the German industrial regions. With day and night strategic bombing campaigns, the air force leaders believed that airpower alone could destroy the Germans' ability and will to make war. As a result of this directive, the air commanders reported directly to the Combined Chiefs of Staff and resisted coming under Eisenhower's command. In addition to their beliefs about the effectiveness of their strategic bombing campaigns, they also fought inter-service rivalries to maintain their independence from the ground forces. This separate command structure clearly violated the principle of unity of command that Marshall and Eisenhower felt so strongly about. It was critical element of the plan that the air forces shift their efforts from strategic bombing to gaining air superiority and isolating the assault area if the plan was to succeed. Eisenhower took his case to the Combined Chiefs and threatened to resign if he did not have control over the air forces. In a compromise, he was not given direct command but did get to have operational control. Although he would have preferred a direct command relationship, operational control would give Eisenhower the ability to exercise the principle of unity of command. Yet there was one more complication. Eisenhower's key air commander, Leigh-Mallory, was disliked by both British and American strategic air commanders alike. So, as another part of the compromise, the direction for the bomber forces would be exercised through Eisenhower's deputy, Air Marshall Tedder. This was only one of the many command issues that Eisenhower had to contend with throughout the war, but it clearly demonstrated that he could be a tough commander when the situation required him to be firm.

With the compromise in place, the air commanders went about their work to support the invasion. They planned and executed what became known as the Transportation Plan. The objective of the plan was to destroy key rail and transportation facilities and networks. This would restrict the Germans' ability to move reinforcements to the battle area. The Allies wanted to isolate the battlefield from Germany's reserve panzer armies. However, to deceive them as to the exact location of the attack, they had to engage targets up and down the coast. They also wanted to destroy the German Air Force to prevent them from interfering with the landings. By the time D-day arrived, the Allies had obtained air superiority over the coast of France. The German Luftwaffe would not pose a threat on D-Day.

The Deception Plan

Another part of the operation was an elaborate deception plan, which was intended to confuse the Germans and prevent them from committing their panzer reserves. The code name for the deception plan was Fortitude. With the Germans anticipating that the Allies would make their main effort at the Pas de Calais—the shortest distance from England to the Continent—the Allies capitalized on their assumption. They built a fictitious army in England to reinforce this view. American General George S. Patton was put in charge as the army commander. He was a good decoy because of the Germans' belief that he was the best Allied field general. However, the primary reason that Patton had been given this assignment was political. It was Eisenhower's way of dealing with the repercussions of the slapping incidents in Sicily where he had publicly humiliated several soldiers who were in field hospitals suffering from battle fatigue. Sidestepping Congressional demands that Patton be sent back home in disgrace, Eisenhower now capitalized on Patton's flamboyant personality to reinforce the narrative of a major threat to Calais. General Marshall deferred to Eisenhower's judgment to deal with Patton however he wanted from his perspective as the commander who was responsible for the invasion. Consequently, Ike reprimanded his friend and appointed him commander of an army that existed only on paper. This allowed Eisenhower to temporarily bench one of his best commanders until the political winds shifted, and the move conveniently played into the deception effort.

To deceive the German intelligence agents, dummy installations with tents were set up in England so that they would think that there was a real army under Patton's command. Models of tanks and trucks were parked in fields nearby so that aerial reconnaissance would confirm the positions of troop concentrations. Bogus radio traffic was routinely sent out over the airwaves with the knowledge that it would be intercepted but would also add to the deception. Although Patton was on a short leash, he could not resist making speeches and appearances with various groups. This additional visibility also added to the deception, although on at least one occasion Patton's remarks again got him in trouble. In a speech to a women's club, his comments about the destiny of the British and the Americans to rule the world insulted the Russians. Nevertheless, Eisenhower still retained him as critical to the war effort. Once the landings took place in Normandy, the hope was that the Germans would believe that these were simply a diversionary assault. They wanted them to believe that the main attack was still coming from Patton's army at the Pas de Calais where they would need to hold their panzers in reserve.

While General Patton commanded his fictitious U.S. First Army Group, the actual assault forces conducted training at various locations around England. An entire twenty-five square mile area of southern England was evacuated of civilians so that units could conduct tactical training. Soldiers were trained in marksmanship and weapons training. Paratroopers practiced making combat jumps with full equipment. Rangers practiced scaling cliffs similar to the ones they would find at Point du Hoc. Large-scale exercises were conducted at Slapton Sands off the coast of England to let the army and navy practice amphibious operations together. These were some of the lessons learned in North Africa and Sicily. While most units benefited from this intense training, The U.S. Fourth Infantry Division was not so lucky. An unfortunate incident occurred when a German naval patrol torpedoed one of their transports during a training exercise that resulted in the loss of over seven hundred Allied sailors and soldiers. As a testament to the secrecy of the operations, this was not disclosed until years after the war. After many months of training and preparation, the Allies were ready. On the June 4, soldiers began loading on the ships that would take them to their destination from which many would not return. D-Day would soon be here.

Staff Ride Notebook

Q1. One of the key responsibilities for a senior leader is to provide a vision for their way forward. Eisenhower and his key commanders provided their concept for Operation Overlord in a clearly stated plan in advance of the invasion. Does you organization have a well defined vision for the future? How does your organization plan for the way forward? How are plans communicated to subordinate teams?

Q2. In planning the operation, the naval, air, and airborne units all had designated roles to play in support of the main effort of successfully landing Allied armies in France. In what ways do component parts of your organization support the overall mission? How could they be more effective in coordinating their efforts toward achieving a common organization outcome?

Q3. When faced with seemingly insurmountable logistical challenges, Allied planners improvised solutions such as artificial ports, underwater pipelines, and new ways to use their equipment. How are innovations made to solve problems within your organization?

Q4. When the air force commanders challenged his command prerogatives as the Supreme Commander, Eisenhower went to the limit over the issue of unity of command by threatening his resignation. What are the principles that you would stand for as a leader? If you are a leader, what are the principles for which you would resign your position if you did not prevail?

Q5. The Allies capitalized on deception to confuse the Germans and gain a local advantage. Although a deception strategy may not be appropriate for your organization, in what ways do you compete so that you can maximize your advantages over your competitors?

Q6. Training and practice are critical to effective teams. Full-scale rehearsals were held for the Allied assault units so that they could effectively work together and be familiar with what they needed to do under battle-simulated conditions. In what ways does your organization provide realistic training for its teams? In what ways could you make training more effective?

U.S. Army Airborne Assault.
Photo U.S. National Archives

CHAPTER THREE
JUMP INTO THE NIGHT:
D-DAY AIRBORNE ASSAULT

American Airborne

No matter how well the planners anticipated the requirements for the invasion, certain variables remained beyond their control. One such uncontrollable variable was the weather, which had deteriorated significantly just as the armada set to sea. A severe storm had moved into the English Channel with heavy rain and strong winds resulting in high seas and limited visibility. Under these conditions the airborne drops were not possible, the bombers would not be able to acquire their targets, and the landing craft would be swamped before they reached the beaches. The staff and key commanders gathered for a meteorological briefing even as the ships were sailing toward their rendezvous points in the Channel.

Without another viable option, General Eisenhower postponed the invasion for twenty-four hours due to the severe storm. Some of the transports needed to be recalled and refueled while the men waited aboard in anticipation. The recall process was very difficult because the lead ships needed to be notified without tipping off the Germans by breaking radio silence. Refueling also interrupted the loading and departure of other ships that followed later in the invasion sequence. Additionally, they did not have a lot of time to complete this process so that they could be ready to go the very next day. In fact, a few ships were unable to comply with the recall order at all. However, there was a predicted break in the weather that presented a window of opportunity for the Allies.

General Eisenhower was once more briefed by his meteorologist, British Group Captain J.M Stagg, about this new window of opportunity. The decision to proceed or postpone the invasion was a critical decision because the moon and tidal conditions for the assault would only prevail from June 4 to June 7. Another delay might mean a postponement of several weeks or more. This would require a total recall of all the forces now aboard the ships. The men and their equipment were ready to go after months of preparation. General Montgomery argued that a postponement would hurt morale. The other key staff officers who had originally argued against proceeding when the storm came through now agreed with Montgomery. Additionally, a further postponement would also raise the possibility of compromising the invasion plans to the Germans. So after consultation with his key staff and commanders and despite the risks of less than ideal weather, Eisenhower issued the go-ahead order. Thus began the largest amphibious assault ever mounted. Now that the order was given, the ships continued to their respective sea lanes while the paratroopers and glider men boarded their transports on airfields all over southern England. Eisenhower paid one last visit to the American paratroopers just before they boarded their planes.

Just after midnight June 6, 1944, airborne landings commenced with paratroops from the U.S. 82nd and 101st Airborne Divisions jumping behind the American beaches. Simultaneously, the British Sixth Airborne troops were landing in the British and Canadian sector. Airborne units were specially trained to seize and hold key terrain, cause confusion and chaos in the enemy's rear areas, and disrupt their ability to quickly counterattack the seaborne forces as they came ashore.

Additionally, the airborne troops were trained to aggressively take up the fight without heavy weapons or armored forces in support. They expected to be surrounded, cut off from the main force, and required to hold out until relieved. Their missions were to destroy artillery batteries aimed at the beaches and to seize and hold key bridges along avenues of advance. In some cases they were tasked to actually destroy the bridges so that they could not be used by the enemy to bring up reserves for a counterattack. These missions were so crucial to the success of the seaborne landings that Eisenhower had insisted on increasing the size of the airborne force from the original plan even though some of his staff recommended canceling them altogether. General Bradley was counting on them to ensure that the amphibious assaults could take place without the prospect of being driven back into the sea as had almost happened in Italy.

Airborne forces first appeared during the early days of World War II when they were first used by the German Army in conjunction with their blitzkrieg march through France. They also used airborne troops to capture the island of Crete in the Mediterranean. The Wehrmacht, as the German Army was known, succeeded in siezing Crete from the British, but took heavy casualties in the process. Consequently the leadership of the German Army was reluctant thereafter to conduct large-scale airborne operations. Where the Germans were discouraged, the Allies drew a different conclusion. They decided to train large airborne units and integrate them into their future plans. In the United States, Army Chief of Staff General George Marshall was a strong proponent of the airborne concept and he helped to sponsor the organization of the American parachute units. He liked the idea of having highly trained and motivated troops who were capable of executing a "vertical envelopment" and utilizing the element of surprise. Airborne soldiers were all volunteers, received special "jump pay" for the hazardous duty, and exhibited an aggressive fighting spirit, an élan not found in other units. Thus, when the Allies invaded North Africa, they utilized units from the 82nd Airborne to capture key airfields as Operation Torch unfolded.

Then again during Operation Husky, paratroopers from the 82nd Airborne jumped in behind the beach in advance of the Allied landings when the invasion of Sicily was launched in 1943. They were hampered by bad weather, inadequate coordination, and lack of training with the army air corps. As previously noted, due to miscommunications, a confusing chain of command, and nervous sailors in the Allied fleet, the paratroopers were the unfortunate victims of friendly fire as the air corps pilots proceeded to their landing zones in darkness. Mistaken for enemy aircraft, the troop carriers were engaged by anti-aircraft fire from the ships while they flew over the beaches to their drop zones. These unfortunate circumstances were the reason that some of the senior Allied commanders were convinced that the airborne operations in Normandy should not be conducted at all.

One of the more vehement detractors of the planned airdrops was British Air Chief Marshal Leigh-Mallory, who called this a "highly speculative operation."[14] Citing the problems from past operations, he anticipated extremely high casualty rates, perhaps in the range of 70 percent, and tried to convince General Eisenhower to cancel this part of the plan. He advocated bringing the airborne units in over the beaches as reinforcements.[15] Although Eisenhower also had serious concerns, he decided to allow the airborne operations to proceed as planned. As the supreme commander considered the risks, he also remembered that despite their problems, the paratroopers had still caused panic and confusion among the enemy forces. Even with casualties from the jumps and the glider landings, small groups of determined soldiers had held off larger units that were moving to oppose the beach landings. He knew that it was necessary to secure these key avenues of advance behind the assault beaches and prevent an anticipated German counterattack from reaching the immediate battle area. As the operation unfolded, Eisenhower's judgment would prove correct. Leigh-Mallory later apologized to Eisenhower when the airborne casualties, although high, did not come close to his predictions. He was sorry to have added to the burdens of the supreme commander at that critical time leading up to the invasion.[16]

On the night of June 5–6, the conditions over the Cotentin Peninsula were difficult for the approaching fleet of C-47 Dakota transport planes. Although the storm from the previous day had now somewhat eased, the wind conditions were still severe for conducting safe parachute landings. This was the largest airborne assault ever attempted, and although the troop carrier pilots had flown many practice runs with the paratroopers to overcome the problems from earlier operations, this was the first time that many of the pilots had flown an actual combat mission. Unfortunately, they were still not well-trained for night formation flying, especially under radio silence. Over eight hundred aircraft from the U.S. IX Troop Carrier Command were flown in tight "V of V" formations to deliver the troops. The night sky was filled with aircraft in a massive formation. It was nine planes wide and stretched back toward England for three hundred miles.[17] Night formation flying was difficult enough; however, as they crossed over the beaches from the English Channel, they also flew into an unexpected cloud bank. Since they were under orders to maintain radio silence, the pilots could not coordinate what they would do next. Once they flew into the cloud bank, some pilots went for altitude while others dropped below to look for clear sky and to avoid hitting the other planes in the formation. The result was that the tight formation now scattered over the peninsula.

The Germans had by this time been awakened by the earlier arrival of the pathfinders. Pathfinders were special volunteer teams of paratroopers who were dropped in advance of the main assault. Their job was to mark the landing zones with lights and radars. When the main body of troop carriers arrived, the pilots flew into a maelstrom of heavy antiaircraft fire. Some of the planes were hit and immediately caught on fire or crashed. Many pilots who were already disoriented from the cloud bank broke formation altogether. Some sped up in an attempt to avoid the German flak, but the additional airspeed added to the risk of injury for the jumpers. As the troopers jumped from planes that were going faster than they should have been, the violent exit caused many to lose their equipment, including rifles and other weapons. As had happened in Sicily, many paratroopers were misdropped beyond their intended drop zones. Others were injured or landed without critical equipment to do their job. Paratroopers were scattered all over the peninsula, often miles from their planned landing sites. Many landed in isolation and others formed mixed groups rather than linking up with their normal units. As they hit the ground, if they were lucky enough not to be injured or killed, they were confused, isolated, and without much of their critical equipment, including weapons and ammunition.

Shortly after the first paratroopers were dropped in the American zone, another wave of glider borne infantry were scheduled to land around 0300 as reinforcements with heavier weapons. Although the British used the heavier Horsa gliders than the American Waco gliders, both were of rather flimsy construction. They were simply canvas wrapped on an airframe. The glider pilots had only one chance to land safely once they were released from their three-hundred-foot tow rope. As the gliders were flown over their intended landing sites, they experienced the same problems as the earlier troop carriers, especially the heavy antiaircraft fire. However, because gliders are not powered, they could not take any evasive action. Additionally, the pastures that were the landing sites were lined by thick hedgerows as well as German emplaced obstacles. The hedgerows were earthen banks that lined the fields with thick hedges and trees growing in them. The hedgerows also created natural defensive positions for the Germans. The man-made obstacles were called "Rommel asparagus," which were twelve-foot poles that were tipped with mines and dug into the middle of the pastures. Many of the gliders literally crashed into either the hedgerows or obstacles instead of the gentle, controlled crash landings that were practiced. The less fortunate glider troops were injured or killed upon landing. In the confusion, some gliders crashed into the English

Channel never to be seen again. The lucky ones, like their paratrooper brethren, were confused and disoriented when they landed. It was an inauspicious start to the greatest invasion ever planned.

Nevertheless, as Eisenhower had hoped they would, a few of the units landed more or less intact according to plan. Most importantly, junior officers and NCOs began to exercise leadership and initiative by organizing small groups. Ad hoc units began to form. Soldiers from mixed units linked up under the command of an officer or NCO who they probably did not know. Despite the initial challenges, all of these soldiers had been extremely well-briefed on their intended objectives. Understanding the plan and overall mission, they proceeded as best they could to get the job done by supporting whatever mission was assigned to them by their new leader.

For the 101st Airborne, that meant securing the four causeway exits off Utah Beach. These were the only exits through a marshy area behind the beach that had been flooded by the Germans. The Wehrmacht intended to canalize the advancing Allied troops into narrow lanes off the beaches so that they could be attacked with artillery and automatic weapons. It was up to the 101st Airborne to harass, neutralize, or eliminate the artillery batteries sited on the beach and the causeways.

Typical of those batteries was the one located at Brecourt Manor about one thousand meters north of Ste. Marie du Mont and ready to fire on Utah Beach. Four 105-mm howitzers were protected by a force of approximately fifty German soldiers. The mission to attack was given to Company E, Second Battalion, 506th Parachute Infantry Regiment in the early morning hours of June 6. The original company commander was not available because he was killed in a plane crash during the initial jump, so the acting company commander, Lt. Richard Winters, took charge with a reinforced squad of twelve men who had assembled. After a quick personal reconnaissance, Lt. Winters assigned a machine gun crew and several others to lay down suppressing fire while he led the rest of the team in a flanking attack and charged each gun in succession. As they overtook each gun, they destroyed it with explosives. Normally this would have required the full company of 150 men, but despite the odds they succeeded by using surprise and shock action in an aggressive attack.[18] In the process, Lt. Winters also captured maps and documents showing all of the German defenses in the area. This proved to be an important stroke of luck for the intelligence staff at his headquarters. For his actions in leading the assault while outnumbered five to one, he was awarded the Distinguished Service Medal. Years later, this action was featured in the book *The Band of Brothers*, written by the noted historian, Stephen Ambrose, and was later made into a television miniseries by filmmaker Tom Hanks.[19]

Meanwhile, the 82nd Airborne had the critical mission of seizing the crossroads in the town of Ste. Marie Eglise. They were also tasked to secure key bridges over the Merderet River at la Fiere and Chef du Pont. Their mission was to prevent German reinforcements from counterattacking the beachhead. The village of Ste. Marie Eglise was the site of a junction of the road network that controlled the area. By seizing this key terrain, the Americans could prevent the Germans from reaching the landings at Utah Beach. When the initial jumps were made there was a fire in Ste. Marie Eglise that illuminated the paratroopers as they were landing.[20] Villagers and German soldiers were manning a bucket brigade to put out the fire. As the paratroopers floated to earth, the Germans took them under fire. Many were killed or wounded by the German garrison living in the village. Yet there were enough paratroopers who quickly recovered and made a hasty attack, and soon they had possession of the town. This was the first town to be liberated in France.[21]

Not long after, two battalions of additional troops who landed farther away assembled on this objective. The senior commander on the scene ordered them to dig in and prepare to defend against a counterattack. While the paratroops were digging defensive positions around the town, other members of the 82nd Airborne were defending the bridges that they had seized over the Merderet. The surprised Germans began to regroup and started their counterattacks as they were trained to do.

Determined paratroopers held these positions as well as several other isolated pieces of key terrain where groups of two hundred to three hundred men had assembled. Now they would simply have to hold out until they could be relieved by the troops coming across the beach. For some of them, this would be up to four days later, but they were trained to fight in isolated units. The training and the esprit de corps made the difference and the paratroopers held their ground.

Although the senior officers of both the 82nd and 101st Airborne Divisions had made the jump into Normandy with their respective units, they generally fared no better than the soldiers under their command. For much of the day, they were unaware of where their units were located, whether they were achieving their objectives, or what their status was in general. With very limited communications they were unable to exercise normal command and control. This led General Maxwell Taylor, commander of the 101st Airborne, to comment "never have so few been led by so many" when he and a number of his officers found themselves among a relatively small group of enlisted men. It was the training and skill of the junior officers and noncommissioned officers that carried the day. The generals simply struggled to get their units organized. For the most part, soldiers and junior leaders did not need to be told what to do because they were thoroughly briefed on the plans. They knew their key objectives and exercised the leadership to get the job done. Although they were more often outnumbered and disorganized, they still accomplished their missions. Consequently, the airborne units saved many lives on Utah Beach as the U.S. Fourth Division came ashore later in the morning. Fortunately they also suffered fewer casualties than some of the pessimistic forecasts by Air Chief Marshal Leigh-Mallory.

British and Canadian Airborne

As with the landings in the American sector, the British and Canadian landings were preceded by glider and airborne assaults in the early morning hours. The British Sixth Airborne siezed key objectives that included the bridges over the Orne River and the Caen Canal. Securing these bridges was necessary to provide rapid access for the seaborne troops to the avenues of approach to Caen. The first troops to land in Normandy were a glider borne force led by Major John Howard. Their gliders were released from their tow planes just minutes after midnight. Most of his 181 man unit landed safely intact within a short distance of their objective. Their silent approach in the Horsa gliders caught the German defenders by surprise. After a short but violent firefight, the bridges were captured with only a few casualties. The small force radioed success shortly before 1 AM but now had to hang on against determined German counterattacks until they were relieved.

The first relief force planned was part of the Fifth Airborne Brigade, who jumped shortly after the gliders had landed. Like their counterparts in the American zone, the British paratroopers were misdropped and landed at some distance from their intended drop zones. Units were intermixed and leaders had a difficult time trying to regroup. Knowing that their mission was to relieve the glider troops at the bridges, the paratroop leaders assembled as many men as they could and took off for their intended objectives. When the under strength force of the Seventh Parachute Battalion arrived to relieve Major Howard's group, they got there just in time to repel a determined German counterattack. The quick action of the paratroop leaders allowed the British to maintain control over the key bridges that were crucial to General Montgomery's plan of moving quickly inland to capture Caen.

Other bridges over the Dives River were to be destroyed by Canadian paratroopers to prevent potential German counterattacks with panzers. Just like the other airborne units throughout Normandy, the Canadians were scattered over a wide area with many of their troops landing at a great distance from their intended drop zone. Once again intensive training and strong junior leadership paid off. Not waiting to assemble the entire force, small unit leaders gathered mixed groups of soldiers and proceeded to their objectives. Complicating this mission was the fact that many of the engineers and their explosives were not immediately available. The paratroopers improvised demolitions by using mines for makeshift explosives until the engineers arrived. In keeping with the aggressive nature and training of the airborne forces, determined attacks by small groups using what they had available at the time ultimately succeeded, and the bridges were blown.[22] German panzers would now need to take alternate routes delaying their arrival to the battle.

While the action around the bridges was taking place, other paratroops under the command of Lt. Col. Terence Otway were preparing to take the guns at the Merville Battery. This gun emplacement was a serious threat to the fleet and the invasion forces coming over Sword Beach. It was imperative that the guns were silenced before the invasion commenced. Similar to the other critical targets, the Merville Battery was bombed by the air forces, but this did not achieve the intended effect. Over one thousand bombs were dropped on the position, but only fifty landed within range. Surprisingly only two bombs actually hit the battery![23] So the task of neutralizing the guns fell to the Ninth Parachute Battalion's 750 paratroopers. As with the airdrops across the rest of the zone, the weather conditions conspired to cause widespread misdrops for Otway's force. Only about 150 of them were able to assemble by 0300 hours. This left them with only two hours to accomplish their mission. If they did not signal a successful assault, the cruiser HMS Arethusa would engage this target.[24]

Despite the fact that he was missing about eighty percent of his unit, his assault guns, and other vital pieces of equipment, Lt. Col. Otway moved out toward his objective. The original assault plan called for a small glider force to support the attack on the Merville position by landing on top of the fortifications. When Otway arrived at the objective, he issued orders to commence the attack anticipating the arrival of the glider force. The gliders never arrived, as unfortunately they, too, missed their target. So now it was up to the few paratroopers to make the attack. Fortunately for the paratroopers, before Otway gave the attack order, some of his troops who had arrived at the objective early had marked their way through a minefield that protected the German gun emplacement. Once the attack order was issued the troops were able to quickly move into the inner part of the fortification because of the minefield markings. With a violent and determined assault, the paratroopers successfully accomplished their mission despite their depleted numbers. To the surprise of the assault force, the intelligence was wrong and the anticipated heavy 150-mm guns were not there; however, there were some smaller 75-mm guns that were taken out of action. Although the attacking force had taken about fifty percent casualties, they had taken possession of the Merville Battery, and beach landings in the British zone could now proceed without interference from these guns.

Staff Ride Notebook

Q1. Perhaps one of the most significant decisions made by Eisenhower was to proceed with the invasion despite the weather conditions. He made the decision based on the best information available but could not be sure that the improved forecast would prevail. What are the critical factors that he considered in making this decision? How do you make decisions when only limited information is available?

Q2. One of the ways that military operations are successful is through innovations in doctrine and tactics. One such innovation in World War II was the use of airborne units to make vertical assaults. In what ways does your organization capitalize on innovative technologies in your industry?

Q3. Various factors conspired to make the airborne assaults disorganized. Yet the junior leaders seized the initiative and proceeded to accomplish most of their assigned missions. How well are junior leaders in your organization prepared to assume greater responsibility if the need arises? What can be done to prepare them for such a possibility?

Q4. Many of the airborne units arrived without vital equipment or weapons. Yet they improvised to accomplish their mission. How well can your organization respond when vital systems or equipment are not available? Do you have backup plans in place? Have they been exercised?

Q5. During the initial airborne operations, the senior leaders were unable to communicate or exercise control. Yet they trusted their subordinates to take initiative and do the right thing with minimal interference. How do senior leaders in your organization react during a difficult situation?

Omaha Beach Assault: American troops landing under fire.
Photo U.S. National Archives

CHAPTER FOUR
COURAGE UNDER FIRE:
D-DAY BEACH ASSAULT

American Beaches: Utah and Omaha

At 0200 hours on June 6 the soldiers from the U.S. VII Corps and V Corps were getting ready to board their small boat landing craft that would take them to beaches on the coast of northwestern France. The VII Corps, led by the Fourth Infantry Division, would land on the right flank of the Allied invasion beaches to assault Utah Beach. They would be supported by airborne infantry who were dropped behind the beaches in advance. Likewise the men comprising the U.S. V Corps, led by the U.S. First and 29th Infantry Divisions along with Rangers from the Second and Fifth Ranger Battalions, were climbing down the cargo nets that were strung aside their transports. The V Corps objective was a ten-kilometer crescent shaped stretch of beach code named Omaha and later known as Bloody Omaha. General Bradley had handpicked the veteran First Infantry Division, the Big Red One, because of its prior combat experience in the landings in North Africa and Sicily. The Omaha assault was also supported by Rangers attacking a promontory known as Point du Hoc. It was here where suspected gun emplacements that overlooked the beaches needed to be neutralized. Utah and Omaha were the westernmost two of the five invasion beaches. Altogether the five beaches spanned some fifty miles of the Normandy coast of France.

As they climbed into the assault boats, many of the troops were already seasick and fatigued. They had boarded their larger transports the day before for the anticipated June 5 invasion. Now that the invasion was rescheduled for June 6, the weather had improved; however the sea and wind conditions were still more difficult than any that they had experienced in their training exercises. The U.S. Navy commanders, who were responsible for transporting the troops heading for Utah and Omaha, decided to anchor twelve miles off the coast instead of only seven miles as recommended by their British naval commander-in-chief. By exercising their independent judgment, they wanted to protect the transports from German coastal artillery. This meant that the troops would have to endure a longer run into the beach in the heavy seas. As the troops boarded the assault boats by climbing down the cargo nets, they had a difficult time knowing when to jump as the small craft bobbed between the waves. A few were injured as they simply fell into the Landing Craft Assault (LCA) boats. Others were killed as they were pinned between the assault boats and the transports. They were among the first American casualties on D-Day. As they crammed into the boats with over eighty pounds of equipment, they each had their own private thoughts and fears as they prepared to make the run onto the beach. Those who were not already seasick quickly succumbed to the illness with the odor of sickness in the air. As some of the waves crested or sprayed over the sides of the boats, men had to use their helmets to bail out excess seawater along with the remains of their breakfasts from just an hour before. Unfortunately, some of the landing craft would not make it because they capsized or swamped before reaching their destination.

On both beaches, the assault divisions would be joined by specialized engineer units who had the mission of destroying the beach obstacles and clearing mines. These special missions were critical to the success of the landings so that subsequent groups could land without their boats being destroyed at the water's edge. While the infantry made their assaults on the beach, the engineers were expected to destroy obstacles that would be underwater at high tide. Hidden from view, they would cause damage to the oncoming waves of boats carrying reinforcements. Technically this was a job for the navy. According to the doctrine, it was their responsibility to deliver the army troops safely to the beach and clear the obstacles; however, since there were insufficient numbers of trained naval demolitions specialists, the army supplemented the naval demolition teams with their own special engineer brigades.

The assault boats carried groups of thirty-one men with all their equipment. When they were in the landing craft, there was little room for them to move. They carried their own personal equipment and weapons, which included three days worth of rations and ammunition. Some also lugged crew-served weapons such as mortars and machine guns. They also had specialized equipment for breaching the minefields and barbed wire entanglements. The crew-served weapons included base plates for the mortars, tripods for the machine guns, and extra ammunition for both. In the dark hours of the early morning, the landing craft circled up at their rendezvous points in the assembly areas and prepared to make their run onto the beach. The small boats tossed in the sea swells while they circled up at the assembly area to wait for the rest to arrive.

While the landing craft were assembling, minesweepers were clearing and marking lanes for the ships to pass. The minesweepers had the critical task of breaching the suspected German naval mines, which were the first line of defense for Hitler's Atlantic Wall. One of the concerns was a new type of pressure sensitive mine that was designed to explode when a ship passed overhead. Naval mines could effectively destroy the landing craft and their vital cargos of men and equipment before they even reached the beach. Many of the transports, minesweepers, and landing craft were from the British and Allied navies. The American Navy did not have enough resources in minesweepers, transports, or warships because of competing requirements in the Pacific. The American Navy had primary responsibility for taking the war to Japan in the central Pacific. Despite the "Germany first" strategy, that's where much of the American fleet and all of their aircraft carriers were located. So Operation Overlord was much more complex than just a typical joint army–navy operation. It truly stretched the limits of planning and coordination as a combined operation that involved forces from the various Allied nations, primarily America, Britain, Canada, France, and Poland.

As the landing craft assembled, American Army Air Corps and British Bomber Command pilots were taking off from airfields all around England with their bombers and fighter planes. The bomber missions were to provide a preassault bombardment that would destroy the beach defenses. Fleets of American B-24 and B-26 bombers that normally flew daytime bombing raids deep into Germany were now being used for precision bombing missions to destroy hardened targets, German built concrete bunkers and gun emplacements protecting the beach. This was a difficult task given the technology of the time and also because air-ground support doctrine was still evolving.

Aerial beach bombardments were made on all the beaches; however, as between Utah and Omaha, there were some critical differences in the plans. First, the flight patterns for the bombers on Utah ran parallel to the beach, whereas those on Omaha were perpendicular. Second, the planes used on Utah were the medium B-26 Marauders, whereas the heavy B-24 Liberator bombers were used on Omaha. Third, the attack procedures were different in each case. The Ninth Air Force came in to attack Utah at a much lower altitude, four thousand to six thousand feet, and used smaller bombs that would not cause craters, which would impede vehicles. The Eighth Air Force, which was trained for strategic bombing missions, flew at about sixteen thousand feet over Omaha and carried larger payloads. These factors would have a material impact on the success of each of their missions.

As the American planes took off in the dark, it was inherently a more difficult mission because the pilots were used to flying daylight raids over Germany. Night formation flying was by definition more challenging and it was further complicated by cloud cover that still lingered over the English Channel. Nevertheless, the sheer numbers of aircraft and their potential destructive power was what the Allied generals hoped would obliterate the German defenses so that the troops could quickly punch through to targets further inland. On Utah Beach, almost three hundred planes dropped over 4,400 bombs. The destructive force totaled over one million pounds of explosives. A Ninth Air Force study concluded that fifty-nine percent landed within five feet of their targets with many direct hits or at least within the minimum bursting radius to have an effect on the target.[25] Their low level, parallel attack was more risky to the pilots but proved very effective.

In contrast, as the Eighth Air Force pilots approached Omaha at a higher altitude to deliver their deadly payloads, they were hampered by cloud cover that obscured the beach. The pilots also knew that the assault boats were inbound to their objectives, but with the poor visibility they were not exactly sure of their progress. To avoid risking harm to friendly troops, the bombardiers delayed dropping their payloads, and due to their perpendicular attack angle, this delay caused almost all of the bombers to fly over their intended targets. Most of the bombs fell harmlessly well behind the beach defenses, leaving them unscathed and fully manned. This was one of the early mishaps on Omaha Beach.

Meanwhile the Navy had also been tasked to provide a ship-to-shore bombardment as insurance that the hardened German positions would be destroyed. In the Pacific theater, the Navy would generally provide a ship-to-shore bombardment of over three hours in advance of a landing and perhaps even longer. At Normandy, the plan was to have a shorter but more intense preparation considering the availability of both air and naval assets. General Montgomery also hoped that a shorter bombardment would also achieve some element of tactical surprise. He reasoned that an extended bombardment would have signaled the intended landing site and allowed the Germans to start bringing forward their reserves.

Additionally, the plan called for landing troops in the American zone shortly after daybreak at 0630 hours. The senior commanders wanted to have a full day to not only capture and destroy the beach defenses but also maximize the amount of time available to bring in reinforcements throughout the day. With the longer periods of daylight in the summer, this would give them well over twelve hours to secure the beachhead. However, since the navy insisted on starting their shore bombardment when they could see the targets, there was only less than an hour available for them to do their work before the first troops would step ashore.

Just off of Utah Beach, the warships of Task Force U were set to begin their beach saturation bombardment at 5:50AM. As the early morning daylight broke over the English Channel, the eighteen war-ships under the command of Rear Admiral Morton Lyndhom Deyo, USN, were spotted by the Germans and immediately taken under fire. With the element of surprise gone, the fleet began their bombardment about fifteen minutes early. Among the Task Force U warships was the battleship USS Nevada, which had been damaged and grounded in the Japanese surprise attack on Pearl Harbor. It had since been repaired and now it was part of the powerful Allied battle group consisting of five cruisers, ten destroyers, and several other smaller ships from Brit-ain, America, and the Netherlands. Each ship was given predesignated targets to engage based on the extensive aerial reconnaissance that had been done over the preceding several months.

Another eighteen warships comprised the battle group of Task Force O led by Admiral John L Hall Jr., USN, just off Omaha Beach. Among the warships there were the battleships USS Texas and USS Arkansas with their huge sixteen-inch guns firing from about four miles offshore. As their massive shells flew to their targets overhead, the sounds of the bombardment was deafening to soldiers in the approaching assault boats. However, they also took comfort in the knowledge that the beach defenses would be pulverized by both the air corps and the navy, but this was not actually to be the case as they would discover shortly. Also included with the battle group of Task Force O were two light cruisers from the French Navy and six smaller destroyers from the U.S. Navy. Due to their smaller size, they came within less than two miles from the beach. The destroyers would play a critical role later in the day.

As with the air corps mission, the navy's mission was complicated by limited visibility in the early morning light. It was also hampered by smoke from brush fires now burning on the beaches from the bombardment and by the low cloud cover. The direct fire from the naval guns normally worked best with adjustments from naval shore parties, but they were not yet landed. So as a practical matter, the fire control officers on the ships had a difficult time identifying and engaging targets, most of which were skillfully camouflaged by the German defenders. The combination of all these factors resulted in a preinvasion naval bombardment that had limited effect. Most of the German beach defenses on Omaha Beach survived the air and naval bombardments. The massive fireworks display simply helped raise the morale of the troops as they passed by the ships firing their powerful salvos.

As the assault troops neared the beaches just before H-Hour, there was one final opportunity to destroy the defenses with landing craft that were modified to fire rockets just off the beach. Although these rockets were awesome to watch and let off an ear piercing sound, they were also extremely inaccurate. The rocket landing craft also tossed about in the sea swells, which destabilized them as firing platforms. Although they were supposed to be calibrated to hit their targets, these weapons were as ineffective as they had been demonstrated during the assault training. Most of the rockets missed their mark and many fell harmlessly into the water. Consequently, the task of punching through the beach defenses would be left to the infantry.

As the first waves of infantry approached the beach, the plan called for specially designed tanks to arrive simultaneously and provided extra fire support. The specially designed tanks, known as DD tanks for their special duplex drive, were supposed to "swim" their way onshore. The dual drive allowed them to move in water and also use their tracks when on land. They had been the creation of British General Percy Hobart who designed armored vehicles for special missions. He also designed some tanks for mine clearing and others to carry portable bridges to span craters or ravines. These special mission tanks were collectively known as "Hobart's funnies." The DD tanks also featured a canvas shroud that was raised to allow it to float while the special drive shaft powered a propeller in the water. They were supposed to be launched about three miles from shore and "swim" their way to the beach. On a good day, they would manage about four miles an hour; however, this was not a good day with the surf still up from the storm. Many of the DD tanks did not make it to shore, especially those destined for Omaha.

On Utah Beach, the first unit to touch French soil was the Eighth Infantry Regiment led by Colonel James van Fleet, who had graduated in the same West Point class as Eisenhower and Bradley. His immediate objective was to break through the beach defenses. He then planned to quickly link up with paratroopers from the 101st Airborne who had been fighting behind the beaches since the early morning hours. Accompanying Colonel van Fleet was the Fourth Infantry Division assistant commander, Brigadier General Teddy Roosevelt, Jr., who at age fifty-six was considered an old soldier. Most of his troops were either in their late teens or early twenties. He had pleaded with the Fourth Division commander, Major General Ray Barton, to go in with the first wave to boost the morale of the troops. Roosevelt would land carrying just a cane and no weapon while wearing a soft cap instead of a helmet. As luck would have it, the strong ocean current had carried the small boats about a mile south of where they were supposed to land. After looking at their maps, Roosevelt and Van Fleet soon realized that they were in the wrong place; however, Roosevelt quickly made a decision to start the war from where they had landed rather than trying to get to the intended landing site. So without any delay, the Eighth Infantry began to move inland and engage the German strong points guarding the beach.

The Utah sector of the Atlantic Wall was defended by the 709th Division of the German Army. The 709th was one of the static divisions. It was tasked to defend about fifty miles of shoreline with twelve thousand men. Averaging thirty-six years of age, most of them were much older than the American soldiers. Static divisions were often of inferior quality. Their units also included wounded veterans from the eastern front and even some captured Russian and Eastern European soldiers who opted to "volunteer" for service in the German army rather than linger in a POW camp. Since the 709th had a large sector to defend, this immediate sector of Utah Beach was defended by only a battalion-sized group. Moreover they were only prepared to defend from prepared strong points placed at intervals along the coast rather than conduct spoiling counterattacks as would be done by a mobile unit. When the troops from the Fourth Division landed, the Germans were still recovering from the shock of the naval and air bombardment, which had been much more effective than at Omaha. The defenders initially resisted, but they were soon demoralized facing a much larger force. After about an hour, the beach defenses started to crumble. Meanwhile, many of the DD tanks that were launched for Utah did manage to make it to shore. With the help of their increased firepower, the Americans now began to overwhelm the defenders and move inland.

The Fourth Division's primary objective after getting past the beach defenses was to link up with the paratroopers. Behind Utah Beach were lowlands that were flooded by the Germans to restrict movement off the beach. The German plan was to use their artillery to blunt the attack as the Americans congregated on the beach and on the four causeways that lay behind it. The task for the 101st Airborne was to secure the causeways so that the Fourth Division would be able to move rapidly inland and avoid being bottlenecked on the beach. Once the linkup was made, the paratroopers could get support from the seaborne force with their tanks and heavy weapons.

As the troops moved off the beach, they had no idea whether the paratroopers had succeeded in their mission to secure the causeways. Nevertheless, they moved ahead as planned and assumed the best. What they found was that the paratroopers had not only secured the causeways but had also destroyed much of the German artillery that would have devastated the landings on Utah. As the follow on regiments landed, they were able to move directly over the causeways. General Barton also sent one battalion up the beach to continue to take out the remaining strong points where the division was supposed to land originally. Simultaneously, the special engineer troops went to work clearing beach obstacles and stopping only occasionally when they were intermittently shelled by artillery. Consequently, the mines and obstacles were removed for the benefit of the reinforcements that would land on Utah over the following days and weeks. Although they had originally landed in the wrong place, the rest of the plan for the Utah sector was falling into place. This was not the case on Omaha.

Shortly after 0630, the first waves of infantry landed on Omaha Beach. They were immediately met with intense automatic weapons and artillery fire that had been sited on the beach. The first troops to land on Omaha were from the 16th Infantry Regiment of the First Infantry Division and the 116th Infantry of the 29th Infantry Division. Additionally, a Ranger force landed on the western end of the beach in support of the 29th Division. The First Division was a veteran division that had participated in the landings in North Africa and Sicily. General Bradley tasked them to lead the assault because of their experience. The 29th Division was a National Guard division that had never seen combat before but had been training for the assault for over a year. Despite the experience and intensive training, in neither unit could these soldiers have imagined the ordeal that they would have to endure.

Omaha was the best defended beach on the Normandy coast. The crescent shaped beach extended for ten kilometers and had four major exits or draws that led off the beach. The draws were important because they were the key to getting the vehicles off the beach quickly. Guarding the exits, the Germans had constructed concrete reinforced fighting positions, widerstandsnests, from which they sited automatic weapons with grazing fire along the beach. The Germans had also placed barbed wire entanglements and minefields in between their positions to contain the assault. Rising up from the seawall were bluffs that were 100 to 150 feet high. Beyond the bluffs were several small villages that were built along a road that paralleled the beach.

As the ramps dropped from the landing craft, the Germans immediately engaged them with machine guns, mortars, and artillery. In the very first wave, A Company, 116th Regiment in the 29th Division was completely destroyed at the water's edge. Officers and noncommissioned officers were positioned near the front by the ramps to lead the troops off the boats. They were among the first casualties. Many troops jumped over the side of the landing craft to avoid being shot down on the ramp. As they jumped overboard, they immediately sank in water that was over their heads. Many of them were unable to drop their equipment, and with the extra weight they drowned in the surf. Those that were only slightly wounded or the lucky ones who made it off the ramps without being shot sought cover behind the beach obstacles. Once they landed, they still had almost three hundred yards of beach to cross before they reached the seawall.

Since this area of the coast was a likely site for an invasion, Rommel had ordered obstacles tipped with mines emplaced across the entire stretch of tidal area to prevent landing craft from entering the beach. The engineers had the mission to blow them up as the first waves landed just after low tide. If they accomplished their mission, subsequent waves could land without interference because the rising tide would cover the obstacles from view. When the first wave was ineffective, the engineers that survived the onslaught had difficulty doing their work. Wounded infantrymen and engineers were using the obstacles as the only protection from the deadly fire pouring onto the beach. Consequently, few of the obstacles were destroyed and the tide continued to rise.

After action reports and interviews with survivors describe the chaos that reigned on the beach that morning: "The men recognized that they were coming straight into the designated landing points. They were at the sides looking toward the enemy shore. What they saw was an absolutely unblemished beach, unpocked by arty or bomb fire and wholly barren of shingle or any other cover. The first ramps were dropped at 0636 in water that was waist-deep to over a man's head. As if this had been the signal for which the enemy waited, the ramps were instantly enveloped in a crossing of automatic fire which was accurate and in great volume. It came at the boats from both ends of the beach....Within 7–10 minutes after the ramps had dropped, 'A' had become inert, leaderless and almost incapable of action. The company was entirely bereft of officers....In those first 5–10 confused minutes when the men were fighting the water, dropping their arms and even their helmets to save themselves from drowning, and learning by what they saw that their landing had deteriorated into a struggle for personal survival, every sergeant was either killed or wounded....It is estimated by the men that one-third of 'A' remained by the time 'B' hit the beach....Two of the men, Pvts. Shefer and Lovejoy, joined a group from the Second Rangers, who were assaulting over the cliff to the right of 'A', and fought with them through the day."[26]

As the tide was rapidly rising, the wounded were drowning in the surf. The next waves of assault boats were coming in as scheduled. Soon the beach began to get crowded. New arrivals landed among the wounded while destroyed landing craft burned at the water's edge. With heavy sea swells, most of the DD tanks on Omaha never reached land. Of the thirty-two tanks launched for the beach, only two of them made it; the others sank in the Channel. Their crews were swimming to stay alive, but the incoming landing craft were under orders not to stop to pick up the survivors. Their mission to get the assault troops to the beach was the priority, and the survivors would have to wait until they made the return trip back out to the larger transports.

What made matters worse for the Americans on Omaha was the presence of the German 352nd Division. This was a highly rated combat unit of the German Army that was not supposed to be there. Intelligence had predicated that the beach would be defended by roughly a battalion-sized element of the 716th Division, which was rated as one of the static defense units that were poorly equipped and trained. Allied intelligence reports put the 352nd in the area of St. Lo, which was approximately twenty miles further inland, but undetected, it had been moved forward as part of a training exercise. Now the beach was defended by at least twice as many Germans, including these higher quality troops. Unlike Utah, the plan for Omaha was quickly breaking down. It appeared that the Germans would be able to stop the invasion at the water's edge as Rommel had anticipated.

For the balance of the morning, the beach assault appeared to be stalled. Small groups and individuals kept trying to move forward. Desperate men courageously struggled to move for the cover of the seawall, but they also had to contend with heavy loads of equipment that they carried on their backs. Their commanders should have learned from the training exercises that the initial assault troops should not be burdened with extra equipment. Although they had learned other valuable lessons during the rehearsals, they failed to make this important adjustment. Despite attempts to protect them, weapons were jammed as they were clogged with sand and seawater. Nevertheless, throughout the morning small groups of individuals from mixed units made it to the "shingle." This was a rock ledge where the beach ended and the escarpment that stretched to the heights above began. The seawall offered some slight protection from automatic weapons fire, but the survivors who reached the wall were pinned down. Eventually the few officers and noncommissioned officers who survived assumed leadership and began to encourage those taking comfort behind the shingle to clean their weapons. They then organized themselves into ad hoc assault teams to breach the next line of defenses. They gathered Bangalore torpedoes to blow holes in the concertina wire and create gaps leading to the high ground. Yet they still had to work their way through minefields before they reached the top.

Meanwhile, communications with the ships offshore were virtually nonexistent. Most of the naval shore parties had become casualties along with the infantry whom they supported. Initial reports to General Bradley were not good. He was contemplating calling off the attack on Omaha and withdrawing survivors from the beach. Alternatively, he thought about redirecting the follow up waves to Utah Beach, which by comparison was a textbook assault. However, this would have created another problem because it would have left a large gap in the line connecting Utah with the British and Canadian beaches: Sword, Juno, and Gold. The Germans, who were the masters at the mobile counterattack, could then penetrate the gap with panzers and defeat the Allies in detail. In order to get a better idea of the situation, the V Corps commander, General Leonard T. Gerow, dispatched his assistant chief of staff to make a run into the beach area by boat and get an accurate status report. Meanwhile, despite the initially grim reports, General Bradley decided to hold off on his decision until he could get a clearer picture of what was happening.

As the American infantry was being decimated on Omaha without support from either their armor or artillery, the navy came to the rescue. Defying orders not to move into the immediate beach area, the captains of the big ships took matters into their own hands. Ignoring the possibilities of grounding their deep water ships within range of German coastal artillery, the captains of the destroyers steamed closer to shore where they could get a better view. They then took it upon themselves to engage the concrete protected German positions that were guarding the exits off the beach. Using their big guns they brought direct fire onto the German positions from one thousand yards offshore. Unlike the landing ships outfitted with the rockets, destroyers were much more stable firing platforms. In full daylight, their direct fire was also much more accurate and deadly. At great risk to their own ships, they were able to destroy or suppress the German gunners so the American infantry could continue their advance.

When the naval gunners were engaging targets, they did not have communications with the ground troops. Consequently they could not tell where some Americans had gained the high ground. Unfortunately, some American soldiers became the victims of this friendly fire, but many more lives were saved because the navy destroyed many of the concrete gun positions. Infantry commanders would later give much credit to their navy brethren for coming to their aid when they needed it the most.

In other places along the beach, the infantry continued to take casualties from automatic weapons fire that had been sited on the minefields. Some of the most intense fire was leveled in front of the Vierville exit facing the soldiers of the 29th Division. When senior leaders arrived around 0730, they immediately exhorted men to move off the beach. Officers such as Brigadier General Norman Cota, assistant division commander of the 29th Division, and Colonel George Taylor from the First Division provided personal examples of courage by standing in the open while exhorting their men. Their personal leadership under fire was inspirational to all those around them including the Rangers. General Cota is reported to have encouraged the Rangers to continue their assault with the words "Rangers lead the way." This would become the Ranger motto.

On the eastern end of the beach, the veterans of the Big Red One were experiencing the same determined German resistance as their counterparts in the 29th Division. Like General Cota, Col. George Taylor, regimental commander, provided personal leadership for his men of the 16th Infantry to get the job done. He rallied those who were paralyzed by fear and sought shelter wherever they could find it on the beach. He challenged his men by famously saying, "Two kinds of people are staying on this beach, the dead and those who are going to die. Now let's get the hell out of here."[27] By his personal example he motivated soldiers of all ranks to get moving. Without needing to be told, many individuals and small unit leaders began to take their own initiative to continue to press the attack. The success of the assault would be determined by captains, lieutenants, and sergeants rather than colonels and generals. It was individual soldiers who did what needed to be done.

Some of the units were fortunate to land in between the exits off the beach. Since the Germans built their fortifications to defend the draws, the automatic weapons fire in these areas was less intense. One of the units to land in such an area was G Company, Second Battalion, 16th Infantry, First Infantry Division. They landed around 0700 hours between the St. Laurent and Colleville exits led by Captain Joe Dawson. He was one of the first off his boat, which was fortunate for him. Moments after he stepped off the ramp, his landing craft was hit and those who had not already stepped off were killed or wounded. Without hesitation, he led the rest of his men to the bluff and began the climb to the top in between the draws. Although they took some casualties, they made slow but steady progress toward the top. Captain Dawson was later awarded a Distinguished Service Cross (DSC), America's second highest award for gallantry, for his actions on D-Day.[28]

Noting their progress, G Company was joined by survivors of E Company. They had taken significant casualties when they landed in the first wave. The group from E Company was led by Sergeant Phillip Streczyk, who was also awarded a DSC. Observing the chaos on the beach, navy destroyers led by the USS McCook began firing mid morning at virtually point blank range on the German pillboxes. With the additional fire support, the Big Red One soldiers reached the top of the bluffs around noon. In the late morning, reinforcements from the rest of the division also began to come into the easternmost sectors code named Easy and Fox. While the reinforcements came onto the beach, those on the top of the bluffs attacked the German positions from behind. Since the Germans were preoccupied looking out to the beach area, they were taken by surprise. Although fighting continued through the rest of the day, several of the draws were open by the afternoon. The troops were moving to their assigned objectives, which were the villages on the bluffs—Colleville, St. Laurent, and Vierville-sur-Mer.

There are numerous stories of personal courage exhibited by small groups led by brave men to get off the beach. A few of them received the nation's highest decoration for courage under fire, the Medal of Honor, but many more acts of individual heroics were unreported because those who witnessed them also became casualties. By the end of the day, all the beach exits had been opened. More than thirty thousand troops and vehicles had begun moving inland off Omaha, but they were still well short of their planned objectives. At the end of the "longest day," the exhausted troops dug in for the night. The veteran First Infantry Division, which had been hand-picked by General Omar Bradley for its experience, lived up to its reputation. The untested 29th Division and the Rangers also fought valiantly and proved their mettle under fire for the first time. However, the price of their success was high. Over two thousand died and over twice that many were wounded. Despite these horrendous casualties, the Americans had succeeded in breaching the Atlantic Wall.

Rangers at Point du Hoc

One of the most daring parts of the Overlord invasion plan was the assault on Point du Hoc, a promontory situated between Utah and Omaha beaches. This cliff strategically overlooks both beaches. Intelligence reports concluded that the Germans had placed a six gun battery of 155-mm howitzers on top of Point du Hoc in reinforced concrete bunkers. These weapons would not only be able to cause havoc on the beaches but also could engage the fleet as it delivered the men and supplies ashore. There were over three hundred suspected or known enemy gun batteries on the target list for D-Day. The guns at Point du Hoc were number one on the list because they were such a threat.[29] It was imperative that these gun emplacements be put out of action to avoid disrupting the assault over the beaches. This task was given to Companies D, E, and F of the Second Ranger battalion under the leadership of LTC James Earl Rudder. They would conduct an assault on the position by scaling the thirty-meter high cliffs from the sea. Once on top of the cliffs, they would capture and destroy the guns. This mission was so critical that the rest of the Second Rangers along with the Fifth Ranger Battalion were tasked to assault the western end of Omaha Beach as a backup plan. If the Ranger assault up the cliffs failed, they would attack from behind and flank the position from the beach.

The Rangers were an elite light infantry team specifically assembled for special missions. They were all volunteers who had been hand-picked for the intensive Ranger training program. The U.S. Army Rangers were modeled after the British Commandos, which were also special assault units. The name Ranger predated the American Revolution. During the French and Indian Wars in North America, Major Robert Rogers led special light infantry units known as Roger's Rangers that were experts in unconventional small unit tactics. They supported the British against the French and Indians as scouts and raiders. Now, the British Commandos trained the American Rangers because they had more recent experience with special warfare techniques. They had been conducting reconnaissance missions and raids since the beginning of World War II along the Atlantic Wall from Norway to France.

In August of 1942 the Canadian Second Division, supported by a force of British Commandos and a small Ranger force from the American First Ranger Battalion, conducted a large-scale raid on the port of Dieppe. The purpose of the raid was to gain experience in landing a large amphibious force ashore, test the German defenses and reactions, and provide a boost to Allied morale by taking the fight to the enemy. The port of Dieppe on the French coast was covered by gun emplacements from both sides of the harbor. The main assault would be made by the Canadians coming in at high tide and first light. The task for the Commandos and Rangers was to support the Canadians by taking out the guns. Unfortunately, there was minimal naval gunfire suppression for the main attack and no use of Allied bombers to soften the defenses. As a result, the Canadians took severe losses. Approximately sixty-eight percent became casualties, including almost one thousand killed out of a total force of five thousand. Although the Canadians had made a valiant effort, they had learned the hard way that a direct assault against a prepared defense with minimal fire support is generally a costly strategy. This lesson was carried forward when plans were made for Operation Overlord. The beach landings at Normandy incorporated bombardments by air and naval forces. They also found out that the Germans at Dieppe had proven to be tough and determined defenders.

In the months following the Dieppe raid, the Second and Fifth Ranger Battalions began to train in North Devonshire, England. The U.S. Assault Training Center had been set up to impart lessons learned from prior experience. The Ranger training was considerably more rigorous than the training for normal infantry units. Rangers were put through the grinder with a difficult physical training regimen, extensive training on small unit tactics, and weapons training with weapons from both the U.S. and German arsenals. All of this extra training was not only to prepare them for difficult missions but also to instill an élan not found in typical units. Their rigorous training made each man a highly skilled light infantryman and forged them into a cohesive team. Additionally, they practiced for this particular mission by scaling cliffs in Britain that were similar to those found on the Normandy coast. Special equipment was designed specifically for this mission. This included grappling hooks launched from rockets as well as special ladders from the London Fire Department mounted on the assault boats.

While they clearly planed to use more firepower, they also wanted to be careful not to tip their hand on the location or timing of the invasion. Several weeks in advance of the anticipated assault, the U.S. Army Air Corps bombed the Point du Hoc cliffs. They also bombed other targets to distract attention from the primary objective. They made four bombing runs beginning in April and ending on June 4 just before the landing. The plan also called for a heavy naval bombardment from the fleet employing the fourteen-inch guns of the USS Nevada. One last bombing run was scheduled twenty minutes prior to the arrival of the Rangers. Even with this massive fire support, heavy casualties were expected while accomplishing this critical mission.

The assault up the cliffs was scheduled to begin three minutes after the naval bombardment ended. However, as fate would have it, the strong tidal current carried the assault boats further to the east by about a mile. As they came close to the shore, LTC Rudder realized that they were coming in at the wrong place. Technically the Navy was responsible for delivering the Rangers to the right place, but now LTC Rudder issued the order to change course, travel parallel to the beach, and proceed to Point du Hoc. This exposed the boats to fire from the shore and further delay.. As they navigated to the correct position, they ran a gauntlet of fire that sank one of the boats. While this was happening, two destroyers, USS Saterlee and HMS Talybont, observed what was happening. They came in closer to shore to lay down suppressing fire for the Rangers. They arrived at the cliffs forty minutes late. The original plan called for D Company to assault from the western side facing Utah while the other two companies came in from the east; however, with the delay and loss of one of the boats, LTC Rudder directed all the remaining nine boats to land on the eastern side of the cliff that faced toward Omaha. It would be from there that they would make the climb to the top.

At about 0710, the first Rangers hit the beach. To begin the assault, grappling hooks were fired from the boats to secure climbing ropes to the top of the cliff. Additionally, several of the boats deployed the climbing ladders provided by the London Fire Department. As is true in all battles, what actually happened departed from the original plan. Some of the grappling hooks did not reach the top, whereas others failed to catch hold. The attached ropes had become so soaked with seawater that it made them heavier than they were in practice. The ladders also did not work as planned, but one brave Ranger climbed to the top of one to provide suppressing machine gun fire while his fellow Rangers climbed the ropes. While exposed to exploding grenades and automatic weapons fire coming from atop the cliff, some of the Rangers completed the climb to the top within the first five minutes of their landing. Once a few had succeeded, then the others quickly followed. As they arrived at the top, they moved out quickly in small groups of three to six Rangers to carry the attack to the Germans.

When they overtook the German concrete bunkers, the Rangers were surprised to find that no guns were emplaced. Instead, they found telephone poles that simulated the guns. Without skipping a beat, they quickly moved out to start patrolling the area behind the Point. Their secondary mission was to cut the road that ran parallel to the beaches so that the Germans would not be able to bring up reinforcements and counterattack either Omaha or Utah. As they continued patrolling further inland, several Rangers led by First Sergeant Len Lomell stumbled upon the guns that they had expected to find earlier. To their surprise, the guns were unguarded. They quickly took immediate actions to render the guns inoperable by destroying the sights with their rifle butts and placing termite grenades on the traversing mechanisms. Other Rangers destroyed a cache of ammunition that was located nearby. Once the guns were destroyed, the Rangers set up a defensive perimeter to control the road and wait for their expected reinforcements coming inland from the beach.[30] Communication from the point to the ships offshore was very limited; however, LTC Rudder was able to report that they had destroyed the guns. He also requested reinforcements, ammunition resupply, and help to evacuate the wounded.

The original plan had called for the Ranger force to be relieved by the end of D-Day, but because of the stiff resistance at Omaha, their relief would not arrive for several days. Meanwhile, Rudder's message was received by the fleet. A former Ranger, Major Jack Street, who was on the staff of the fleet commander, organized an effort to get some supplies and men to the point. Exercising initiative, he brought several boats with much needed ammunition, food, and a handful of reinforcements. They also were able to evacuate some of the more critically wounded Rangers back to the ships so that they could be further evacuated to hospitals in England.[31] This allowed the Ranger force to continue to hold out against significant counterattacks by the Germans. Meanwhile the Fifth Rangers and the remainder of the Second Rangers were making their way inland from Omaha Beach. Joined by elements of the 29th Infantry Division, they were finally able to make it through around noon on June 8 to relieve Rudder's force. Of the 225 Rangers in the original assault force, only 90 were able to report for duty when the relief force arrived. The other 135 who were killed or wounded in the effort had paid the heavy price to accomplish their mission with initiative and daring. They overcame unbelievable odds and a variety of unplanned challenges, and having done so, the Rangers earned their place in history. Their bold and determined action added to the Ranger reputation, and they lived up to their new motto of "Rangers lead the way."

British and Canadian Beaches

The British and Canadian assault took place on the other end of the Normandy coast between Port en Bessin and Ouistreham, a stretch of about twenty-five miles. The British Second Army under the command of Lt. General Miles Dempsey landed at the beaches that were code named Gold, Juno, and Sword forming the left flank of the Allied assault. Dempsey, a veteran of Dunkirk, had also commanded units making amphibious landings in the Sicily and Italian campaigns. His Second Army's primary objective was to breach the beach defenses, move rapidly inland to link up with the airborne units, and secure key terrain and airfields on the Caen-Falaise plain. The key terrain in the eastern zone included the city of Caen and high ground controlling the airfield at Carpiquet. The city of Caen was located about ten miles inland from Sword Beach on the far left flank where critical road junctions controlled a German access of advance to the landing areas. On the right flank of the British zone, the objective would be the city of Bayeux behind Gold Beach. Bayeux was also a transportation hub that needed to be controlled in order to link up with the Americans coming in from Omaha. The link up was important to consolidate a continuous beachhead so that German counterattacks could not penetrate the boundaries between armies. Boundaries between units tend to be weak points because they require more coordination to defend. Assuming that the British could capture their objectives, they could threaten a breakout and advance from the vicinity of Caen onto Paris. They would also protect the left flank of the invasion against a German counterattack with their panzer army from Calais. With a secure left flank, the American

First Army could move inland, cut off the Cotinen Peninsula, and capture the critical port city of Cherbourg. The Allies needed a deep water port to continue the buildup by bringing in more reinforcements and maintaining the logistics pipeline to the United States.

The key to General Montgomery's plan for the British and Canadian forces emphasized speed. He wanted the Second Army to move quickly to capture the key objectives. Aggressive action to advance inland would allow them to relieve the British paratroops and defend against counterattacks by German panzer reserves that intelligence predicted were most likely to come at this part of the battle zone. Just prior to the invasion, Montgomery briefed his senior officers above the rank of Lt. Colonel with the following guidance: "Great energy and 'drive' will be required from all senior officers and commanders. I consider that once the beaches are in our possession, success will depend largely on our ability to be able to concentrate our armor and push fairly strong armored columns rapidly inland to secure important ground or communications centers. Such columns will form firm bases in enemy territory from which to develop offensive action in all directions. Such action will tend to throw the enemy off his balance, and will enable our build-up through the beaches to proceed undisturbed; it will cut the ground from under the armored counter attack…. Inaction and a defensive mentality, are criminal in any officer—however senior." [32] Spearheading the British assault would be the British 50th Division on Gold Beach, the Canadian Third Division on Juno Beach, and the British Third Division on Sword Beach.

Similar to the plan for the American sector, the beach defenses were scheduled to be destroyed by a naval and air bombardment. In the early morning hours of June 6, over one thousand planes from the Royal Air Force delivered over five thousand tons of bombs in the British sector.[33] This was followed by a naval bombardment from the Royal Navy that lasted a little over an hour-and-a-half, as much as four times as long as the comparable bombardments on the American Beaches. They had more time to conduct their bombardment because the British landings were scheduled to begin about an hour after the American landings. This was partly due to differences in the tides and the need to let them rise above the offshore reefs. It also reflected the hard lessons learned by the Canadians during the Dieppe raid. They would not forget the importance of massed fire support prior to the assault to weaken or destroy the fortified beach defensive positions. With this lesson in mind, the warship in the Eastern Task Force set about their work.

Much like the preinvasion bombardment in the American sector on Omaha Beach, the effects of these bombardments did not meet the planner's expectations, but unlike Omaha Beach, the German beach defenses were not reinforced by first-rate troops. The beach defenders in the British zone were part of the LXXXIV Corps of the German Seventh Army. They were limited to the 716th Division, one of their static units that defended from fortified positions, and the 736 Grenadier Regiment. Only a small part of the crack 352nd Division that defended Omaha also defended the area behind Gold Beach. The initial beach assaults by the British–Canadian force went reasonably well and according to plan. As they moved inland, they began to meet more determined resistance from strong inland defensive positions that slowed their advance. Later in the day the Germans would also reinforce their defenses, especially behind Sword Beach with the powerful 21st Panzer Division. This would disrupt the British advance on Caen.

With more than an hour before the landings were scheduled to begin on Gold Beach, the naval task force consisting of six battleships, two monitors, and twenty-two cruisers began their bombardment.[34] Both the U.S. Army Air Corps and Royal Air Force completed bombing runs as the fleet began to engage known gun batteries at Mont Fleury, Ver sur Mer, Arromanches, Vaux sure Aure, and Longues.[35] The most important of these was the battery at Longues. Simultaneously, the smaller destroyers fired on strong points located directly on the beaches themselves. As on the American beaches, the DD tanks, which were designed to "swim" to the beach, were launched about five thousand yards offshore. They were scheduled to arrive at the same time as the assault troops. A final barrage of rockets from specially designed landing craft was fired at the beach and targets just behind it.

Gold Beach was about ten miles in length, but because of the difficult terrain, only about half the stretch was useable for landings. From Port en Bessin to Arromanches, the coast was dominated by high cliffs, so the landings only took place in the center and eastern parts of Gold Beach. The 50th Division attacked with the 231st Brigade in the center and the 69th Brigade on the far eastern side of the beach. Despite the heavy use of naval and air bombardment, many of the German strong points survived. Across the sector, there were at least a dozen reinforced concrete widerstandsnests with automatic weapons and guns of various sizes prepared to defend the beach. A particularly stubborn defense was put up by the WN 37 at the village of Le Hamel. The heavy seas once again swamped some of the DD tanks, however, more of them survived than on Omaha. The British also used specialized "flail" tanks to clear the minefields. These were specially designed tanks with chains that would flail in front of them to detonate mines and clear pathways. Other tanks were specially designed with flame throwers for assaulting pillboxes. With the arrival of more armored units, the assault broke through the beach defenses. By noon most of the troops were moving inland except for the immediate vicinity of Le Hamel. There the determined defenders held out until late afternoon. After the beach defensive positions were eliminated, troops advanced to the main road between Bayeux and Caen.

Also on Gold Beach, the 47th Royal Marine Commando landed ninety minutes behind the 231st Brigade with the mission of passing thru the first waves to assault Port en Bessin from the rear. Located on the extreme right flank of the British zone, this port would need to be secured so that they could accomplish their primary task of the linking up with the Americans on Omaha. As their landing craft approached the beach, four out of their fourteen boats became casualties when they hit mines on the underwater obstacles and were shelled by onshore artillery. Those boats that made it to the beach were carried further to the east by the same strong tidal current that plagued the smaller boats on all the beaches. Since they landed further from their objective, the commandos had to fight through more of the German defenses and they got behind schedule. As a result, they only reached the outskirts of Port en Bessin on D-day. The link-up with the Americans would have to wait until the next day.

By the end of D-Day, the units of the 50th Division had led the way for the British XXX Corps on Gold Beach. They had successfully breached the beach defenses and landed a force of twenty-five thousand soldiers. They were moving inland toward their objectives, and in fact, they perhaps could have captured Bayeux as planned. However, after running into stiff resistance from a German counterattack, the commanders decided to dig in short of their objective. The 231st Brigade was able to secure the western end of the beach around Arromanches, where they would construct an artificial harbor to bring in reinforcements and supplies in the days ahead. The artificial harbors were known as Mullberries. They were an innovative British solution to the problem of not having port facilities until Cherbourg could be captured by the Americans.

The British I Corps conducted the assault on Juno and Sword Beaches. The corps commander, General J. T. Crocker, assigned the missions on Juno to the Canadian Third Division and on Sword to the British Third Division. The Canadians were tasked to capture the strategically important airfield at Carpiquet and the towns along the way from the beach. The British, landing on Sword, were tasked to link up and relieve the airborne units that had captured key bridges across the Orne River and Caen Canal and then take the city of Caen. After the initial assault, both the Canadians and British were to link up and close the four-kilometer gap between the two beaches. Like the other landing sites, they were scheduled to receive ample support from the fleet and air forces with preassault bombardments.

The Canadian landings on Juno were sequenced to begin even later than on Gold and Sword. This meant that the tide would be higher and that the troops and supporting armor would have a shorter beach to cross and less time to be exposed to automatic weapons fire. With the tide coming in fast, the beach quickly narrowed to less than a hundred yards. Offsetting the apparent advantage of a shorter distance was the fact that beach obstacles would be hidden underwater. This made it more risky for the landing craft because many obstacles were tipped with mines. Almost predictably, a number of assault craft and vehicles became casualties to these hidden hazards and then came under artillery fire. Due to the narrow beach, vehicles and men began to pile up. As the beach became congested it created an even more inviting target for the German artillery. The leaders knew that they had to get off the beach and get moving. So, with naval gunfire support from the fleet and direct attacks by the initial waves of infantry, the beach defenses were neutralized by mid morning. Then engineers began to open up the beach exits.

On Sword Beach the picture was similar to Juno with congestion on the beach causing delays. One difference was the success of the "swimmable" DD tanks. Thirty-one out of a total of forty DD tanks actually made it to shore. They arrived with the initial waves of infantry to provide supporting fire on the strong points. However, a number of them got bogged down on the beach and they added to the congestion. At high tide the beach narrowed to just thirty yards, and as more troops and equipment arrived, the bottlenecks got worse. The British Third Infantry soon slowed down their advance because they were waiting for their supporting armored units to get off the beaches. As noted by historian Carlo D'Este, "in the first two-and-a-half hours of the assault the Second British Army had managed to land over thirty thousand men, three hundred guns, and seven hundred armored vehicles."[36] As units started to stack up, the commanders decided to advance with the infantry without waiting for the armor support.

On their advance inland, they ran into some heavily fortified positions that had survived the Allied bombs. One of these fixed fortifications was named Hillman. Hillman was the location of the headquarters for the 736th Infantry Regiment. It was constructed with thick concrete and featured several protected gun emplacements, interlocking automatic weapons, and minefields surrounded by barbed wire. The troops began their attack by breaching the barbed wire with Bangalore torpedoes, but without tank support, their light weapons had little effect. Even when the tanks arrived later, it still required placing explosive charges right against the concrete to blast an entrance open. The fighting continued until late in the day. The British finally succeeded in capturing Hillman, but by then it was too late to advance further onto Caen.

Meanwhile the Germans had commenced a counterattack with the 21st Panzer Division. General Maracks, commander of the German LXXXIV Corps, now realized that Caen was the British objective. The 21st Panzer Division had been prepared to move early in the morning but was awaiting further orders. Late in the day they were finally ordered to counterattack on the western side of the city. About four in the afternoon they ran into the British force coming in from the beach in the vicinity of Bieville. After a violent clash, the Germans pulled back and both sides decided to dig in for the night. Some units of the 21st Panzer, however, did make a penetration all the way to the sea by exploiting the gap between the Canadians on Juno and the British on Sword. The German commander who spearheaded the penetration was awaiting further orders when at about nine in the evening a flight of 250 planes towing gliders flew over the beach. He believed that this was another parachute assault that would cut them off, but the gliders were actually reinforcing the British Sixth Airborne further inland. Fearing that he was about to be cut off, the German decided to withdraw his units and consolidate their defense around Caen. Despite landing a major force on D-Day, the British would be fighting for the next month to capture Caen.

Staff Ride Notebook

Q1. When the first waves of the Fourth Division arrived on Utah Beach, BG Roosevelt realized that they had landed in the wrong place. Faced with a decision to continue from there or reboard the landing craft to go to the correct location, he quickly made the decision to continue. He proved his value "leading from the front." How important is it for leaders to be at the point of action? When should they intervene to influence the action? When should they not intervene?

Q2. When the Rangers who assaulted Point du Hoc reached their objective on the top of the cliff, they found no guns emplaced. Yet they continued on with their secondary mission and subsequently found the guns. How important is the ability to persevere in the face of obstacles in accomplishing the mission? Would your team be able to continue on with their work if faced with an unexpected event? How can you prepare your team to effectively deal with the unexpected?

Q3. When the first waves of assault units landed on the beach, most of the officers and NCOs became casualties. Junior NCOs and enlisted soldiers stepped up to take charge. How ready are the junior people in your organization if they need to step up in a crisis? How can you prepare them to be able to take charge if needed?

Q4. In order to have additional firepower on the beaches, the British modified tanks known as DD tanks to "swim" to shore. They also developed "flail" tanks to breach minefields. These along with other innovations such as the Mulberry harbors were attempts to adapt to specific situations. How effective is your organization at developing innovative solutions. When the solutions don't work as planned, as in the case of the DD tanks, how are the sponsors of those ideas treated? Are they encouraged or discouraged to try again?

Field Marshal Rommel inspects beach defenses at Normandy.
Photo U.S. National Archives

CHAPTER FIVE
DETERMINED RESISTANCE:
SURVIVING THE LONGEST DAY

Since the bliztkrieg in 1940, the Germans had occupied northern France and the Low Countries. Following their lightening strike into northern Europe and after loosing the air war known as the Battle of Britain, Hitler canceled Operation Sea Lion, the German planned invasion of Great Britain. Alternatively, he ordered defenses prepared along the North Sea coast from Norway to the Atlantic coast of France. This became known as the impenetrable Atlantic Wall designed to defend the continent against an inevitable Allied landing. They knew that if the Allies were to win the war, then they would have to retake Hitler's "Fortress Europa." Although the Germans anticipated the invasion, they had over time rotated many of their best units and men from France to the Russian front as the operations in the East became protracted. Initially, the Atlantic Wall had not been hardened with mines and obstacles as had been advertised, but this didn't matter because the Allies did not have the resources to mount an attack anyway.

The Germans also had other problems besides the inadequacy of the physical fortifications. Their command structure in the west was confusing because it diffused authority among various commands. Key reserve formations were tightly controlled directly under Hitler's authority rather than the local commanders. Additionally, the naval and air forces did not report to the commander-in-chief west, but through their own separate chains of command. The Germans were further challenged by the fact that their senior officers had different views about the best strategy to defend against the invasion. This was compounded by a massive Allied deception effort, Fortitude, to confuse the Germans about the Allied intentions. All of these factors would contribute to the slow reaction by the German commanders when the invasion came on D-Day. Nevertheless, the German army had well-trained soldiers who could fight tenaciously against a numerically superior force and who had combat experience in doing so on the Russian front.

The overall German commander in the west was General Field Marshal Gerd von Rundstedt. He was sixty-nine years old, which was much older than most of the senior officers on either side. As a professional soldier, he supported the traditional German approach to defensive tactics. His plan was to repel the invasion by allowing the landings to take place and then strike with strong counterattacks as the invasion force moved inland. The German Army was very good at conducting counterattacks into the flanks of an assault to stop an aggressor in their tracks. They had perfected these tactics over the years, especially on the Russian front. By allowing the Allies to land and then move inland, the German army would also be beyond the range of the Allied naval gunfire when they made their counterattack. Since the Allies had both air superiority and strong naval forces, this would at least minimize one of the major Allied advantages in firepower over the battle space.

Von Rundstedt's command, OB West, included two army groups, a panzer army group and a parachute army. These commands included fifty-eight combat divisions, but over half were static divisions, which meant that they did not have the mobility to launch aggressive counterattacks. Only twenty-four were rated as strong enough for duty, if needed, on the Russian front.[37] Since the invasion of

Russia in 1941, many of the units in the West were either depleted for replacements or rotated from Russia to France for retrofit and rest. Other units were either newly formed or had been organized with captured equipment and "volunteers" from other fronts. They were led by German officers and noncommissioned officers, but the soldiers were unmotivated and untrained captives who often could not even speak German. Thus many of these formations were not the same high quality of men and equipment as those formations that participated in the blitzkrieg in May 1940. The most effective German units were with the panzer army, the armored forces. These were positioned in the area of the Pas de Calais where the Germans expected the attack to take place. Calais was the shortest distance across the English Channel from the British Isles, offered the most direct route to the German heartland, and had the best deep water ports. Here the panzer units were being held in reserve and under the direct control of Hitler himself even though they were assigned to OB West. Since these were their most important units, Hitler did not even trust his most senior commanders with the authority to commit them on their own initiative.

Serving under Von Rundsted was Field Marshal Erwin Rommel, the "Desert Fox." He had gained fame as the commander of the Africa Corps in North Africa. There he had skillfully held off the British Eighth Army and later the Americans with limited resources. His repeated appeals to the German high command for reinforcements of men and equipment as well as supplies of ammunition and fuel were unfilled because of commitments elsewhere, notably the Russian front. Those requests that were filled were often disrupted by the British Navy in the Mediterranean and never reached his panzer army. The campaigns in North Africa then became a war of attrition when the Allies continued to pour men and material into the theater while the Germans and their Italian allies could not replace their losses. Ultimately Rommel was relieved due to illness and to save one of Hitler's favorite generals from capture. The Africa

Corps later capitulated to the overwhelming combined British and American force.

Nevertheless, Rommel had demonstrated his remarkable skill as a field commander. This was not lost on the British, especially General Montgomery, who was the commander of the British Eighth Army for much of the time that they engaged the Africa Corps. Rommel had also previously been the commander of Hitler's personal guard before the war, where he gained the respect of Hitler himself and developed a personal relationship with the German dictator. Rommel had also earned a reputation as a daring and unusually capable officer during the First World War when he was also decorated for heroism. Later, during the blitzkrieg across France in 1940, he commanded one of the leading divisions, where he added to his reputation as a bold and decisive leader.

With Rommel's reputation for boldness and daring, Hitler assigned him first as the inspector general to assess the defenses of the Atlantic Wall. When he arrived in France he found that the defenses were totally inadequate. After issuing his report to the German High Command and having recovered from his illness, he was appointed Army Group B commander of the German armies in northern France. As army commander he reported directly to von Rundsted, but he also had the privilege of a Field Marshal to communicate directly with Hitler if he desired without going through his chain of command. With his characteristic drive and intensity, he immediately set to work fortifying the coastal defenses. His strategy was to defeat the Allies on the beaches when they came ashore. He built reinforced concrete strong points known as widerstandsnests at key avenues of approach. He planned a defense in depth with prepared positions in defensive belts arrayed five to six miles inland. At the beaches he ordered literally millions of mines installed with various steel and concrete obstacles above and below the high water line in the tidal flats. These obstacles were covered with automatic weapons and preplanned artillery fire. Additionally in the fields he placed what became known as "Rommel asparagus." These were sharp wooden stakes tipped with land mines designed to prevent glider and parachute assaults. In the first six months of his command, Rommel's soldiers laid three times the number of mines as had been emplaced during the past four years.[38] Although he worked his soldiers hard, they were also highly motivated knowing that they had one of Germany's best generals as their new commander. His mere presence was what the military calls a force multiplier because his leadership instilled confidence in the troops.

Learning from his experience in Africa, Rommel knew that if the Allies were permitted to gain a beachhead, they could immediately reinforce their initial landing with a vast amount of men and equipment. He also knew from firsthand experience the devastation that the Allied air forces would bring to the battle. If the Allies were permitted to secure a beachhead, they would eventually be successful. Given their vast resources in men and equipment, it would be too late to stop them once they were established. Rommel's plan was to disrupt and destroy the invasion at the water's edge with a forward defense of obstacles and mines. He positioned his forces near the probable landing sites and wanted to back them up with a mobile reserve that could quickly move to push them back into the sea. In his memoirs, *Normandy to the Baltic*, General Montgomery acknowledged Rommel's intent as follows: "Rommel, who was no strategist, favoured a plan for total repulse of an invader on the beaches; his theory was to aim at halting the hostile forces in the immediate beach area by concentrating a great volume of fire on the beaches themselves and to seaward of them; he advocated thickening up the beach defenses, and the positioning of all available reserves near the coast."[39] Rommel knew that if he could succeed in disrupting the attack, it would be very unlikely that the Allies would mount another assault in the near future. The task was simply too complex and resource intensive.

On the morning of June 6, the Germans were slow to react to the initial assault. There were a variety of reasons why they did not react quickly. These included the impact of the Allied deception on German intelligence estimates, the German command structure, and other chance circumstances. Although the invasion was correctly anticipated, German intelligence still thought that the main Allied effort would be made at Pas de Calais. This assumption was reinforced with the successful Allied deception effort, Fortitude. The Fortitude ruse convinced the Germans, including Hitler himself, that Normandy was merely a diversionary attack and that the main attack was to come later. The deception plan featured three possible Allied attacks: one in Norway, one in Normandy, and a probable main assault at Pas de Calais.

In order to perpetuate the ruse, the Allies had prepared dummy installations around southern England, complete with mock tank and vehicle parks. They also added phony radio traffic to confuse the Germans. Adding to the charade was Eisenhower's decision to assign General George Patton as commander of this phantom force. Since Patton had bested the Germans in North Africa and Sicily, his reputation added to the credibility of the story. The Germans never suspected that Patton's assignment was primarily due to his personal behavior in Sicily. Ike specifically warned Patton to keep a low-key profile when he reassigned him; however, his flamboyant personality would not permit him to do so. He once again made a public gaff while speaking to a women's club in England. At what was supposed to be an off-the-record speech, he inadvertently inflamed the Russians by suggesting that the British and Americans were destined to rule the post-war world. His remarks were reported in the British press and these reports added to the story line of another Allied army under Patton's command prepared to open a second front at the Pas de Calais. Consequently, the Germans kept many of their best panzer formations in the vicinity of Pas de Calais awaiting the main Allied invasion even well after D-Day. Hitler retained personal control over the authority to use these forces, and this would prove to be a disastrous decision for the field commanders. He would not use these units for many weeks after the initial invasion.

The Fortitude deception also pinned down large numbers of German forces in Norway. The British had been conducting raids on several of the fjords to perpetuate the possibility of an Allied strike in that direction. They had some success with the raids, including sinking a German warship anchored in a Norwegian harbor. The British Navy routinely patrolled the North Sea while Allied ground forces stationed in Scotland for training as part of the buildup of the invasion force also provided a potential threat to Norway. The deception became more elaborate when the British uncovered a network of German spies. By threatening them with prosecutions, they turned them into double agents. This forced them to cooperate with the Allies and report information to German intelligence that supported the deceptions. Thus, the Germans were convinced that an invasion of Norway was a real possibility, and they kept a sizable force in Scandinavia instead of redeploying them elsewhere.

In addition to the Allied deception efforts, the German command structure also contributed to the confusion on D-Day. As previously noted, the panzer reserves were placed under the personal direction of Hitler himself. They could only be released for action under his authority alone. When the Allied seaborne forces landed just after daybreak, Hitler was still asleep at his headquarters in the mountains of southern Germany. Although still not fully convinced that this was the main attack, Field Marshal von Runstedt was experienced enough to put in an immediate request to the German High Command to release the panzer units. He had already issued alert orders to some of the units and was now looking for Hitler's concurrence. To Runstedt's consternation, none of Hitler's generals would awaken him to report what was happening in Normandy. Hitler was not made aware of the situation until later in the day.

By chance, Rommel was also away from his headquarters. He was back in Germany for a short visit home and a planned meeting with Hitler himself. Convinced that the Allies would not launch their attack in the stormy weather on June 4, he decided to visit his wife for her birthday. He had also planned a meeting with Hitler to try to convince him to give control of the panzer reserves to his boss, Runstedt. Without Rommel on the scene, his Chief of Staff General Hans Speidel was slow to give orders. Rommel did not learn of the invasion until four hours after it began. It took Speidel more than eight hours to be in touch with Rommel to update him on the invasion.[40] Further complicating the German command situation, other senior officers were away from their posts attending a war game planning conference in Brittany. Then there was also a birthday party for General Eric Marcks, the LXXXIV Corps commander of the German Seventh Army. It was in his sector that the paratroopers from the American airborne units had landed. Once the paratroopers were on the ground, they immediately began to disrupt the communications networks by cutting telephone wires and blowing up key installations. After this, the Germans' ability to communicate effectively only continued to get worse. Initial reports were confused. This is common in the "fog of war" while the situation is developing. The Allies played into this confusion by also dropping "dummy" paratroopers. These were small scale replicas of paratroopers that were rigged with explosives to simulate gunfire when they hit the ground. Since they landed in darkness, it was difficult to distinguish them from real paratroopers who were engaged in firefights and only added to the general confusion. All these factors caused the Germans to experience "command paralysis" until later in the day.

The paratroopers were also assisted in their tasks by the French Resistance, known as the FFI (Free Forces of the Interior). After the Germans had defeated the French Army in 1940, hundreds of brave French men and women decided to resist the German occupation. At first only small groups and individuals took it upon themselves to strike out against their occupiers with small acts of resistance. This was very dangerous because those who were caught were tortured or executed by the Gestapo, the secret police. Nevertheless, as the occupation continued, so did the resistance. Over time the resistance groups grew with support from the British and Americans. British intelligence and the American Office of Strategic Services (OSS) provided weapons, explosives, and radios as well as small teams to help coordinate the resistance efforts. By 1943 many of the desperate groups had been organized under the banner of the FFI and they were routinely sabotaging railways, bridges, and communications. By 1944 they committed hundreds of acts of sabotage every month and were having a significant impact on the Germans' ability to transport troops and supplies. Although they were not told about the date of the invasion for security reasons, they were given various codes and targets by the Supreme Headquarters. Utilizing coded messages, including some that were broadcast by the BBC, the FFI were periodically instructed to carry out tasks. Initially, the Allied high command dismissed their efforts, but by the eve of the invasion they realized how effective the Resistance had become. Their courage and daring contributed significantly to the confusion on D-Day. Further, by sabotaging critical infrastructure, they limited the Germans' ability to shift their forces for a counterattack against the invasion forces.

Complimenting the efforts of the resistance to disrupt the Germans were the preinvasion attacks by the Allied air forces. By executing the Transportation Plan during the lead-up to D-Day, the Allied air efforts disabled key transportation hubs and facilities. This not only significantly complicated the task of the German defenders but also contributed to the efforts to neutralize the Luftwaffe fighter command. The Transportation Plan called for the destruction of the railways and bridges that would be used to transfer reserve formations to the battle area. Marauding Allied fighter bombers also attacked airfields and other military targets of opportunity.

The Allied strategic air commanders viewed this plan as a distraction from their bombing campaigns against the German heartland. They had been conducting a relentless campaign under the direction of the Combined Chiefs of Staff around the clock. The strategic bombing campaign was jointly executed by both the British Bomber Command and by the American Eighth Air Force flying missions from airfields in England. The British Bomber Command flew nighttime missions against population centers, whereas the Americans flew daylight missions against strategic industrial targets. The British area bombing was an attempt to break the will of the German people to continue supporting the war. The Americans were trying to hit war material production facilities such as the ball bearing factories in Schweinfurt and engine manufacturing facilities. Additionally the American 15th Air Force flew missions from Italy against the oil production sites to strangle the flow of petroleum products to the German Army, Navy, and Air Force. The overall objective was to reduce the ability of the Germans to replace their battlefield losses in critical weapons and supplies. The strategic bombing campaign had the added benefit of forcing the Germans to position their fighter squadrons in the homeland to protect their cities and factories. Although these bombing missions were costly to both sides, the Allies could more easily replace their losses of both planes and aircrews, whereas the Germans could not keep up.

By May 1944 the German Air Force was reduced to combat ineffectiveness. Both the Americans and British began using the P-51 Mustang, one of the best fighter planes of World War II in 1943. It had a longer range than other fighter planes and when built with the British Rolls Royce engine was one of the best performing planes in the air. The new pursuit squadrons were exceptionally effective at defeating the German fighters as they flew extended missions to protect the bombers during the first half of 1944. "On January 1, 1944, the Luftwaffe had had 2,395 single engine fighter pilots on active duty.... Over the next five months, the Luftwaffe lost no fewer than 2,262 single engine fighter pilots—equivalent to 99 percent of the number present for duty at the beginning of the year." [41] Consequently the Luftwaffe fighter forces were drastically reduced and the new replacement pilots were not trained. On D-Day the Allies would have unchallenged air superiority over the battlefield.

The strategic bomber commanders were strongly committed to the idea that they could force the Germans to surrender, which would avoid the need to invade at all. They continued to resist coming under the control of the supreme commander until Eisenhower threatened to resign, which forced Churchill and Roosevelt to pressure the Combined Chiefs of Staff to compromise. When the argument over the Allied command structure for the air forces was resolved it gave the authority for direction of the strategic bombing missions to the supreme commander. Although he had sought a direct command relationship, the ability to simply direct their missions satisfied Eisenhower. In April he directed them to implement the Transportation Plan. Although the bomber commanders still disagreed with this approach, they executed this plan perfectly. The plan not only hit targets in the Normandy area but also areas farther up the coast including Pas de Calais and Belgium so as not to give away the point of attack for the invasion. By May they focused on attacking the rail transportation systems and destroyed over five hundred locomotives. They next destroyed bridges across the rivers and canals. The combined effect reduced the rail shipments to thirty percent of the January levels.[42] Additionally, by June 7 the Free French Resistance had destroyed twenty-six rail trunk lines that could be used to bring German reinforcements into Normandy. Altogether they cut rail lines 486 times in the month of June.[43] By D-Day, the beaches were effectively isolated from the rest of France. The Germans would experience great difficulty bringing reinforcements forward, especially during daylight hours when the Allied fighters ruled the sky over Normandy.

Despite the numerous issues facing the Germans in Normandy on D-Day they were still a formidable force. Over six million mines had been sewn across the Normandy coast. Concrete reinforced resistance nests and strong points guarded probable landing sites, and inland obstacles had also been prepared on likely airborne drop zones. In the field they had almost 1.9 million troops, over 3,300 artillery pieces, and 1,343 tanks ready to do battle.[44] Unfortunately for the Germans, their naval and air forces were no match for the Allied juggernaut, but their ground forces were prepared to put up a fight. Had it not been for their own self-inflicted problems of command and the success of the Allied deception efforts, the Allies might not have succeeded. D-Day was not a preordained victory for the Allies. They had to give it everything they had and then some to overcome not just the German Army but also the vagaries of weather, difficult terrain, and the "fog of war" to achieve success.

Staff Ride Notebook

Q1. What is the concept of unity of command? How did this apply to both the German and Allied forces? Does your organization practice the principle of unity of command to ensure a team effort?

Q2. What were the Allied deception plans and how did they impact the Germans? How did the German intelligence contribute to their response to the invasion? How did Allied intelligence contribute to their invasion plans? How does your organization use market intelligence to support its operations?

Q3. The FFI (Free French of the Interior) Resistance forces complemented the Allied army, navy, and air forces as a force multiplier. Does your organization use volunteer or supplemental organizations to help achieve their goals? How can you leverage customers, suppliers, or other stakeholders to help?

Q4. The Allies targeted key infrastructure such as railways and bridges. They also isolated the battlefield and eliminated the threat of the German Air Force. How does your organization use its resources to minimize the strengths of your competition? Are their ways that you could approach the marketplace to ensure dominance?

Victorious Allied troops in Paris
Photo U.S. National Archives

CHAPTER SIX
THE BREAKOUT, THE FALAISE GAP,
AND THE LIBERATION OF PARIS

By the end of D-Day, the Allies had landed over 150,000 troops on French soil. They had succeeded in establishing a lodgment on all five invasion beaches. Yet they had failed to attain their D-Day objectives according to General Montgomery's plan. Furthermore, there were gaps between some of the beachheads, and progress inland especially from Omaha was minimal. The Rangers on Point du Hoc were isolated and fending off counterattacks. German artillery still ranged on the beaches. The "longest day" had come to an end, but the Battle for Normandy was only beginning. What follows is a summary of the rest of the campaign that ended in August almost ninety days after it had begun.

The first task for the Allies was to close the gaps between the beachheads and to penetrate further inland. Gaps existed between Sword and Juno, Gold and Omaha, and Omaha and Utah. As previously noted, the breach between Sword and Juno was actually penetrated by a German panzer unit that subsequently retreated on the evening of June 6 because they anticipated being cut off. The British and the Canadians were able to hook up the next day. Also on June 7, the British who arrived on Gold Beach were able to link up with the Americans who came in on Omaha. This link-up was originally planned for D-Day, but they were delayed by the stiff defense put up by the same German 352nd Division that had caused problems on Omaha. The link-up between Omaha and Utah would take longer. American troops advancing west from Vierville-sur-Mer took two days to relieve the Rangers at Point du Hoc, the promontory between the two American beaches. It took several more days for the airborne units to take the town of Carentan and effectively form a continuous front for the Americans. The Germans stubbornly held on to their real estate and effectively used the hedgerows to mount a defense in depth. Once the beach link-ups were made, the Allies continued the drive inland to gain maneuver room and safe areas for supply dumps.

The drive inland from the beaches was a slow tough slog. The natural obstacles favored the defense. The hedgerows of the "bocage" countryside in Normandy provided natural defensive positions for the Germans. Additionally, the German units relied on automatic weapons that were more effective than the comparable U.S. weapons. In particular, German units had better quality machine guns, model MG-42, which had a higher rate of fire. They could be placed in the hedgerows so that a few machine gun crews could hold up a much larger force by firing from mutually supporting positions. They learned how to control the fields with interlocking fire from firing positions contained within the hedgerow. From there they could retreat if necessary. The Americans were forced to assault these positions while exposing themselves in the open to gain the few hundred yards to the next hedgerow. If the Germans were not killed or wounded in the assault, they simply fell back to the next hedgerow to repeat the process all over again. Meanwhile the Americans continued to take casualties, many of whom were now replacement troops who had not received the benefit of the intensive training provided to the assault units prior to D-Day. Furthermore, many of the experienced leaders had also become casualties. There was no time for on-the-job training for either the new soldiers or junior leaders joining the units that were in contact with the enemy.

Nevertheless, the Allies continued to punch away as the German resistance stiffened. Following the initial confusion on D-Day, the Germans regrouped and fought tenaciously. As noted by the respected military historian Max Hastings in his seminal book on the battle for Normandy, *Overlord*, "the inescapable reality of the battle for Normandy was that when Allied troops met Germans on anything like equal terms, the Germans almost always prevailed." [45] Their effective resistance was also remarkable since the Allies had complete air superiority and, while they were still within range of the fleet, were able to rely on accurate naval gunfire support. As a testament to the tenacity of the Allied armies, they were able to expand the lodgment so that by June 12 they had consolidated all the beachheads into a single front that extended inland from ten to thirty kilometers from the beaches. They also installed artificial harbors at both Omaha and Gold beaches. These innovative facilities ensured that they could continue to bring additional reinforcements and supplies. By D-Day+6, over 325,000 troops were ashore and by D-Day+12, General Montgomery was planning additional offensive operations to break the German resistance.

In the American sector, Major General Joe Collin's VII Corps was advancing to cut off the Cotentin Peninsula and attack the deep water Port of Cherbourg on the end of the peninsula. On June 15 they attacked across the neck of the peninsula and by June 18 had isolated the German garrison in Cherbourg. On June 22 he attacked north with three divisions to secure the port and by June 26 had accepted the surrender of the German commander. With their stubborn resistance, they had bought some time for German demolition teams to do some significant damage to the facilities just before they surrendered. Nevertheless, the Allies finally had a deep water port. This was now even more important because a severe storm had caused significant damage to the artificial harbors the week before.

Meanwhile, the American V Corps under Major General Leonard T. Gerow was attacking south with the objective of securing the town of St. Lo. This was a strategically important town because it was another transportation center. The slugfest in the "bocage" continued as more reinforcements arrived. Joining the V Corp in the push south was the VIII Corps and the XIX Corps. St. Lo would finally fall into American hands when the 29th Division, which had been the first to arrive at Omaha Beach, finally entered the city on July 18 just as the remaining Germans were withdrawing. After capturing St. Lo, the 29th would be rotated back to a rest area having been in continuous combat since they landed on Omaha Beach on D-Day.

While the Americans were making steady progress in the western end of the battle zone, the British were facing stiff resistance from several German panzer divisions. Rommel had rejoined the battle as the commander on D-Day+1 after returning from his ill-fated visit to Germany just before the invasion was launched. Hitler still refused to release panzer units from the Pas de Calais area partly because of the success of Operation Fortitude. The Allied deception plan still was working to convince him that the main attack would occur at Calais. Meanwhile, Rommel, who was now back in Normandy, committed the panzer units that he had under his control for an immediate counterattack. Attacking in the British zone, these German units fought tenaciously and denied the British and Canadians from reaching their D-Day objectives of Caen and Carpiquet, respectively. Consequently, Montgomery planned another attack. He chose to attack first on his western flank toward Villers Bocage on June 12 with the British XXX Corps. Participating in the assault was his famed Seventh Armored Division. The Seventh Armored Division had been with him in the desert in North Africa when he had previously successfully fought with Rommel. After several days of fierce combat, the attack stalled when the British were counterattacked by German panzers including the huge Tiger tanks. With this attack stalled, Montgomery planned his next operation, code named Epsom. The objective was to concentrate a penetrating attack just west of Caen on June 26. This attack would be spearheaded this time by the British VIII Corps. It was planned with an advance air bombardment and naval gun fire support, but due to bad weather the attack was postponed. When it was finally launched, it quickly stalled in the face of determined German resistance. Consequently, Montgomery planned to launch his third operation, Charnwood. With massive air support he planned to take Caen with several Corps attacking together. On July 9, British forces secured the northern part of the city after four weeks of fighting from when they landed. Montgomery would later claim after the war that although these attacks did not achieve all of their objectives, they had the effect of containing the bulk of the German armored forces in the British sector so that the Americans could plan a breakout in the West.

Meanwhile, on July 3, Hitler had replaced his commander-in-chief west. Field Marshal von Runstedt was relieved by Field Marshal Hans Gunther von Kluge. Since he had been forewarned by Hitler and the German general staff, von Kluge arrived in Normandy with the preconceived notion that von Runstedt and Rommel were projecting an attitude of defeatism through their repeated requests for reinforcements. Hitler had actually met with von Runstedt and Rommel on two separate occasions during June to hear them out. Each time they met and also in their communications to the Fuhrer Headquarters they emphasized the problems they were facing: enemy air superiority, the Allies' powerful naval gunfire support, the vast amount of war material and reinforcements flowing into the beachhead, and the effectiveness of the Allied airborne forces.[46] Hitler interpreted these comments as defeatism rather than realistic assessments. To his credit, von Kluge made frontline inspections upon his arrival in France. He wanted to see for himself the situation they actually faced. He later agreed with Rommel that the German Army was being hard pressed and sustaining significant casualties with only minimal replacements. Given these continued losses, the odds were not in favor of a German victory. Faced with this reality, von Kluge did not consider this defeatism. His conclusion was similar to Rommel's, and he thought that they should begin a tactical withdrawal to consolidate their lines and preserve their remaining forces. Then on July 17 Rommel was severely injured when his staff car was strafed by an RAF fighter plane. This was a major setback for the Germans as they lost one of their most effective commanders. Von Kluge was now not only CIC West but also the temporary army group commander for Army Group B.

While the fighting raged simultaneously in Normandy, Italy, and on the Russian front, some disaffected Germans plotted to overthrow Hitler. They desired to seek a truce with the Allies before their country was destroyed. Among the plotters was Colonel Count von Stauffenberg, who was a staff officer and had access to Hitler's bunker. On July 20 there was an abortive attempt to assassinate Hitler when von Stauffenberg placed a bomb in the command bunker in East Prussia. The bomb was hidden in a briefcase that he placed beneath Hitler's map table at a conference with Hitler. It was moved by another one of the staff officers by chance and placed behind one of the heavy legs of the table. When the bomb exploded, this shielded Hitler from serious injury. Rommel was later implicated in the bomb plot. Although he might have been sympathetic to ending the war on favorable terms, he was not one of the plotters. Nevertheless, while he was recovering from his war wound, he was forced to commit suicide by the German High Command as retribution for his alleged involvement in the plot. The Reich's most famous Field Marshal chose suicide to protect his family from further consequences and for his cooperation he was given a hero's funeral. While the investigations continued to route out other plotters, Hitler had quickly recovered from relatively minor injuries. Ignoring the realities of the present German position in Normandy, he ordered Von Kluge to counterattack and also not yield any more ground in the West. This "no retreat" communiqué was Hitler's usual order to his generals in the field.

If Hitler had not issued his attack order, von Kluge and the senior German commanders in the field would have likely begun to retreat and shorten their lines. As a military expedient, this would have been an effort to consolidate their remaining units while preventing a possible encirclement by the Allies. However, due to the recent attempt on Hitler's life and the subsequent investigations that were implicating hundreds of officers and other officials in the plot, von Kluge complied with the order against his better judgment. He did not want to risk raising suspicion that he was somehow involved in the plot. Without consideration for the tactical realities on the ground, the German commanders began planning for the attack as directed.

Toward the end of July, two new Allied attacks were planned, one in the British zone named Operation Goodwood and one in the American zone named Operation Cobra. Both attacks were supported with massive air and artillery bombardments. This was now the typical Allied tactic given their overwhelming firepower and air superiority. The objective for Goodwood was to capture the southern part of Caen and the surrounding environs so that the British and Canadians could get into the open country in the direction of Falaise. The objective of Cobra was to punch through the German defensive line in the western part of Normandy and open the door for the American armored forces. The Americans planned to activate the U.S. Third Army under General Patton. They felt that he could break out into the open country beyond the hedgerows with tanks. General Bradley wanted to use the mobility of the American armored and mechanized formations to attack the German flanks and rear. Both of these attacks were planned for late July and as such they were intended to be mutually supporting.

Goodwood would go first. The British Second Army under Lt. General Miles Dempsey massed over 2,500 tanks for the assault to the east and southeast of Caen. On the morning of July 18 a series of massive bombing raids on the German positions was the first phase of softening up the defenses. The air raids by both the British Bomber Command and the U.S. Army Air Forces were followed by a tremendous artillery and naval gunfire bombardment. Following the bombardments, three British armored divisions and several independent brigades began to break though the German defensive lines. The German frontline defenders conducted a fighting withdrawal to the south while von Kluge sent available reinforcements to the battle. Soon the British armor had outrun their supporting infantry. This left them vulnerable to German antitank weapons, including the extremely effective German "88s." These antiaircraft guns were devastating when used in an antitank mode. The British then began to sustain serious tank losses and the attack finally ran out of steam several days after it had begun. The British were now about ten kilometers south of Caen, but by July 26 they halted any further advance south for the time being.

Meanwhile, General Bradley attempted to kick off Operation Cobra on July 24. Again the plan called for a massive bombardment of the German frontline positions by the Allied air forces. At the last minute, the attack was postponed for twenty-four hours due to weather, but the lead aircraft did not get the word. Unfortunately they released their bombs, and some fell short into the American lines causing friendly causalities. The attack was officially launched again the next day with an unfortunate repetition of the tragic bombing incidents resulting in more American casualties. Despite their repeated use in a ground support role, the strategic bombers were not well-suited for close support missions.

After regrouping from their misfortune, the U.S. VII Corps mounted its attack into the breach. There they met initial determined German resistance despite the massive aerial bombardment. The VII Corps was joined the next day by VIII Corps and together they finally breached the German defenses with their armored units. On August 1 Bradley activated the Third Army. General Patton had quietly been brought to Normandy. The Germans still thought he commanded the fictitious First Army Group in England and was poised to strike at the Pas de Calais. Bradley tasked Patton with leading the breakout into southern Normandy and Brittany and thus gave him the opportunity to get back into the fight. Patton wasted no time. He brilliantly led the exploitation and kept the pressure on the German armies. In fact, his lead elements outran their communications. At times, their locations were unknown to Third Army as they made their audacious pursuit.[47]

Complying with the Hitler's directive and as directed by von Kluge, the German Seventh Army attacked at Mortain in early August 1944. This was a last ditch attempt to retake the Contentin peninsula and cut off the Americans while they were advancing further south. Unlike the American attacks, the German attack was not preceded with an artillery preparation in an attempt to gain surprise. However, the Allies had been tipped off to this pending attack through the ULTRA intercepts of German communications. The ULTRA program was a top secret program run by British intelligence; they had broken the German communications codes and listened in on their radio messages. This was so secret that its existence was not revealed until almost thirty years after the war. With some advance warning and courageous determination by the Americans, who in some cases were surrounded, the German attack was defeated.

When the Germans attacked west at Mortain, it created an opportunity to encircle the German Army and trap them in a battle of annihilation. General Bradley immediately recognized this opportunity. Bradley now commanded the 12th Army group consisting of both the First and Third U.S. Armies. He proceeded to coordinate with General Montgomery, who was still the overall land forces commander as well as commander of the British 21st Army Group. With the success of Operation Cobra and the breakout of the Third Army under Lt. General Patton, Bradley recognized that by ordering the First and Third Armies to attack northeast he could cut off the Germans' line of retreat. While the British advanced south from Caen in the direction of Falaise they could close the noose. This would prevent the Germans from escaping east across the Seine river to safety. Bradley implored Montgomery to have the British continue their drive from their position just south of Caen to link up with the Americans. With Montgomery's agreement, on August 8 Bradley directed the First Army led by Lt. General Courtney Hodges to advance in the direction of Flers. Meanwhile Patton's Third Army would circle north to Argentan.

On August 10, Patton's XV Corps led by Major General Wade Haislip attacked toward Argentan with two armored divisions in columns abreast. He placed the newly arrived French Second Armored on the left and the American Fifth Armored to the east on the right. The plan called for a rapid advance northward using the mobility of the armored forces and bypassing if necessary any pockets of German resistance so that they could rapidly reach the objective. Each of the armored forces was followed by an infantry division, the U.S. 90th and the U.S. 79th, respectively, who would clean up any remaining resistance along the axis of advance. In the face of the strong Allied armored advance the German units were retreating north anyway. Most of them were now depleted from the weeks of heavy fighting without adequate replacements or logistical support. The U.S. infantry units, which were less mobile than the armored divisions, followed in their wake as fast as they could but were quickly outpaced by the advancing tank units. By August 13 the XV Corps of the Third Army had reached Argentan but was ordered to halt their advance by General Bradley. He wanted to avoid running into the Canadians and British as they advanced south through Falaise.

Meanwhile, the U.S. First Army was advancing northwest from just south of Mortain where they had contained what was the Germans' last gasp offensive of the campaign. The First Army advance tightened the noose further by compressing the pocket that contained the remaining German forces that were now severely depleted. The First Army advance would also protect the flank of Third Army. This left the First Army advancing while the Third Army halted at Argentan. Patton wanted to continue to attack anywhere he could find Germans. He convinced Bradley to allow him to use the remainder of his army to attack east. This was unfortunate in that the Canadians had run into some tough resistance in front of Falaise and perhaps the Americans should have continued to advance north from Argentan. The Canadians renewed their attack on August 14, and finally captured Falaise on August 16. Now only fifteen miles separated the Canadians from the American XV Corps.

On August 17 Montgomery ordered the Canadians to once again attempt to close the gap. This time they were joined in the effort by elements of the First Polish Armored Division. However, by then the Germans had realized that their situation was no longer tenable. The German commander, von Kluge, had finally obtained Hitler's permission to issue a retreat order in an attempt to save what was left of their army. As the Germans retreated thru the gap, Allied aircraft and artillery units began to maul those fleeing east. When they came under attack, most units abandoned their equipment. The massive bombardments took their toll. Those who did not surrender were most likely to become casualties. Despite their reputation for mobile warfare, the Germans used horses to haul their weapons, particularly artillery. Many of these horses were also killed which added to the carnage. Now on orders from Montgomery, the Americans resumed their advance north from Argentan. On August 19 the Allies linked up at Chambois about seven miles north of Argentan and the gap was finally closed. Any Germans who remained in the Falaise pocket were trapped. Amazingly, the German Fifth Panzer Army and the Seventh Army had barely avoided total annihilation. Yet, they had abandoned almost all their heavy weapons and sustained tremendous losses. Actual loss estimates vary, but during the course of the campaign, over 200,000 German soldiers were killed or wounded while another 200,000 were taken prisoner. Of those taken prisoner, 135,000 surrendered between July 25 and August 25.[48]

The Germans who had escaped retreated across the Seine and were heading back toward Germany. The Allies mopped up remaining resistance and moved on to take Paris. Paris had been declared an open city by the German commander to avoid unnecessary destruction. On August 25 the Allies entered Paris led by the French Second Armored Division and the American Fourth Infantry Division. The Battle of Normandy was officially over.

Staff Ride Notebook

Q1. After the Allies had consolidated their beachhead in Normandy, they were still short of many of their D-Day objectives, including capturing the city of Caen. Yet they persisted in their operations until they finally achieved a breakout in the west following COBRA. Through their resilience and persistence they finally achieved their objectives. Do you remember a situation that you have personally experienced, whether in business or your personal life, where resilience and persistence made a difference in the outcome?

Q2. The Germans were handicapped by the insistence of the highest levels of their command structure to pursue strategies and tactics that were counter intuitive to the best judgments of their commanders in the field: Rommel, von Runstedt, and von Kluge. When is it appropriate for the most senior leaders in any organization to override their field commanders? On what basis should such judgments be made? How should senior leaders react when they are directed to execute strategies that they don't support? What methods should senior leaders use to ensure that they are effectively informing the most senior leaders who are removed from the day-to-day events?

Q3. The closing of the Falaise gap completed the Battle of Normandy. Yet the decision by Bradley to halt Patton's army at Argentan remains a controversy to this day because it allowed some of the Germans to escape before the gap was closed. Arguments favoring his decision include the avoidance of friendly fire casualties as the two Allied forces advanced on each other and the fact that he had already stretched Patton's forces to get there. Yet many historians believe that had the gap been closed sooner, either by a more aggressive Canadian and British drive south or by allowing Patton to drive further north, the result would have been the complete annihilation of the German army in Normandy. Although it is easy to second guess this decision after the fact, it also reflects the tension between the British and American senior commanders to fully cooperate. Montgomery led Bradley and Patton to believe that he could more easily advance south. This did not happen quickly. Bradley could have pressed Montgomery for permission to continue Patton's attack north, but their egos got in the way. How can leaders avoid suboptimal performance by competing elements within their organizations?

PART TWO
VICTORY PRINCIPLES

General Eisenhower presents awards to soldiers of the US First
Infantry Division, "The Big Red One," who distinguished
themselves during the Omaha Beach Assault on D-Day
Photo U.S. National Archives

The story of D-Day is one of the most interesting stories of World War II. It was the decisive battle in the European theater that made the Allied victory over the German war machine possible. As a massive amphibious invasion, it was also a highly complex operation both in size and scope. Amphibious operations are extremely risky military operations to mount until the assault is consolidated in a secure beachhead. The assault forces landing on the beach are in danger of being thrown back into the sea when they are the weakest and least able to exploit their combat power.

Operation Overlord was no exception. Looking back from the vantage point of over sixty years, one easily can misunderstand the risks involved and the challenges faced by the Allies against a determined enemy. Victory was not guaranteed at the time, and even the supreme commander, above all, understood the risks. He penned a message in advance to be released to the press in the event that the Allied landings were unsuccessful. In his prepared message he offered to take full responsibility if the Allied invasion had failed.

The cross-channel attack was literally years in the making before it evolved into Operation Overlord. It required the development of a strategic option of a "second front" among the major Allied powers: America, Britain, and Russia. It also involved coordination with Canada and the French, Dutch, and Polish governments-in-exile. The Allies needed to form a joint and combined headquarters under a supreme commander to plan and execute the operation. They had to coordinate the activities of not only the several nations but also the army, navy, and air force that each of them brought to the fight. Detailed planning was required to maximize the use of the ground, air, and naval forces from the several nations into a cohesive force to break through the formidable German defenses.

The assault forces needed to be organized, equipped, trained, and marshaled so that they could be delivered under fire on a heavily defended shore. Once they landed on the beaches, the successful execution of the plans required unbelievable courage under hostile fire with strong leadership at every level of the command. Only the combined efforts of literally hundreds of thousands of individuals working together could break through the Atlantic Wall and defeat the formidable foe that fought from prepared defenses.

So what were the keys to their victory? What made this a successful operation? What are some of the key lessons that their stories illustrate? What lessons can be learned that are useful even today?

By examining the events of June 1944 in Normandy one can see examples of leadership in action. There are examples of both success and failure. Each unit has its own story about the part that they played in the overall plan. Further, each soldier, sailor, and airman had his unique perspective. Senior leaders obviously had a critical role in planning and preparing the units that participated. Their perspectives were from the highest levels of government and military organizations. However, the successful execution of the plan was less dependent on generals and admirals and more so on the actions of thousands of lower ranking individuals down to the privates, sergeants, and lieutenants. They were the ones who led the charge up the beaches or jumped into the fight from perfectly good airplanes. It was their initiative, tenacity, and courage under fire that made the difference.

I use the acronym VICTORY to categorize some of these lessons. Although I have labeled these the "Victory Principles," they are not a magic formula for success. They are rather a simple framework to organize some lessons. Each of the letters represents a key concept that leaders used to bring them success in 1944. I have selected stories from Operation Overlord that illustrate how they used each of these principles. Although these concepts are illustrated in the context of the D-Day story, they are just as applicable today as they were then.

Much has changed since D-Day with the introduction of our modern technologies such as computers, the Internet, jet planes, and cell phones. Regardless, the one thing that has remained more or less constant for thousands of years is human nature. An awareness of human nature is the basis on which all good leadership principles depend.

What makes these principles important is that they transcend time and place. Leaders use them to successfully lead their people. They were just as relevant when Alexander and Hannibal were leading their armies in ancient times as when Eisenhower was preparing to launch D-Day. Although you and I are not likely to lead an operation of the magnitude of Operation Overlord, the success principles are applicable for any leader who wants to bring success to his or her team or organization.

Also included are some brief examples from the "business battlefield" that show how these principles are used in commercial and nonprofit enterprises. There are almost an infinite number of examples to choose from, but I have picked some that I believe best illustrate the application of the principle in either a business, nonprofit, or government agency setting. I also address how you can use many of these principles in your personal life as well, your personal quest. Finally you will also note that these principles tend to be mutually supporting. For example, when you look at applying the principles of innovation and learning they may actually be applied to draw lessons from adverse circumstances. Often the best lessons learned are the result of a setback; to overcome the adversity, you need to apply the principle of resiliency. As you review these examples, perhaps consider how they are often mutually supporting. So let's begin with the first principle, vision.

CHAPTER SEVEN
VISION

A LEADER MUST PROVIDE A COMPELLING VISION FOR
HIS OR HER ORGANIZATION THAT DEFINES FUTURE
SUCCESS AND TRANSLATES INTO A PLAN OF ACTION.

One of the most important tasks for organizational leaders is to set forth a compelling vision of where they intend to lead their organization. This is true regardless of the size of the organization. Whether it is leading a country, an army, or a rifle platoon in combat, successful leaders set forth a vision of their plan for the future. This principle of vision applies to commercial enterprises, charitable organizations, and any other group that has a common purpose. The effective leader must tap into the group's common cause and inspire people with a vision of future success. It is a natural human instinct to want to be on a winning team. Winning begins with the vision of how that is to be accomplished so that everyone on the team can pull in the same direction.

It has been said that a victorious commander fights two battles: The first is envisioned in his mind before engaging the enemy; the second is the actual battle itself. The vision of how the battle will be won is the first key to victory. It is important to note that the primary responsibility for defining vision is with the organizational leader, usually the one who finds himself or herself in a formal role of leadership: the unit commander, the company president, the CEO, or the executive director of a nonprofit.

However, the successful leaders do not create the vision by themselves. Successful leaders involve their people in the process. In the military, successful commanders will often enlist their subordinates in a council of war or in the process of formal staff planning. The important task of defining the vision cannot be accomplished in a vacuum— when it is done this way, it is usually not successful. So how do those who find themselves in positions of organizational leadership leverage other leaders within their team? How do leaders craft their vision?

First, they are good at listening and observing. They listen to what others on the team are thinking. They carefully observe what is happening in the context of their environment. They look both internally and externally to better understand the context and the challenges. In the case of the military, commanders will make inspections to their units to assess training, the status of equipment, and the morale of the troops. Inspections along with reports from their subordinate commanders and staff will give them an internal view of their team and its capabilities. Commanders will also rely on military intelligence and support from outside agencies to get information about their external environment. This information will help them to understand factors such as the terrain, weather, and capabilities of the opposing forces they will engage. In the U.S. Army there is a concept called the estimate of the situation that would be used and which includes an analysis of the mission, enemy, terrain, troops available, and time (METT-T), In commercial environments, leaders will seek out market intelligence about their competition, alternative products, and their customers. The better they know their competition and the "terrain," the better chance they have of creating a compelling vision for their own organization.

Next, leaders involve their people. A good leader will engage his or her people in the development of the vision, which helps instill organizational "buy-in." Usually it is not possible to have everyone participate in this process unless it is a small organization. Smart leaders will identify a critical few who can help them craft the vision and set the strategic direction. Among the "critical few" participants in this process may be individual contributors as well as those charged with a formal position of leadership. In this context, leadership is less about a formal organizational position and more about influence, whether formal or informal. It is important that these people not only help craft the vision, but also sell it to the rest of the people on the team when the time comes to muster support.

Once again, in the context of a military operation, this will involve the commander's staff and subordinate commanders. The commander will engage the staff by sharing his or her intent and objectives while considering various courses of action. Subordinate commanders will provide input directly to the commander or through their own staff officers who coordinate with the senior headquarters staff in their functional areas of expertise. After receiving the staff analysis, the commander will decide on the course of action to accomplish the mission. In the context of a nonmilitary organization, the process of choosing a course of action and strategic direction may be more democratic; however, all successful organizations will decide on a clear view of their future direction and communicate it to their employees, stakeholders, and customers.

With a view of the future and the strategic direction, the next logical step is to plan the details—a plan of action. You must be able to answer the question "How do we get from here to there?" Here again, smart leaders involve their people in the process. They may involve additional people who were not part of the original vision group but who are chosen for their planning expertise or special knowledge. Often those with functional responsibilities understand the requirements and possible solutions best. Enlisting experts on your team to help plan the details will make the strongest possible plan to make the vision come true. As with the initial visioning process, the inclusion of more people in planning will create more organizational momentum to execute the plan. Involving experts will also avoid mistakes that would be obvious to those who have more detailed knowledge of the operating environment and the capabilities of the team. Finally, involving experts on the team provides a level of confidence with others in the quality of the plan and the underlying strategies.

Once a plan is crafted, it is the responsibility of the leader to communicate with the team. Strong leaders will make sure that everyone understands the plan, their role within the plan, and what they need to do to make the vision come to reality. Success is only possible when everyone on the team understands the mission, the objectives, and the concept of the operation. Leaders ensure that everyone is onboard by briefing the plan to the team. It is human nature for people to want to be included and to do the right thing; however, they can only play their part in executing the plan if they fully understand their role. People on a team also tend to perform at a higher level when they not only understand their own responsibilities but also those of the others on the team. Depending on the circumstances, they may not need all of the details that their teammates require for their specific role, but it is extremely useful for everyone to understand the overall organizational goals and the vision of how those are to be achieved together. This is how leaders harness the power of a compelling vision for their organization. It gets everyone pulling in the same direction and toward common goals. It is how they accomplish their mission.

Examples from Operation Overlord

How is the first VICTORY principle, vision, illustrated in the context of Operation Overlord? There are many ways in which the clear and compelling vision contributed to the success of this operation. From many possibilities, I have selected several good examples that demonstrate this principle. The first one is the overall development of the war strategy by the Allied political leaders. Their vision set the stage. It provided the context for the planning to put the forces and resources in place to make success possible in the first place. The strategic vision provided the framework for the commanders to envision plans for the invasion and subsequent operations. It also allowed subordinates to develop their own vision of individual unit actions as part of the overall strategy. Let's begin with the overall strategic vision.

During World War II, the Allied political leaders periodically met to formally discuss their strategic vision. Sometimes it was simply Roosevelt and Churchill, and sometimes they met with their Russian counterpart, Stalin. Occasionally, they would even invite other Allied leaders to join them. It was at such conferences that the overall strategies for the conduct of the Allied war effort were decided. The Allied political leaders usually included their senior uniformed military officers and trusted civilian advisors at these meetings. For the British and the Americans, their senior level military leaders were known as the Combined Chiefs of Staff. The American Chiefs of Staff were led by General George Marshall, whereas the British Chiefs were led by Field Marshall Alan Brooke. Often the Chiefs met separately during the course of the conferences and subsequently made their recommendations to the political leaders. Sometimes they all met together depending on the topic.

There were often instances where the chiefs could not agree on the appropriate course of action. It was then the responsibility of the political leaders to make the final determination. An example of this type of decision is the "Germany first" strategy that was agreed upon between Roosevelt and Churchill at the Arcadia Conference. Simply put, the Allied leaders decided to make the primary effort to defeat Germany first while making their best efforts in the Pacific to contain Japan. Although the Allies would attempt to block further Japanese aggression and regain the strategic initiative in the Far East, their priority was to avoid detraction from their main effort in Europe. This was decided even though the United States had been the victim of a surprise attack in the Pacific by the Japanese Navy at Pearl Harbor. Following the unprovoked Hawaiian attack, American public opinion was strongly against Japan. Sentiments for a counterstroke in the Pacific ran high with the American public. Thus the vision of the "Germany first" strategy was a bold one for the American president.

From the very beginning of the U.S. involvement in the war, General Marshall was an advocate for an early strike into the heartland of Germany. His British counterparts argued for a more measured approach recognizing both the limited forces available at the time and the untested American combat units. What ultimately resulted was the North African invasion, Operation Torch. Due to the differences of opinion within the staffs, the ultimate decision was made by President Roosevelt and Prime Minister Churchill.

This example illustrates how Roosevelt and Churchill as the political leaders were ultimately responsible for defining the vision for prosecuting the war effort. Although the vision was theirs to decide, they relied heavily on their uniformed military leaders and civilian advisors to help define the direction. Once decided, then many more people—civilian and military—began to craft the detailed plans required to successfully execute the vision. It not only included specific military plans but also mobilizing the industrial base in the United States to provide the equipment and the logistical support required to succeed.

It also illustrates how involving experts from the entire team can often result in a better vision. Specifically, had the Americans been left to decide on the vision by themselves, they would not have decided on an invasion of North Africa as their first strike. Perhaps they might have even decided to put "Japan first." However, the British were correct in their assessment of the military preparedness of the Allies to mount a cross-channel attack at this point in the war. Their influence enabled Roosevelt and Churchill to make a sound decision after listening to both sides of the argument. The cross-channel attack was postponed, and the invasion of North Africa was conceived.

Another example of setting the strategic vision was at the Tehran Conference. This was when the "big three" political leaders met in late 1943 and decided to open up a second front in Western Europe. This time, the Americans had vigorous support from the Russians to advocate the direct approach by invading Nazi-occupied France. They argued that the quickest way to victory was to force the German army to fight in both the east and west simultaneously. Throughout most of the conference, the British still argued for a more indirect approach through the Balkans. Churchill and his chiefs were influenced by the memories of their horrendous losses during the stalemates while waging the trench warfare of World War I. They were also concerned about the abilities of the combined Allied forces to successfully conduct a difficult and complex amphibious operation. Churchill vividly remembered the failed Allied landings from the First World War at Gallipoli when he was the First Lord of the Admiralty. The losses from this unsuccessful amphibious assault were horrendous. Realizing that they were not going to convince their partners otherwise, Churchill agreed to the vision that enabled Operation Overlord. Once the political leaders had set the strategic direction for the war effort, they left almost all of the details of the invasion plan to their subordinates, but it was now possible for all the Allies to move ahead with a unified vision.

Planning for the invasion itself is yet another example of leaders developing a vision. In this case it was the Allied commanders' vision for conducting the cross-channel attack. In order to begin planning the invasion, the Combined Chiefs appointed a staff under General Morgan to flesh out the details. They initially conceived a plan with a three-division assault on a narrow front supported by limited airborne forces. They based this plan on the available resources and best available intelligence at the time.

When he was appointed as supreme commander, General Eisenhower quickly determined that three divisions would not be powerful enough to crack through the Atlantic Wall. His experience in North Africa and Sicily helped him envision what would be required. After consulting with General Montgomery, they together developed a new vision for a stronger invasion force. Their new vision called for a five-division assault over a fifty-mile wide stretch of coastline supported by three airborne divisions. Their new vision called for a simultaneous attack in force across a broad front so that the Germans would not be able to concentrate their reserve panzer forces for a counterattack.

Once they outlined the direction, otherwise known in the military planning process as the "commander's intent," their staffs then went about coordinating the details. General Eisenhower then arranged for their plan to be briefed to all the major subordinate ground, naval, and air commanders at General Montgomery's headquarters at the St. Paul's school in London on April 7, 1944. Also in attendance at the briefing were the Prime Minister and the King of England. Each of the prime commanders for the ground, naval, and air forces briefed their part of the plan.

At the conclusion of the briefing, General Eisenhower invited questions and feedback. He encouraged opposing views to be brought forward because he knew that debate and loyal opposition from his staff would result in a stronger plan. Some of the feedback he received up until the eve of the invasion questioned the wisdom of the airborne operations. The air commander Leigh-Mallory and some others feared they would sustain great numbers of casualties among the airborne and glider units. He based his opinion on the significant problems with similar operations in North Africa and Sicily. Yet Generals Montgomery and Bradley made their case for using the airborne units to seize key terrain and protect the beach assaults. After considering all their input, Eisenhower decided to proceed with the operations as originally planned. The final plan for the Operation Overlord vision was set by the supreme commander.

The principle of vision can also be found in the combat actions at lower levels of command. One example is the assault on Pegasus Bridge. This mission was assigned to Major John Howard's British airborne glider force. The bridge was critical for controlling movement of troops over the Orne River and Caen Canal behind Sword Beach in the British sector. The British needed the bridge to advance on the city of Caen, which Montgomery had planned as his D-Day objective.

Also, by controlling this bridge, the British could prevent a German counterattack against the Allied left flank.

When the mission was assigned, Major Howard began to plan his vision of the operation. He envisioned a rapid and violent assault using the element of surprise. A glider force landing at night offered the possibility of a silent approach to deliver the assault force near the objective. His intent was to surprise the German sentries guarding the bridge and quickly overwhelm them before they could react. Howard translated his vision into a plan that was practiced by 180-man strong force that would carry it out. The entire team was briefed and the plan was rehearsed. It is a good example of how everyone on the team was aware of the mission, the objective, and the overall concept of the operation.

As the D-Day invasion began, Howard's force was among the first ones to land in occupied France. Although part of the force did not land near the objective as planned, the remainder quickly accomplished their mission and secured the bridge. They then prepared to defend it until a relief force could reach them from the beach. The vision in the form of the commander's intent was flawlessly executed despite problems along the way. It clearly illustrates how a team can succeed even when faced with obstacles if everyone knows what is expected of them.

There are numerous other examples of the principle of vision applied to other actions during the invasion. Every part of the plan called for a clear vision on how specific units would accomplish their mission. Whether it was the Rangers at Point du Hoc, the navy task forces providing preassault bombardments, or the air corps transport pilots delivering the paratroops, each team had to understand their mission and how they would succeed. They needed a clear picture of what needed to be done and had to plan accordingly.

Examples from the Business Battlefield

The examples above are all based on military operations, but a vision is no less important for other organizations in different fields of endeavor. People must be inspired by the vision if the leader expects them to commit to the plan. The team should be engaged in defining the vision and creating the plan when possible. In this way, everyone on the team knows what to do and how they can be successful. That's the power of a compelling vision.

Whether you are a leader of a large company, a small business, or simply a team of volunteers for a nonprofit, you must have a compelling vision of the future. You can probably think of hundreds of companies or organizations that have been successful as a result of a compelling vision. Many large businesses today have grown because the founders at one time articulated a vision of the future that employees, investors, and customers believed. This is also true of nonprofit organizations too. Let's take a look at some brief examples.

Although the automobile industry has fallen on very tough times recently as the price of oil has gone up and the economy has slowed, the major auto manufacturers are good examples of how a compelling vision was important to the growth of those companies when they were founded at the beginning of the twentieth century. For example, Ford Motor Company in its early years grew rapidly as a result of the vision of Henry Ford. His vision outlined how he intended to make automobiles affordable for the common man by using assembly lines with workers who specialized in assembling various components of the Model T. From the time it was introduced in 1908 until the last one rolled off the assembly line, more than 15 million Model T Fords were sold. Mr. Ford also included paying his workers a livable wage as an incentive for them to help him bring his vision to life. His persistence and foresightedness enabled Ford Motor Company to grow rapidly in the early days of the automobile industry as Ford produced his cars for the mass market.

Meanwhile, Ford's competitors at General Motors began to grow their company by having an organizational and marketing vision. After several years of political infighting, Alfred Solan eventually led the way for GM's growth. He offered a vision of a company that combined the power of multiple brands each targeted at different markets. He combined this marketing concept with his organizational structure. His vision for GM was one where the manufacturing platforms and the parts suppliers were all owned by the same company creating synergy among the group. This vision of a conglomerate of different automobile brands with the efficiency of mass purchasing power led General Motors to become a manufacturing powerhouse and one of the most trusted global brands of the twentieth century.

Coincidently, both Ford and General Motors contributed to the World War II war effort as part of the arsenal of democracy. They retooled their assembly plants and produced thousands of trucks, tanks, and planes for the Allied powers. After the war, it was the German and Japanese car manufacturers who built companies such as Mercedes, BMW, Toyota, and Honda into powerful rivals to these American firms through their own vision and commitment to quality. At first, their products were often not as good as the either Ford or GM, but they persistently stuck to their vision of producing quality automobiles. By the beginning of the twenty-first century, their vision had become a reality as each of them produced products that met or exceeded consumer expectations of quality and luxury. Now with a renewed vision of fuel-efficient cars, Toyota rivals GM as the world's largest automobile manufacturer. Meanwhile, GM and Ford are restructuring to implement a new vision of high efficiency automobiles to compete with Toyota and other global competitors. How well they succeed or whether they will succeed at all will depend on the ability of the current leaders of these organizations to articulate and implement a new vision for success over the next decade.

Other enterprises have also grown into mega companies by executing the power of a visionary concept. McDonalds, Wal-Mart, and the

Special Olympics all were started and led by visionary leaders. For example, McDonald's succeeded in becoming one of the largest restaurant companies in the world through the vision of its founder, Ray Kroc. He started with one restaurant in Illinois that was modeled on the McDonald brothers' concept of their successful California hamburger stand. Kroc then built an empire of franchised and company-owned stores with his vision of a restaurant chain that offered fast food with consistent quality, speed, and service from clean restaurants all across America. Now there are McDonald's restaurants not only in America but also around the world. Even though menu items vary in different countries, the visionary concepts on which the company was built still guide their operations.

After running several retail store concepts including his neighborhood 5&10 cent store, Sam Walton opened his first Wal-Mart in Rodgers, Arkansas, in 1962. His vision as a retailer was to provide his customers products at consistently low prices. "The Lowest Prices. Guaranteed!" became their marketing byline. This described the vision of the value proposition for his customers. Within five years, the company had grown to twenty-four stores. Walton began to use the group purchasing power of a large retailer to constantly source products at low prices. As his enterprise grew, he also developed efficient distribution and transportation systems to keep prices low. As computers became available, he leveraged these systems to track purchases and restock his stores more efficiently than any other competitors. The commitment to his original vision has been the driving force behind the company that today is the largest retailer in the world. Wal-Mart now operates in thirteen countries with almost seven thousand stores and is continuing to grow its operations based on the vision set forth by founder Sam Walton back in 1962.

In 1968 Chicago teacher Anne McGlone Burke approached Eunice Kennedy Schriver to support the idea of a Special Olympics. Burke was a physical education specialist who had a vision of enhancing the self-esteem of special needs children by having them compete in athletic events. Schriver was the sister of President John F. Kennedy and was supportive because she had a sister with intellectual disabilities. With financial help from the Kennedy Foundation, the first events were held that year with more than one thousand competitors. Since then, the concept has grown and the participation has increased. The Special Olympics are now officially sanctioned by the International Olympic Committee. More than 2.5 million athletes now train for Special Olympics competitions in over 180 countries around the world. International competitions in both summer and winter sports are now held every two years similar to the Olympics. What began as a vision to help some kids in Chicago has grown into a worldwide organization that is not only dedicated to helping athletes with intellectual disabilities improve their physical skills and self-esteem but also is now a force for social change.

Each of these enterprises began with a compelling vision. The fact that they were able to grow into leading global organizations within a relatively short time is a tribute to the power of the visions set forth by their founders. Obviously not everyone with a vision can succeed on the same scale as those in these examples; however, none of these enterprises would have reached the heights of their success without a powerful vision of the future. Look around and you will find lots of examples of organizations both large and small that have succeeded over time because someone had a vision and took action on it either to start or grow an organization.

Your Personal Quest

Whether you are in a formal position of leadership or simply an individual performer, you can still apply the VICTORY principle of vision. You can be a leader in your own life and perhaps not only get what you want but also inspire others to succeed as well. I am a firm believer that leadership is not defined by a position. It is more about what people do and what they believe. Many people go through life without a vision of where they are going or how they intend to get there. There are lots of people who wish for things, such as a better job, more sales, or a new house. On a personal level they could be wishing to have a better relationship with a spouse, friends, or family. The difference between a wish and actually achieving any of these is simple: You need a plan and a goal. The best way to get these is to develop them with a vision of your future. If you can describe your desired future state in terms of a strong vision, then you can set goals and put plans in place to achieve it.

So how do you articulate your personal vision? For many people this may be a difficult task. Some people don't really have a clue about where they want to go in their lives, and just thinking about it gives them a headache. Others haven't even given it any thought. If they did, they might be able to reach inside themselves to articulate what may have been there all along but not articulated. Still others might need to do some research. This might involve getting feedback from people they know and trust. It might also involve just working through a process of self-discovery.

Ask yourself questions like

- What are my personal values?
- Do I have a personal mission, and if so, what is it?
- What value can I contribute to my company, my community, or the world at large?
- What do I like to do?
- How do I like to do things?
- What makes me happy?
- Who do I want to be with most?

By asking these kinds of questions, you can begin to peer into the future. The more you contemplate, the more likely you will be able to more clearly see your future. You will then be able to write it down and clearly articulate it for yourself and others. Some people like to write this in the form of a personal mission statement that they can share with the world. With a personal vision of your future in mind, you will be able to set goals and put plans in place to make it a reality.

It is clear that all successful organizations and individuals have a vision of the future. Some people or organizations may have a more compelling or inspiring vision that will be reflected in how successful they will become. Martin Luther King described his vision in his famous "I have a Dream Speech." John F. Kennedy described his vision for manned spaceflight when he challenged America to "land a man on the moon and return him safely to Earth by the end of the decade." They each inspired millions of people around the world. If you want to be a real leader, make sure that you have a clear vision of the future for others to follow. You may have to convince a lot of people about your vision, but this goes with the territory of being a leader. The starting point for all successful leaders is a compelling vision.

Staff Ride Notebook: Vision

Q1. Does your organization have a compelling vision of the future? Who crafts the vision in your organization? Do the right people have input or are they just told what to do after the plans have been made by senior leaders?

Q2. Once the strategic direction is set in your organization, how do the details get planned? Is planning done by a group, a committee, or simply the leader? What would be an appropriate method for your organization? Is the planning in sufficient detail to execute or is more information often required?

Q3. Who approves the plan? How does the plan get communicated? To whom does the plan get communicated? Are the people who need to know thoroughly briefed?

Q4. What one thing would make planning more effective in your current organization?

EXERCISE: Remember a time when you were involved in a successful undertaking as a member of a team or organization. Was there a compelling vision? Write out the details of how future plans were developed and carried out. What worked in that situation? What could have been done differently to make it even better?

EXERCISE: If you are in an organizational leadership position, write out the steps you would take to craft the organizational vision. If you already have a vision, describe the process that you used to get there. What went well? What could you do differently? How could you improve it even today?

EXERCISE: Do you have a personal vision? What is your personal mission in life? What is your great work? What is your plan to carry it out?

CHAPTER EIGHT
INNOVATION AND LEARNING

SUCCESSFUL LEADERS PROMOTE INNOVATION
AND LEARNING WITHIN THEIR ORGANIZATION
AND TEAMS. THEY ARE INTELLECTUALLY
CURIOUS AND LIFELONG LEARNERS.

Successful organizations focus on innovation and learning. They have a culture that rewards measured risk-taking and innovation. They adapt new technologies to solve problems and perform better. They also avoid punishing failure when it occurs in pursuit of innovation. Punishment is the quickest way to kill innovation. Others will quickly note the consequences for those who were brave enough to try but failed. Instead of punishment, successful leaders focus on learning. They learn quickly from either success or failure. When mistakes are made, they adapt quickly to avoid the same mistakes in the future. They make learning a part of their organizational DNA. They not only learn from their own successes and failures but also from those of others. They are quick to note best practices and make them a part of their own practices.

Innovation and learning are the keys to long-term success of any organization. They allow organizations to adapt in a dynamic environment. The one thing that is always true about operational environments is that they are forever changing. Now it also seems that the pace of change is accelerating more than ever before. These trends have been with us throughout history, but until recently the magnitude of changes was not as challenging as it is today. Every year brings innovative technologies in the broadest definition to almost every endeavor. Organizations and their leaders have always been challenged to adapt these new innovations to provide themselves a competitive edge. With the dawn of the twenty-first century, the number of innovations and the pace of change have been greater than ever. Now the additional challenge for leaders is not only how to adapt new technologies but to decide which ones are relevant for their future success. Every organization is faced with limited resources, and choosing the wrong innovations and technologies can just as easily derail success as choosing the right ones will propel it. Sometimes it is difficult to decide which are more important especially when innovative trends are emerging. The key to making the correct decisions is innovation and learning.

Examples from Operation Overlord

Military organizations in particular have developed reputations for learning and adaptation. These capabilities are necessary for success on the battlefield. They need to quickly learn what works and what is not working. They often need to do this in real time to defeat the enemy. This organizational competency, learning agility, is reflected in how quickly they can adapt to the enemy's tactics, weapons, or resources. This reality is a military necessity. If they fail to learn and adapt, they will not prevail on the battlefield. They must be nimble enough to learn from their own success or failure as well as their adversaries. They must adapt their best practices throughout their entire organization to prevail on the battlefield.

The campaigns from World War II offer a number of examples of how the military used innovation and learning to succeed and win.

They also offer a few lessons on the consequence of not learning from experience. The following examples illustrate the military's skills at innovation and learning. The examples demonstrate how they

- Observed the outcomes of early engagements and learned how to adapt technologies and tactics to future operations
- Innovated solutions to overcome obstacles by using and modifying new equipment and weapons
- Sometimes missed learning opportunities, which resulted in tragic consequences

The first example is the use of airborne forces to provide another dimension to the battlefield, the vertical assault. The Germans were actually the first to successfully use large-scale airborne forces. They started with the opening of the blitzkrieg campaign on the western front. German airborne units were used to secure key positions such as fortifications and bridges in advance of their main invasion into the Low Countries and France. At the start of the war in the west, they dropped highly trained airborne troops on key targets in the Netherlands and Belgium. They paved the way for the armored forces that were quickly coming behind them. They literally opened the door for the panzer units.

Their skill in using this technique was also noted by the Allies when the Germans launched their invasion of the island of Crete in the Mediterranean. Although the attack on Crete resulted in heavy casualties for the Germans, the Allies learned that they also needed to develop their own airborne capability. The Allies subsequently launched airborne attacks in both North Africa and Italy. However, their use of airborne and glider units in Sicily proved to be as problematic as it had for the Germans on Crete. Due to poor coordination, lack of training, and also some factors beyond their control, the airborne troops did not land near their intended targets. Furthermore, they also sustained a high number of casualties due to friendly fire. Despite these unfortunate incidents, they learned from these operations. When the airborne operations were incorporated into the Overlord plan, they took care to more deliberately coordinate the plan to avoid friendly fire casualties. They painted special markings on the aircraft, three large white and two black invasion stripes on each wing, so that friendly aircraft could be easily identified from the ground or sea. They also changed their approach patterns to the landing zone to avoid flying over friendly ships or troops where possible. During Operation Overlord, they still experienced casualties from other factors beyond their control, such as high winds and enemy fire, but they were successful in avoiding friendly fire casualties from the fleet on their approach to the drop zones. Further, other lessons were learned about recognition once on the ground. In the 101st Airborne Division, each soldier was issued a small clicker as a means to challenge and authenticate friendly troopers in the darkness. The challenge of one click was to be answered by a response of two clicks. Alternatively the entire force used a verbal challenge and password: "Thunder" and "Flash." Although these techniques were not always effective, they did illustrate the ability of the planners to learn and adapt from previous operations.

Another example of the military's propensity for innovation and learning was apparent on the beaches in the form of specialized vehicles. The amphibious DUKW trucks had worked reasonably well in Sicily and were used again at Normandy. However, due to the much higher sea swells, some of these slow moving vehicles became swamped only to sink in the English Channel. Perhaps they should have understood the limitations of these vehicles better because they had used them in training; however, the fact is that they developed specialized equipment to get troops ashore and were willing to experiment with new solutions.

Additionally, they used specially designed amphibious tanks in an attempt to get heavy weapons support to the beaches. The Allies had learned from their failure during the raid at Dieppe. There they learned of the need for tanks on the beach in support of the assault infantry. Thus, they developed specially modified Sherman tanks that could operate both in water and on land. These duplex drive (DD) tanks achieved mixed results for the same reasons that were problematic for the DUKW. The Allies certainly got high marks for their innovative efforts, but perhaps they should have been better prepared to deal with the limitations. In fact, some of the Naval officers actually defied orders to deliver their cargo of DD tanks much closer to shore. Although this did not happen everywhere, it did make a difference for some and demonstrates the ability to learn and adapt in real time.

Other innovations included modified tanks that had "flails." These were chains that would spin in front of the tanks to detonate mines. Their purpose was to breach minefields by safely detonating the mines to create passable lanes. As the mines exploded harmlessly, troops and vehicles could follow in the path of the tank. Still other tanks were modified to shoot a fiery stream of napalm, a form of petroleum jelly. Essentially these were giant flame-throwers used to incinerate bunkers and fixed fortifications. These innovations were mostly used in the British sector because it was British General Percy Hobart who experimented with these concepts.

In the American sector, a good example of learning and adaptation was the use of a makeshift dozer blade welded to the front of a tank. This allowed them to bust through the hedgerows—thick vegetation that bordered the Norman fields. An American sergeant decided that a toothlike blade could be made from the iron obstacles that littered the beaches. He had one made and welded it onto his own tank. Then he demonstrated how it could cut into the hedgerows and minimize friendly casualties. This gave the Allied troops the ability to make their own openings into the fields and avoid pre-sited machine gun fire. Since the natural openings were usually covered by automatic weapons and mortar fire, the ability to quickly make another opening was a life-saving innovation. Soon more tanks were being outfitted with makeshift dozer blades. This is another example of an innovation made in real time during the course of the Normandy campaign.

Learning and innovation were not limited to the Allied side alone. The German military also learned and adapted too. One of the best examples was the use of the deadly German 88-mm antiaircraft gun. This was one of the most versatile and effective weapons on either side during the war. It was not only an effective antiaircraft weapon but also perhaps even more effective as a direct fire antitank weapon. The Germans quickly learned that this gun could be used in a ground mode to take out tanks or defeat hardened positions such as reinforced pillboxes. Although this was not its primary purpose when it was first fielded, much to the chagrin of the Allied armies the German "88" was perhaps one of the best tank killers on the battlefield.

The Germans also had one of the best machine guns with their MG-42. It was more reliable and had a higher rate of fire than comparable Allied weapons. The Germans learned how to use them with great effect during the battles in the "bocage"—the hedgerow country. The MG-42 crews emplaced their weapons in mutually supporting positions covering the Norman fields surrounded by the hedgerows. The German army that had previously earned a reputation for its swift and violent counterattacks effectively adapted their tactics in the "bocage" by taking advantage of these natural defensive positions. This allowed them to fight a defensive battle when their mobility was restricted by superior Allied airpower. Allied soldiers also quickly learned to distinguish the sounds of an MG-42 and take cover quickly.

Despite the propensity of armies to learn and adapt, there were also instances where lessons were not learned. One example of a lesson that was not learned concerned the amount of the equipment carried by the Allied assault troops on D-Day. Generally the troops were burdened with more equipment than necessary during the assault phase. This not only made it hard for them to move across the beach but also cost many of them their lives when they stepped into deep water and could not get free of their burden. Most troops carried about eighty pounds of equipment, and some of them even carried more. As they conducted their preinvasion rehearsals, they should have learned that

154

assault troops only needed what was absolutely necessary for the immediate attack on the beach, primarily weapons and ammunition. Once the beach assault succeeded, then they could have been resupplied with rations, more ammunition, and other items such as entrenching tools and tents. This demonstrates why it is important to rehearse operations and conduct periodic reviews.

Over the years since the Normandy campaign, many military organizations around the world have more formally embraced learning as a core competency. Before modern war, the concept of learning was a less formal practice, but in modern military organizations it is embraced as part of the culture. In particular, U.S. military organizations have often been cited for their techniques used to conduct after action reviews (AAR). An AAR is a methodology used to review operations, capture lessons learned, and pass these along to other units. At the conclusion of an operation or training exercise, leaders assemble their soldiers to review what happened. They discuss the mission, what went well, what did not go well, and what can be done to improve similar operations in the future. By routinely learning after each operation, units and soldiers improve their future performance.

The U.S. Army has also tried to institutionalize learning in a variety of ways. For example, they have established a "Center for Lessons Learned" at the Command and General Staff School at Ft. Leavenworth, Kansas, to study and publish lessons learned from operations. They have incorporated vigorous debriefing exercises as a part of the National Training Center at Ft. Irwin, California, where specially trained opposing force units (OPFOR), battle units about to be deployed overseas in realistic training exercises. They are also leveraging technology such as Internet websites specifically designed for company commanders to share lessons directly from the combat zones in the Middle East with their contemporaries who are about to be deployed into the theater. These various learning experiences help develop more effective units and save lives on the battlefield.

Examples from the Business Battlefield

Let's now take a quick look at some commercial and nonprofit applications of innovation and learning. Consider Apple Inc. and the city of New Orleans. Each of these entities has used innovation and learning to overcome obstacles and adapt to the future. They have learned from their own experience, which includes some degree of failure. Despite the setbacks, they have applied lessons learned from their experience and made appropriate adjustments for the future. Apple and New Orleans are some good examples of innovation and learning in action.

Apple was founded by the visionaries who were able to innovate and learn as they went along. As the founders, Steve Jobs and Steve Wozniak perhaps can be credited with unleashing the personal computer revolution. Although many people both before and after them played distinct roles in making the personal computer the ubiquitous device that it is today, these two men commercialized what was until then a technology that was used primarily by scientists and university researchers. They adapted the technology to devices that could be used by the masses.

Like Henry Ford's vision of making affordable cars, the duo wanted to make personal computers available to the average person. When they launched the Apple II computer it soon became a popular brand among the upstart personal computers in the late 1970s. Then, having observed some innovations such as the mouse and user friendly point and click technologies at Xerox's PARC research facility, they realized that the time had come to bring these products to the mass market. When the Macintosh brands were introduced to the market in the early 1980s, users with limited computer knowledge could put them to use without needing to know how to use programming languages, punch cards, or card readers. Their new products spurred other competitors to jump into the market. This made it possible for another major company, Microsoft, to launch their business by licensing DOS operating software to other manufacturers who made personal computers (PCs) that were built with IBM compatible standards. Soon other brands collectively overshadowed the market share of Apple. The PCs running on the Microsoft Windows operating system outpaced Apple's sales, seemingly to doom the future of Apple as a company. In order to try to regain the lead, Apple's board of directors hired a senior marketing executive from Pepsi to take over operations from Steve Jobs. Wozniak left the company altogether and was later followed by Jobs.

Despite the expertise of their new executive, John Scully, Apple continued to struggle and never could overtake the lead of their rivals. Yet they had a core group of loyal customers. Their Macintosh computers did certain tasks better than their mass market rivals, but Apple continued to struggle with innovating new products. Meanwhile, Jobs went off to build another successful company, PIXAR animation, and produced successful animated movies. Later, PIXAR was sold to a major movie studio while Apple continued to survive due to the loyalty of its customers. Eventually in the late 1990s, Steve Jobs was enticed back to his old company and resumed his role as the leader. Although he might not have been an MBA style manager like John Scully, he did know how to innovate and bring new products to market.

Apple marched on and eventually reinvented itself by building on its technologies. Since the first Apple computers were introduced to the market, the underlying technologies of microchips and memory devices had advanced to be significantly more powerful as well as smaller. Using these devices, Apple introduced the iPod, a miniature device that could hold thousands of music recordings. No longer would it be necessary to carry large tape recorders or CD players to listen to your music. Now you could download songs and make custom albums of your favorite songs. These were all stored on a small device that was lightweight and very portable, the iPod. This eventually led to the Apple Store online, where you could download music for a fee. Apple was now a reinvigorated company.

Their next major innovation was the introduction of the Apple iPhone. Like other electronic devices based on the miniature chip technology, the portable phone had become ubiquitous over time. Once again Jobs saw an opportunity as the line between a phone, storage device, and computer blurred. The introduction of the iPhone has spurred other competitors to introduce phones that offer similar features. They not only serve as a telephonic device but also connect people to the World Wide Web and email. They also serve as a personal electronic productivity device. With the advent of competitors, it remains to be seen if the iPhone will capture a significant market share of the portable telephone market.

However, the remarkable reinvention of Apple Inc. is a great example of an organization that has been able to learn and innovate. Under the leadership of Steve Jobs, they have demonstrated a core competency of being able to recognize and capitalize on market opportunities by adapting new technologies featured in products that empower people to be more productive. Despite the ups and downs over the years, Apple has been able to survive and now thrive under Job's leadership using their ability to innovate and learn. Their penchant for innovation and learning is a terrific example of this victory principle in action in a commercial enterprise.

Now let's look at New Orleans. Many people remember the tragedy of Hurricane Katrina in 2005 that was televised in the news. These images were shown around the world and left an impression of a government unable to respond to the crisis. When the levees broke, much of the city was flooded leaving thousands of residents stranded. The New Orleans football dome became the shelter of last resort for many people who had no way to evacuate before the storm. The dome quickly became overcrowded and people languished in squalor waiting to be rescued. Many of the first responders were overwhelmed by the scope of the disaster and simply left the area for their own safety. The State of Louisiana and the federal government were unprepared. The Federal Emergency Management Agency (FEMA), which normally provided natural disaster relief, was ineffective in their response to the crisis.

These television pictures left a clear impression of a failed government infrastructure as thousands of victims were stranded.

It was difficult to comprehend that this could be happening in a major American city. Officials at all levels immediately started to shirk responsibility and point fingers. The mayor publicly expressed his outrage about support from both the state and federal levels but never mentioned the failings of his own city officials. Likewise the governor blamed the federal government without acknowledging that the state was unprepared to coordinate disaster assistance. The president, who initially remained detached from the situation, left it to the Secretary of Homeland Security who had jurisdiction over FEMA. He pointed to the FEMA director to sort it out, and it soon became apparent that none of them were prepared to provide a response.

As a quick fix, the military was called upon to step in and get things under control. Under the leadership of Army Lt. General Russell Honere, military units were brought in to restore order, rescue stranded victims, and provide relief. Although not specifically trained for this mission, Gen. Honere applied basic decision-making skills to quickly develop a plan and get things moving in the right direction. Although it was a makeshift solution, the situation began to improve, but painful lessons had been learned about governments' ability to handle a major disaster. Unlike 9/11, which was a horrific attack with many more people killed and injured in the southern tip of Manhattan, the disaster area of Katrina extended well beyond the city of New Orleans. The size and scope of the aftermath of Katrina stressed the resources of every level of government.

As weeks and months passed, the tragedy of Katrina moved out of the news headlines. It would occasionally be brought back into focus as issues surfaced with the rebuilding effort. However, behind the scenes the emergency planners had rolled up their shirtsleeves to put new plans in place for future disasters.

After action reviews were conducted to look at what didn't work and how they could fix it. At the local level they focused on evacuation plans that would provide early warning. Transportation plans were made for people who did not have any means to evacuate. They looked at how they could move nursing home residents and deal with hospitals. They also decided that they would not have thousands of people go to a shelter of last resort but would instead harness public transportation and school buses to move residents out of harm's way. At the state and federal levels, they invested in communications equipment so that the various agencies could speak with one another. They also looked at how they could better coordinate their efforts for unity of purpose, and they prepositioned relief supplies that could be brought in quickly after the disaster struck. These may seem like commonsense actions, but for agencies that were unprepared to deal with Katrina, these were major steps forward.

Now fast forward to the 2008 hurricane season when a series of storms hit the Gulf Coast one after the other. One of the first to hit the New Orleans area since Katrina was Hurricane Gustav. Unlike what happened during Katrina, the mayor of New Orleans and the governor of Louisiana were both out front with early warnings and declared mandatory evacuations. The evacuations were executed in an orderly manner. The city had a plan for transporting by bus and trains those who did not own an automobile. First responders were patrolling threatened areas, and policemen stayed on the job. The governor had called on the National Guard, and FEMA was prepared to provide needed supplies that had been prepositioned.

Although the storm was strong, the effects were not as disastrous as they had been with Katrina. Repairs that were made to levees in the intervening years held, and the damaged caused by widespread flooding did not occur this time. What seemed even more evident was the improvement in the governments' response, particularly on the state and local level. Although federal officials also appeared to be prepared, they were not tested in the same way that they had been during Katrina because the damage from Gustav was less severe. It did appear that they would have been prepared to respond if needed.

Not long after, they were required to provide assistance to Texas when Hurricane Ike came ashore in Galveston and Houston. This time the federal agencies were more proactive and better coordinated with the local levels of government.

The moral of this story is generally a positive one not withstanding the rebuilding effort which is still ongoing. Difficult lessons were learned from the experience with Katrina; however, officials developed solutions and applied them with success several years later. Innovations were made to improve communications and coordinate efforts among the various levels of government. This is a good example of how government agencies applied the principle of innovation and learning to improve their disaster response capabilities.

Your Personal Quest

The principles of innovation and learning are also powerful principles for success on a personal level. This is especially true today when the pace of change is much more rapid than it was during the time prior to World War II. Additionally, with the advent of personal computers, the Internet, and cell phones, we are all exposed to more information and interconnected like never before in history. This offers great possibilities, but it also requires that people be adaptive through innovation and learning on a personal level.

We all have a choice: We can either embrace change or change can pass us by. Those who want to succeed in this challenging environment must become lifelong learners. They must continue to explore these new opportunities to apply new technologies in their own lives. They must learn new skill sets to remain relevant in their jobs and realize the personal productivity now available through access to technology and information. They must enthusiastically embrace the concept of being a lifelong learner. Read books, take a class, go to a seminar, listen to a webinar, and explore new technologies.

Another way to personally apply the principles of innovation and learning is to develop the habit of a personal after action review. Whenever you do something that is important at work, in your community, or with your family, take a few minutes to reflect. Consider how well you did, and be honest with yourself. Seek feedback from others when appropriate. Ask yourself

- What did I learn from this experience?
- What went well?
- What did not go so well?
- Could I have done this differently and achieved a better result?
- If I were to do it again, what changes would I make?

Realize that when you are learning a new skill, it is natural that you will not do it well the first time. Skills only get better with practice. Accelerate your learning with more conscious refection and deliberate practice. You can do this either formally or informally depending on the circumstances and your personal preference.

You may also want to keep a journal of your lessons learned and progress you make along the way. This is what I recommend for leaders who want to improve how they lead their organizations. If you are in an organizational leadership role, you can seek feedback on how well you are perceived as a leader from your people, your peers, and your boss. You can do this informally or you can enlist the support of an outside coach to help with the process. Whatever method you choose, success is totally dependent on you. You must be willing to get and evaluate feedback from trusted sources. You must decide if and how you will incorporate the feedback into changes to your personal leadership style going forward. Whatever changes you decide are right for you, you must consciously work toward making them a natural part of your values and behaviors. This may be difficult to do effectively, and frankly, many people do not change. This is either because they don't really want to change or they haven't practiced the new behavior enough to make it a permanent part of their future leadership style. The bottom line is that improvement begins with your decision to innovate and learn.

In summary, these same principles used by the military can easily be adapted to all kinds of situations. Regardless of our field of endeavor, we all operate in a dynamic and changing environment. Change, either on a personal or organizational level is something that we all must learn to deal with effectively. Innovation and learning are skills that allow organizations and people to adapt to new circumstances and discover more effective ways to do their work.

The really good news is that there are powerful networking tools to enhance learning and innovation. Distance learning and sharing information has never been easier. The U.S. Army's example of using the Internet to connect its junior officers is a good one. They have specifically sponsored a site for company level commanders to share lessons learned from the battlefield with each other. You can do the same for yourself or your company. Online communities of interest now abound for other fields of endeavor, too. See if you can find one that works for you. Make innovation and learning part of your skill set.

Staff Ride Notebook: Innovation and Learning

Q1. Is your organization a learning organization? Does your organization learn from other organizations that are similar to yours or from your competitors? Does your organization promote individual learning and skill development?

Q2. What methods do you use to monitor or learn about best practices? How can you learn from how best-in-class organizations operate?

Q3. Does your organization value experimentation? How does your organization generate solutions to problems or new products? Do you normally set a time to test and evaluate new concepts at an appropriate time in the future?

Q4. How do leaders in your organization deal with bad news? Do they tolerate mistakes or do they punish people who take risks that fail?

Q5. How does your organization learn from failure? Does your organization conduct after action reviews to learn what works and what does not?

EXERCISE: Think about a time when you were a part of an organization that was implementing a new approach to business. How was that new approach discovered? What was the process used to train people and to shift to the new approach? What worked well? What did not work so well? How would you do it differently?

EXERCISE: Recall a recent activity or project in your current organization. Did you do anything like an after action review? How did it go? What could have been done differently? If you did not do one, write out the steps you could follow to draw out the lessons learned for the future.

EXERCISE: Think about your own skills and career. What one or two skills would make a big difference in your future success if you were able to either learn how to do them or to do them better? Are these things that come natural to you? How will you acquire these skills? Are you building on your strengths or trying to overcome perceived weaknesses? Write out a development plan for yourself.

CHAPTER NINE
CAPABILITIES: PEOPLE AND RESOURCES

THE TWO CRITICAL CAPABILITIES FOR
ORGANIZATIONAL OR TEAM SUCCESS ARE
THE RIGHT PEOPLE AND THE NECESSARY
RESOURCES. PEOPLE NEED THE RIGHT SKILLS
AND RIGHT TOOLS TO ACHIEVE SUCCESS.

Another key to any successful operation or plan is having the right people and the right tools to get the mission accomplished. People and resources are critical to mission success regardless of the type of organization. Getting critical organizational capabilities in place is a four step process: Ask questions, focus on people, focus on resources, and stress test the system.

Begin by asking questions. In a military organization, a successful leader begins with a mission assessment. He or she will clearly seek to understand the mission objectives upon receipt of an operations order.

The commander will start by asking his or her staff questions such as:

- What is the mission?
- What are the next higher commander's intended outcomes?
- What is the concept of the operation?
- What tasks will be required?

The assessment will consider both quantitative and qualitative requirements. It will focus on the number of things and people. A clear understanding of the mission and the requirements for people and resources is the first step in planning success.

Next, focus on the people. How many people will be needed to get the job done? What are the skill sets needed to accomplish the tasks? Do I currently have the right people with those skill sets? If not, can I train my people, or do I need to find new people? Where can I find people if I need them? People are the engines behind all organizations. It is the responsibility of the leaders to make sure that they have enough of the right people with the right skills in the right places at the right time. In fact, this is one of the primary roles for senior organizational leaders. They are always on the lookout for great people, even when they don't have an immediate need for them. Often a senior leader has more flexibility to hire talented people somewhere within the organization, even in advance of the need. Then when the need arises, they have a pool of talented people to pull from to fill critical positions. After they are hired, great leaders make sure that their people get off to a good start by mentoring them. They also tend to use mission-type orders that focus more on what needs to get done rather than how it is to get done. In other words, they focus on the expected results rather than how the results will be achieved. Once their people understand the mission or the tasks required of them, the commander will hold them strictly accountable to do their job and provide them feedback along the way.

Then focus on resources beyond people. What types and quantities of resources will be needed to get the job done? When will they be needed? Do I need special equipment? Where can I get the resources I need? Are substitutes available for items that cannot be obtained? Who can assist with obtaining the resources? Having the right tools and equipment is crucial to mission success. It is true that if you have great people, they will often find a way to overcome shortages of other resources to get the job done. However, even the best people with the right skills will have much more difficulty and perhaps not be able to do their work if they don't have the right tools and equipment at the right time and place.

Finally, stress test the system. Simulate the plan or an operation to test if you have the right people and resources to succeed. Often this will be done through rehearsals and practice. Time does not always permit a full dress rehearsal, but there are a variety of ways to simulate operations short of a full rehearsal.

The military uses a variety of techniques. For example, one simple way to review a plan is to have subordinates brief back what is expected. This will not only check for understanding but also be a quick way to make adjustments on the fly as necessary. Another way the military rehearses is by conducting command post exercises without troops or field training exercises with only representative units or leaders. Other simple techniques are map exercises or sand table exercises to review operations with key leaders. When time or other resources limit the amount of preparation, then more limited rehearsals might be done on only certain critical aspects of an operation. In today's modern army, simulations are also done using computers to provide virtual opportunities to practice critical tasks. Whichever method is used, the ability to rehearse and practice can be a very powerful method to ensure success. It is often especially important when things go wrong as they often do; unplanned events can unnerve otherwise qualified people and cause widespread confusion. By practicing drills and preparing for unexpected events, people will be much more prepared to simply adapt and carry on with their mission. They gain confidence through rehearsals. They are better prepared for contingencies when given adequate time to think ahead and practice.

Examples from Operation Overlord

How does the story of the Normandy invasion illustrate some of these concepts? Planning for people and resources began well before

General Eisenhower was designated as the supreme commander. The Combined Chiefs of Staff designated General Morgan and a combined staff to begin planning the invasion over a year in advance. When the planning began they needed to simply get information and make an assessment on a wide range of topics. They began by asking lots of questions. Obvious questions were about where to land on the continent, what size force would be needed, and how they would get there. Their inquiries led them to analyze the Channel coast from Norway to France. They looked to intelligence to determine the number and types of German units that were defending the Atlantic Wall and where they were located. They considered the various courses of action, the troops, and the resources that would be available. As the planning progressed, they were able to narrow the focus to specific units, proposed landing sites, and equipment requirements such as landing craft that were needed to get them there.

When the decision to proceed with the invasion was affirmed, the first thing the political leaders focused on was people. Who would command the operation and who would be among the key staff and subordinate commanders? Involved in this decision were not only the political leaders but also the senior military leaders of the Combined Chiefs, General Marshall and General Brooke. Marshall helped Roosevelt with his decision to appoint Eisenhower as the supreme commander. Following his appointment, Brooke worked along with him and Churchill to identify key British officers who would fill the positions for ground, naval, and air commanders. Marshall and Brooke both acknowledged that this was one of their key functions as the senior military leaders. Perhaps their greatest contribution to the war effort was identifying qualified commanders and staff officers to lead the Allied forces. They made it their job to personally know their pool of key officers in their respective military organizations.

When a position was vacant, they carefully weighed each candidate's skills against the requirements for the position. In some cases, as in the case of the selection of General Montgomery for overall ground forces commander, they did not all agree on the best candidate for the job. However, in the case of Montgomery the Americans could hardly argue about his track record of successful command, and so they deferred to Brooke and Churchill in the interest of Allied unity.

This decision illustrates the fact that there may be multiple considerations beyond just the specific candidate's qualifications for selecting someone for a key position. Most often there is not an ideal candidate who meets every requirement of a position. Even a great slate of candidates includes people with individual strengths and weaknesses. Sometimes there is not one specific criterion on which to base a selection, so the final decision for any position is ultimately a judgment call that takes into consideration the whole person and everything they will bring to a given position. The whole person view takes into account both the positive and negative aspects of a candidate's personality, skills, talent, and temperament.

For senior level leaders, successful performance in successive positions of increased responsibility is usually the predictor of future success. Usually military officers will progress through a wide variety of command and staff assignments as they get promoted to higher rank. A track record of high performance in a variety of jobs and circumstances is great way to assess an individual's ability to adapt and perform in future assignments.

Once the appointments were made for the senior command and staff positions, Eisenhower held each of them accountable for their part of the operations. This important lesson reflected the relationship between Marshall and Eisenhower. Marshall had made it clear to Eisenhower that he needed to be strong in holding people accountable. Marshall's warning to Eisenhower was as follows: "He turned to me to say slowly and emphatically, 'Eisenhower, there is one thing that you must understand clearly. Retention under your command of any American officer means to me that you are satisfied with his performance. Any man you deem unsatisfactory you must reassign...or send him home! This principle will apply to the letter because I have no intention of ever giving you an alibi for failure on the excuse that I forced an unsatisfactory subordinate (on you.) I hold you responsible.'"[49]

If they did not perform, it was his duty to replace them; otherwise, Marshall would assume that Eisenhower was happy with their performance. Eisenhower exercised this command prerogative when he removed commanders and staff officers who did not measure up to the task at hand. In doing so, Eisenhower removed some officers whom he had known for a long time, including some he had known since his days at West Point. This included removing General Lloyd Fridendahl after the American defeat at Kasserne Pass in North Africa. Eisenhower also exercised this command responsibility when he reprimanded one of his most aggressive and successful commanders, General George Patton, for his inappropriate behavior in dealing with the combat-stressed soldiers in the hospitals. These were difficult but necessary decisions because the consequences of failure in war were measured in the loss of lives.

The other major organizational capability and primary leadership responsibility is acquiring the necessary resources to accomplish the mission. Once again Operation Overlord is illustrative of this leadership function.

In order to successfully mount the cross-channel attack, the logistical requirements were daunting. This is especially true when you think about the fact that they did not have personal computers to track equipment and supplies. Vehicles, weapons, food, ammunition, petroleum, ships, planes, and thousands of lesser items such as socks, uniforms, and maps were all necessary to field the vast invasion force. One of the most critical items was the assault boat, the LCA, otherwise known as a Higgins boat. These were the flat-bottomed craft that dropped their ramps to deliver the men to the Normandy beaches. They were in short supply and became one of the reasons that the invasion was postponed from May until June. The extra month was critical so that more of these boats could be available. It was also one of the reasons that the original plan called for only a three-division force instead of the five-division force envisioned by Eisenhower and Montgomery. Once they had decided upon the larger force, it was incumbent upon them as leaders to seek out the additional shipping. The additional naval requirements not only included more assault boats but also warships to support the bombardment of two additional beaches, additional transports to get the troops and supplies to the debarkation stations, and additional auxiliary ships such as minesweepers to escort the convoys.

When they increased the size of the airborne operations, they also needed to seek out additional transport planes and gliders. Beyond the planes themselves, they needed to obtain additional petroleum, more maintenance facilities, and airstrips from which to launch the planes, not to mention additional aircrews to fly them. Thus, they made it part of their agenda at the highest levels of the Allied command to obtain these additional assets, even when it meant the need to postpone other operations in other parts of the world. Their efforts as leaders to obtain the necessary resources enabled the invasion to proceed with the larger force. This change in scope likely made the critical difference in a successful outcome for the Allies.

Another example of resourcing was the inter-service fight over the use of the bomber force. The senior air commanders wanted to continue the strategic bombing campaign against Germany's industrial centers, but Eisenhower insisted that they reallocate their missions to directly support Overlord. As a result, they executed the Transportation Plan and destroyed the Germans' ability to reinforce their units in Normandy. Additionally they attacked the Luftwaffe with such vengeance that the German Air Forces were not a factor during the entire campaign. Once again, Eisenhower was successful as an overall commander by focusing on the critical elements of his plan and obtaining the resources needed for his subordinates to succeed.

Once the people and the resources were in place, they needed to test the system. Having previously learned during other operations that the services did not always function well together, rehearsals were conducted at the Assault Training Center at Slapton Sands. Replicas of German fortifications were prepared so that the troops could actually make a practice run on beaches that would approximate what they would encounter in France. Although the practice runs were not made against a hostile force, live ammunition was shot overhead to simulate some of the sounds and chaos of the battlefield. These realistic training sessions did result in some actual casualties despite the fact that they were under controlled conditions. However, the Allied leaders were willing to risk these casualties in training because they knew how important it was to test the men and their equipment under field conditions.

Thus, the planning and execution of Operation Overlord demonstrates how the two critical capabilities of successful organizations—people and resources—made the difference in the outcome of the invasion. Once the requirement for the five-division assault was defined, the senior leaders sought out the right people and resources needed to make it happen. They ensured that rehearsals took place that enabled the various components of the force to work together. When D-Day arrived, the men and their equipment were as ready to go as they could make them.

Examples from the Business Battlefield

Capabilities of people and resources are equally important to business organizations. One of the best known commercial enterprises that has achieved widespread success based on developing people is the General Electric (GE) corporation. Managing talent is a core competency that GE developed over long periods of time. There are many other fine companies who also do a great job with their people, but GE developed a reputation under the legendary leadership of Jack Welsh for focusing on its people. Regardless of the specific division, managing talent became a core competency across all of GE's businesses under his leadership. Welch set the example in selecting and personally developing senior leaders. He made sure that his subordinates carefully evaluated the performance of their people on an annual basis and used his human resources department to assist in the process. When vacancies occurred, especially at the senior levels, their bench strength often allowed them to choose from a slate of several well qualified candidates from within the GE family of businesses. The reputation for developing people has led a number of GE alumni to opportunities to lead other organizations where they have tried to put similar talent management systems in place.

There are other large organizations that have also put an emphasis on talent management. These include Pepsi Corporation and Johnson & Johnson in the United States, and Toyota and IKEA from overseas. All of these leading companies have systems in place to attract, develop, reward, and retain the best people. Although each of these organizations manages its people differently, they all share common principles that are applied to their unique cultures. So, although the critical skills needed to succeed may vary from organization to organization, the commitment and focus on talent management is shared. Each of them in their own way rigorously evaluates candidates before offering an opportunity. These companies each have their own method to "onboard" new hires so that they are acclimated to their corporate culture and their job. They are clear about company goals and what is expected from their people. Their development programs may vary, but the commitment to developing people is a common thread. So is the challenge of providing appropriate rewards and recognition for high performance. Excellent companies in the twenty-first century know that they must have more than a slogan about their commitment to people. They must have human resources systems, policies, and programs in place. Talent management must be an organizational competency that delivers results for customers, shareholders, and employees.

These same companies also know that they must provide their employees with the tools they need to do their work. Having the right equipment is a key factor to engage employees in the work of the enterprise. The best people will hold themselves accountable for good performance. It goes without saying that good people will quickly become frustrated if they don't have what they need to get their job done. If they can't perform at a consistently high level because of the work environment, they will disengage. This will be manifested in a lack of employee commitment and eventually in poor service or inferior products. The best people will eventually leave an organization when they don't have what they need to succeed at a high level of performance. These same principles hold true for nonprofit organizations and government agencies. It is thus incumbent upon the leaders, regardless of the type of enterprise, to make sure that their people have what they need to succeed. The VICTORY principle of capabilities only works when the right combination of people and resources come together.

Another great example of an organization that brought together the right people and resources to get the job done was the super-secret Manhattan Project during World War II. Now declassified, this was the U.S. Government's secret project to develop the atomic bomb. Under the leadership of physicist J. Robert Oppenheimer and Brigadier General Leslie Groves, this complex project brought together over 130,000 people, three primary research facilities, and over thirty other sites to build the first atomic bombs. Although their success ultimately ushered in worldwide problems of nuclear proliferation that we struggle with today, the project illustrates how gathering the right people and resources was the key to accomplishing their mission.

In 1939 many esteemed scientists, Albert Einstein among them, were concerned about the prospects that German scientists were working on an atomic weapon. He wrote a letter to President Roosevelt and urged him to organize an American project to beat them to the finish line. The project was initiated but did not seem to be moving ahead very quickly. At the time there were a variety of scientists around the United States, Canada, and Britain who were working in loose coordination on atomic research. In 1942 Oppenheimer pulled together a conference in California to gather some of the best scientific minds at the time to discuss the feasibility of producing such a weapon. Subsequently, the U.S. Army was given the responsibility for coordinating the project under the leadership of Colonel Leslie Groves. Groves was an engineer officer and was selected for his ability to lead large complex projects. He had previously been in charge of constructing the massive Pentagon building in record time. Groves was promoted to Brigadier General so that he could use his rank to garner the necessary resources. One of his first tasks was to select Oppenheimer as the research director. Oppenheimer pulled together a team of scientists, many whom he knew personally, to work together to solve the riddle of unleashing the power of the atom. Until he gathered his team at Los Alamos, New Mexico, the idea of atomic power was largely the realm of theoretical physicists from around the world. Getting the right people in place was step one in moving the project ahead.

Groves then went about securing additional resources. In addition to acquiring the Los Alamos site, he set up two other sites at Oak Ridge, Tennessee, and Richland, Washington. While the physicists worked on translating the theoretical science into engineering the mechanisms for the bombs, the facilities in Tennessee and Washington were set to work on producing the fissionable material needed for the actual bombs themselves. Groves' hard charging manner earned him the reputation for getting things done. While Oppenheimer kept the research project on track, Groves acquired whatever resources were required. The complete story of this complex project had a number of twist and turns, including an espionage incident, until the first successful test of an atomic bomb in the New Mexico desert in July 1944. For illustration of the VICTORY principle of capabilities, it sufficient to simply say that the ultimate success of the project was directly attributable to the leadership of both General Groves and Robert Oppenheimer to muster the right people with the right skills and resources. Together they forged a team with a common vision and gathered the necessary people and resources to get the job done.

Your Personal Quest

How do you apply the VICTORY principle of capabilities on a personal level? You can start by assessing your own skills and abilities. A realistic and honest assessment of what you do well and what you don't will help you decide how you can best use your skills. Everyone has strengths and weaknesses, and people succeed more quickly and to higher levels of success when they can put their strengths to work. Knowing what your skills are will also help you identify what you might need to do to improve. Many senior managers hire a coach to help them with this task. A coach can provide you with honest feedback that will help you improve where you can or find new ways to use your strengths in other areas. Just like a good coach of a sports team who puts players in positions that leverage their strengths, so, too, a personal coach can help you with your work and life challenges.

Successful people also improve their skills by investing in themselves and staying current in their professions. For some people this means getting an advanced degree such as an MBA or law degree. For others, it might mean getting certified in their profession. For still others, it might mean moving from apprentice to journeyman or from unlicensed to licensed. Some professions such as doctors or lawyers are required to take continuing education classes to maintain their professional licenses. Others such as professional sales people attend seminars or industry trade shows to stay current on the most recent trends in their industry. Finally, others spend time reading professional journals or listening to webinars, home study courses, or simply reading books. The bottom line is that you need to consciously work toward continuous improvement of your skills.

Keep in mind that sometimes you may need to develop a whole new skill set if you plan to advance in your career. The skills needed to lead a large organization are very different from those needed to lead a small team. Although there are some basic leadership skills that apply to both, a senior executive will focus more on setting the organization vision and environment, whereas the team leader will exercise leadership at a much more personal level with the resources provided by senior management. To get from team leader to senior leader, you will consciously need to develop the new skills that are required for senior leadership.

The other way that you can apply this VICTORY principle on a personal level is to make sure that you have what you need in terms of resources to do your job well. Any craftsman will quickly tell you that having the right tools to do a job will make a big difference in his or her ability to deliver a quality product. The carpenter who only has a framing hammer, ruler, and a handsaw will not be able to work as quickly and precisely as another who has a table saw, a laser level, and a pneumatic nail gun. The same applies to any profession. Whether you are an engineer who works on a computer or a photographer who uses a high-resolution camera, the right tools will enhance whatever skills you bring to the job. Ideally when all other things are equal, you want to be the person with the best skills and the best tools to get the best results for yourself and your company. If you don't have what you need to succeed, immediately have a discussion with your boss so he or she can get it for you; or if you are self-employed, you must invest in your business and career to obtain what you need.

Staff Ride Notebook: Capability: People and Resources

Q1. Does your organization have the people and resources it needs to accomplish its mission? How do you currently assess and forecast the people and resource requirements for your organization? How does your organization fill these requirements? Is the process of getting resources easy or complex? Who has the approval authority?

Q2. How well do leaders in your organization know their people? How do leaders assess their skills and talent? How and why are people assigned to new positions? Do senior leaders mentor subordinates?

Q3. Are people in your organization held accountable? How are the top performers recognized and rewarded? What are the consequences for substandard performance?

Q4. How well do the systems in your organization work? Are they responsive to the team, coworkers, and customers? Is there anything that could be done to make them better, faster, or more effective?

Q5. How well do different functions work together to support the overall organization?

EXERCISE: Think about when you have been part of an organization that attempted to accomplish a major activity. Did the leaders identify the requirements needed to get the job done? Did they obtain the people and resources necessary to succeed? Identify how well they did this and if they could have done it better. Where in particular did they not provide the necessary people or resources?

EXERCISE: Do you personally have the skills and tools that you need to be successful in your job? If not, what skills or resources do you need? How do you intend to get them?

CHAPTER TEN
TIMELY DECISIONS: AIME DECISION MODEL

EFFECTIVE LEADERS MAKE TIMELY DECISIONS. THEY
USE A DECISION-MAKING FRAMEWORK OR MODEL.

Another key to victory is the ability to make timely decisions. Often managers or leaders delay critical decisions when they operate from fear of making the wrong decision or not having enough information. General Patton wisely advised: Don't take counsel of your fears. Sometimes it is true that you do need to postpone a decision until better information is available or until the circumstances are more favorable to what you are trying to accomplish. It is unlikely, however, that you will ever have all the information you might like to have before you need to make a decision. When you are the leader, your organization looks to you for key decisions in order to move forward. By not making a decision, the effect on the organization is that you have made a decision, consciously or unconsciously, to hold off. Under those circumstances, your whole organization is mostly just waiting for you to decide something.

People make decisions in various ways. Some perform detailed analysis of the issues before they can decide how to proceed. Others are capable of making decisions solely on intuition, on a gut feeling. Neither of these extremes is consistently effective. Endless analysis often leads to paralysis by analysis, whereas making gut-level decisions based on emotions often overlooks critical facts. To help them make timely decisions, effective leaders use a decision process—a decision model. Using a decision model or consistent process adds a certain level of discipline. Effective leaders do this either consciously or unconsciously, having learned a process that works for them through trial and error. I will present such a model here: the AIME model.

AIME

Although this isn't a specific military decision-making model, AIME parallels the thought process used by many leaders in both the military as well as other professions. The AIME model has four distinct steps that are easily remembered by the mnemonics name itself.

Assess the Situation

The first step is to assess the situation. This can be similar to the METT-T estimate of the situation used by the military. Assessments can either be complex with months of research or simply done in a matter of minutes depending on the situation at hand and the time available.

Initiate a Simple Plan

The second step the decision maker will take is to initiate a simple plan by investigating a possible course of action. The simple plan will most likely be one of the several possible courses of action available. After comparing the advantages and disadvantages of each course of action, the decision maker must decide which one is most appropriate. This can be done either methodically with a complex decision matrix or, as is more often the case, a simple comparison done in a short amount of time followed by a quick decision. The simpler the planned course of action, the easier it is to communicate to those who must implement the decision.

Make it Happen

The next step is the action step—make it happen. Failure to take action will doom even the best decision. Once the decision is made, a leader must make sure that it is vigorously implemented. Paraphrasing General Patton again, a good decision vigorously executed today is better than a perfect decision tomorrow. Communicating the decision often starts this step of the model if your decision requires team support. What Patton means is that once you make a decision get everyone behind it and do your utmost to make it happen. The enthusiastic execution of even a mediocre plan will yield better results than a well thought out one that is not timely. The key is the ability to make timely decisions and follow through with deliberate action.

Evaluate Results

Finally, good leaders follow up on their decisions. They set a time in the future to review the results they are getting based on the decisions. This is embodied in the last step, evaluate. Whereas many decisions are critical, most are not permanent or unchangeable. Even skilled decision makers will discover that a large percentage of their decisions may seem incorrect with the benefit of time. Thus the evaluation step allows a leader to modify, reverse, or push ahead with vigor after observing the effect of the initial decision. Knowing that most decisions can be modified also helps the decision maker to overcome the impasse of fear associated with potentially making a poor decision. Timely evaluation will also allow for a course correction when needed to avoid any further adverse effects of what would have been exacerbated by a poor decision. So, let's look at a few examples of decisions that were made related to Normandy and apply the AIME model for illustration.

Examples from Operation Overlord

First, consider the case of General Eisenhower's momentous decision of when to launch the D-Day invasion. There are few decisions that have such importance. The original target date set for the invasion was in May 1944. However, there was a shortage of landing craft to support the full five-division plan. This fact alone made any date in May unlikely. Additionally there was an unfortunate attack by German E-boats during a training exercise. The E-boats were similar to American PT boats that were more commonly used in the Pacific theater. The attack took place in April on a convoy during a U.S. Fourth Division practice assault drill at the Assault Training Center at Slapton Sands. Nine German E-boats penetrated the convoy defenses while the rehearsal, Exercise Tiger, was in progress. Several troopships were attacked with torpedoes, resulting in the death of more than seven hundred U.S. soldiers. Since the Fourth Division was one of the primary assault units, Eisenhower moved the date for D-Day to early June. This was the next window of opportunity when the tides and moon would be in the correct phase to support the invasion. The troops coming in from the sea needed to arrive just after low tide so the beach obstacles would be visible, and paratroops needed moonlight for visibility.

In early June the troops began moving from their marshalling areas to the awaiting ships. By June 4, the troop ships were loaded and ready to go. Paratroops and airplanes were waiting on the tarmacs at dozens of airfields across England. All were waiting for the supreme commander's final decision to go; however, as the June 5 date for the invasion approached, one of the worst storms in memory moved into the English Channel. The severe weather delivered torrential rain with high wind and waves. Furthermore, the weather forecast was bleak. After consulting his staff and key subordinates, Eisenhower decided to postpone the decision for twenty-four hours. The next day he would have another forecast and hopefully better weather. He postponed the invasion launch with the full knowledge that hundreds of thousands of soldiers, sailor, and airmen would have to stand down to wait another day for his decision. When the staff convened the next day, his initial decision paid off. His senior meteorologist reported a favorable weather forecast for the following day, June 6. After reconsidering his options and consulting again with his staff, Eisenhower made the decision to launch Operation Overlord with the simple words, "OK, let's go." With this decision now made, his subordinates immediately took the necessary actions to proceed with the biggest amphibious invasion in history, and the date of June 6 would forever be remembered as D-Day.

Most people will never be faced with such a momentous decision that has life and death consequences for thousands, perhaps even millions of people. But the process of decision making is similar regardless of the scope and the consequences of the decision. Although this was a decision with monumental consequences, Eisenhower followed what amounted to the simple four-step process of the AIME model: Assess the situation, initiate a simple plan, make it happen, and evaluate results. His thought process can be illustrated by analyzing the decision within this framework.

First, he assessed the situation. Eisenhower sought to get input on the facts bearing on his decision. He consulted his staff and key commanders. From General Montgomery, the ground forces commander, he got a sense of the status and morale of the troops: The troops were ready and anxious to go, morale was high, but it would be difficult to keep them motivated if the landings were postponed until July. From Admiral Ramsey, the naval commander, he got the status of the fleet, their ability to operate in the high seas, and how long their supplies of food and fuel would last. From Tedder and Leigh-Mallory, he learned about the air forces' ability to drop the bombs accurately on target and to deliver the paratroops safely under the severe conditions. Finally, he got the weather report from Group Captain Stagg: Weather conditions were severe, but there was a possible change with a new weather system moving into the Channel.

Armed with the relevant information, he then quickly proceeded to the next step by investigating courses of action to initiate a simple plan. There were three obvious choices: Proceed immediately, postpone for another day, or recall the fleet and cancel the operation until some future date. He carefully considered each option by comparing their advantages and disadvantages. Proceeding immediately on June 5 would likely cause the plan to fail because the ships and planes simply could not operate under the current weather conditions. Postponing the decision for another twenty-four hours was feasible, but beyond that timeframe it was not possible due to logistical constraints for the fleet. However, the alternative of a twenty-four-hour delay did offer the possibility for an improved weather forecast. Finally, delaying the invasion for another month would likely compromise the location and timing of the attack to German intelligence. Furthermore, as General Montgomery indicated, morale and effectiveness of the troops would be difficult to maintain. Once he had considered the comparative strengths and weaknesses of each, he completed a simple plan by deciding on an option: Postpone for a day.

Then, Eisenhower simply communicated the decision right there at his staff meeting. That was all the action required of him as the supreme commander to do the next step: Make it happen. Now his subordinates had the necessary information for them to take the appropriate actions to postpone the invasion for twenty-four hours. Before the meeting concluded, he immediately set up another meeting to evaluate the decision. He knew that his meteorologist, Group Captain Stagg, would have an updated forecast. He hoped that the weather conditions might be more favorable the next day. Since the ships would be required to be refueled and resupplied, he knew he had only one day to make another decision if the operation was to proceed. Thus the time allotted to evaluate his decision was purposely short. Nevertheless, the evaluation step would be the critical key to the overall success of the plan.

At the next day's staff meeting, Eisenhower again followed the process. He got an updated weather forecast from Stagg, which predicted a favorable window of opportunity for thirty-six hours beginning late on June 5. Although this meant that he would still risk less than fully favorable conditions, he went around the table to get another view from his staff. This time, they all concurred that it was possible to proceed despite the risks. With their input, Eisenhower made the final decision, and D-Day was set for June 6. Although this was a weighty decision for the supreme commander, it still followed the same simple process of the AIME decision model.

Now consider another example of a decision made by Brigadier General Teddy Roosevelt, Jr., assistant division commander, Fourth Infantry Division on Utah Beach. He was among the first troops to set foot on French soil. His superior, Major General Ray Barton, had reluctantly agreed to Roosevelt's request to go in with the main assault. This would prove to be fortuitous because the first waves of troops landed in the wrong place. The swift tidal current had carried the small assault boats about a mile down the beach. When BG Roosevelt stepped off his boat, he made a quick reconnaissance. He immediately realized that they were in the wrong location. This called for a quick decision: Should the rest of the division arrive where they just landed, or should they be rerouted to the correct location further up the beach? He decided to proceed from where they had landed. The follow-on forces would come to reinforce Roosevelt and his men and they could move inland together.

This on-the-spot decision was made quickly following a similar process of the AIME model. First, BG Roosevelt quickly assessed the situation: They had landed in the wrong place, yet resistance was relatively light and the troops were able to move inland. Redirecting the assault to the correct location would cause delays and confusion. Thus, the simple plan was to proceed from where they had landed. He made it happen by communicating his decision to the fleet. The Fourth Division assault on Utah proceeded with minimal disruption. As units continued to move inland across the causeways and further up the beach, he evaluated his decision by consulting with the brigade and battalion commanders. Since they met only limited resistance, it was reasonably clear that this was the right decision. Several weeks later, BG Roosevelt suffered a fatal heart attack, but his decisive leadership on Utah Beach earned him a Medal of Honor, which was granted posthumously. He was later interred at the American Cemetery at Colleville-sur-Mere where he rests along with almost ten thousand other soldiers, sailors, and airmen who died in the campaign.

Decision making on D-day was not confined to general officers. In fact, most of the critical decisions were made by sergeants and junior officers. Yet the AIME decision-making model still applies. Take for example the experience of Lt. Richard Winters described in *Band of Brothers* by Stephen Ambrose. As recounted in chapter three of the book, Lt. Winters found himself as the acting company commander for E Company 506th PRI, 101st Airborne Division when his company commander became a casualty during the jump. His battalion commander assigned to him the mission of destroying the German artillery battery at a place called Brecourt Manor. German artillery was dug in there and firing on Utah Beach. With only a fraction of his men available, Lt. Winters did a quick reconnaissance of the German position. He assessed the situation and determined that the fortified gun position was guarded by about fifty soldiers with automatic weapons, including the very effective MG-42 machine gun. He initiated a simple plan whereby part of his small force would lay down a "base of fire" with their own machine gun while the others would maneuver into the trench line assaulting and destroying each artillery piece in succession. Despite being outnumbered, they took vigorous action to make it happen and brilliantly executed their plan. In the process they not only destroyed the guns and prevented more casualties on the beach but also discovered a German map of the area. Upon evaluation it was determined that this map contained the details for other German defensive positions in the area, which only added to the overall success of this mission.

Another example of a decision made in the heat of battle was the one made by LTC Otway in the British sector. His parachute infantry unit was assigned to take the Merville Battery, which posed a threat to the British and Canadian forces landing in the Eastern sectors. Otway's battalion, like most of the airborne units, did not land all together at its designed drop zone. When they attempted to regroup, Otway discovered he had only about twenty percent of his force to attack the fortified position at Merville. He quickly assessed the situation. He basically had two alternatives: One was to commence an immediate attack with those whom he had gathered. The other was not to attack but to allow the fleet to commence firing on the fortification. In fact, this was a backup plan that was previously scheduled in the event that his unit failed to accomplish their mission. Before he made his decision, he encountered some of his soldiers who had breeched the outer defenses surrounding the position. Otway then initiated a simple plan: Conduct an immediate attack with the troops available. Wasting no time, he took action to make it happen by leading a violent but successful attack. As the attack was concluded, his quick evaluation was that they had succeeded in their mission. They were able to communicate their success to the fleet thereby canceling the barrage on the position. Evaluating this action as "mission accomplished," the British troops could now land on Sword Beach without interference from the German artillery at Merville.

Another great example of quick decision making on the beaches on D-day was the heroic work done by the medics attending to the wounded at great personal risk. Due to the overwhelming number of casualties with severe wounds, they were forced to make quick decisions about who they could help and who was likely to die. Otherwise known as triage, this process requires snap judgments in making life or death decisions based on medical expertise. The medics who landed with the 116th Infantry, 29th Infantry Division in the Dog Green sector on the western edge of Omaha Beach were forced to make these tough, life and death decisions under their baptism of fire. A Company landed in the first wave into an inferno of mortar and artillery fire as well as murderous crossfire from machine guns sited on the beach. The medics had little time to react. Within minutes after landing, almost the entire company was either killed or wounded. The company was leaderless as individual survivors desperately tried to save themselves and get to the shelter of a seawall. In this melee, medics moved from one casualty to the next trying to save those they could, but realizing that many were too severely wounded to help. If the medics tried to help the most severely wounded, they would waste not only time but also precious medical supplies needed to help those who could possibly be saved.

Did they go though the AIME decision-making process as they moved along the beach? Perhaps not consciously, but they clearly used a process informed by their medical training and common sense. In retrospect, one can analyze their triage process using the AIME model. Medical professionals, like professionals in most endeavors, tend to be able to make what appears to be snap decisions because they have been trained to immediately recognize the relevant facts and possible courses of action. Their experience and training allows them to quickly assess the situation, decide on a simple plan, and take immediate action. Then they follow up the decision with an evaluation when the situation permits. The AIME model perfectly describes the triage process. It is the same decision-making sequence but in compressed time. These same types of decisions are made virtually every day in emergency rooms in major cities. What might appear to be snap decisions by nurses and doctors are actually very deliberate decisions informed by years of training and their medical expertise.

So, although the AIME model is simply a framework, it represents the logical sequence of steps that successful decision makers use in a variety of situations. The process is the same even when the nature of the decisions is different. Whether it is time compressed, formal, or informal, the same sequence applies: Assess the situation, implement a simple plan, make it happen, and evaluate your decision.

Examples from the Business Battlefield

An example of a key decision made by a business enterprise was Johnson & Johnson's handling of the Tylenol poison scare in 1982.

This example is sometimes used in business schools as a classic case of business decision making during a crisis. At the time, Tylenol had a thirty-five percent market share, and it was one of the most popular over-the-counter pain relievers. Then someone tampered with a few bottles and subsequently there were several deaths in the Chicago area. Faced with a crisis of major proportions, Johnson & Johnson officials, led by CEO James Burke, needed to take action, and there was not much time to react. Further, they did not know if this was an isolated instance in Chicago or if it would happen elsewhere. The company officials quickly assessed the situation. The FBI went to work immediately, but they could not provide any definitive answers. In fact even until today this mystery has not been solved. However, Johnson & Johnson officials quickly assessed the situation. They knew that other people would be at risk of death if there were other tampered bottles on the shelves of drugstores. They moved to initiate a simple plan. Basically, they had several likely courses of action: They could wait and see if other incidents occurred, they could pull all Tylenol products from the shelves of Chicago-area retailers, or they could institute a nationwide recall of all Tylenol products and then proceed to develop a tamperproof bottle to protect consumers. Clearly the first two options were less expensive; however, the last option would clearly prevent any further deaths while protecting the company's reputation. Johnson & Johnson's executives decided on their course of action to initiate a simple plan: recall all their products nationwide. Then they quickly made it happen. Over thirty-one million bottles were collected with a retail value of over $100 million dollars. This was a costly recall but ultimately a wise choice.

After the recall, they evaluated what had happened. They developed the tamperproof bottles and restocked the shelves of retailers. Initially their market share slid to just eight percent, but consumers trusted the brand. Over time they were able to evaluate their decision. The consumer's trust was reinforced with the swift actions of the company to protect consumers, and despite the huge costs incurred, their market share quickly climbed back up. Even today, Tylenol is a respected pain reliever, highly recommended by medical professionals and a trusted brand for consumers. If you go to the Tylenol website, you will find that they promote safety as one of their core selling points. Thus, the decision to recall their products was not only a great decision but also stands today as an example for corporate responsibility in action. Although they did not use the AIME model to make the decision at the time, using the model now to analyze this decision makes it easy to see how their reasoning led them to a good decision.

Literally millions of business decisions are made every day at large and small businesses alike. Many of the decision makers could benefit from using the simple AIME decision model to add discipline to their process. They may need to decide if they should launch a new product, expand into a new market, offer their customers a special sale, automate their operations, or hire a new executive. Each business has unique challenges and available resources and each must make their decisions in their own context.

The leaders who make the decisions need to assess their situation by looking at their own operating environment. They next need to develop their options or courses of action. If they are hiring some additional staff, they will look at their top candidates as possible choices and perhaps have an additional option to delay the hiring altogether. By comparing and contrasting the options, in this case the qualifications of the potential candidates, the decision makers can decide which candidate has the best qualifications for the position. This will lead them to decide on a simple plan for the way forward. Once the decision is made, then it is up to the leaders to make it happen. This may require negotiations with a candidate if it is a hiring decision, or it might mean organizing a project implementation team for implementing a new IT system. Once the decision is made, it must be implemented with maximum effort. For all decisions, it is prudent to set up a time to evaluate the results. For complex decisions, such as implementing a complex IT solution, interim evaluations may make sense to keep the project on track. Regardless, using the AIME model will work for all kinds of businesses or nonprofit organizations. Using the model will sharpen the process for most organizations and allow decisions to be made more quickly and deliberately; the whole enterprise will benefit from having a common language on how to make decisions.

Your Personal Quest

Decision making at a personal level is just as important to you as an individual as it is to an organization. Your personal decisions will impact your success in life. Every day, we face decisions that impact our future. Some might seem insignificant and thus are not ones that we will spend a lot of time wondering about. Others are more important with differing consequences. For example:

- Should I apply to this college or not?
- If accepted should I attend?
- What major should I study?
- Should we have children now or wait?
- Do I accept this job offer or not?
- Where should we buy a house?
- Is this a good deal or not (on this house, car, or whatever)?

On the more important decisions, you will naturally spend more time and think about the consequences. Some people may choose to consult a friend, family member, or other trusted advisor. You might make some decisions primarily based on emotions or "gut feelings," whereas others might be more deliberately based on facts. In part, how you make your decisions will be based on the information and time available. In this sense, you make personal decisions with the same kinds of constraints that are present for organizational decisions.

In every case, having a decision-making model or framework would be helpful for most people. Although there are various models available, including the well-known "Ben Franklin checklist," the AIME model can be a useful model even for personal decisions.

In every case, whether it is personal or organizational, you will want to assess the situation. This involves gathering up relevant facts bearing on the problem. Your sources may vary, but basically you need to get whatever relevant information is available to help frame the problem and its possible solutions. Next, you initiate a simple plan by logically investigating your possible courses of action. My advice is to keep it real simple. For most decisions, generally there are only a few viable courses of action. If you find yourself facing more than five, then you need to first cull the list of possible courses of action down to no more than five, but preferably three. Then you simply compare and contrast the options by looking at the advantages and disadvantages of each. For this step, you might even use your "Ben Franklin checklist" by laying the options side by side in columns on a sheet of paper. Then you would simply list the pros and cons of each one to create a visual for yourself. Of course you can get more sophisticated in your analysis by assigning values to the most important and then adding the totals for each, giving you a numerical result. However, if your gut tells you that the best one is not the highest scoring option, be careful to consider your intuition. In the final analysis, you need to feel good about your decision. If you don't feel good about it from the start, then you will have trouble with the next step: Make it happen.

Once you decide on an option, then you should proceed to implement it quickly. Don't wait for more information or to see what happens next. If you felt that you needed more information then you should have made a decision not to proceed. Once you have decided on a course of action, you owe it to yourself and others to whom you have made commitments to vigorously implement your decision. When you put all your energy behind something, most often you will get the best results. You will not only get better results but you will also find out quickly if this was not the right course of action. This will naturally flow into the final step of the AIME decision model: evaluation.

When you give something your best shot, how you will know for sure if you are succeeding or need to make a course correction? No one makes perfect decisions every time. So if you made a poor decision, get over it quickly and make another decision on where to go next. The knowledge that very few decisions that we make are permanent will help most people who have a fear of making decisions to get on with it. Similar to a spaceship headed to the moon, there are course corrections that are made to hit the target. Marking your calendar for a future time to review the results of an important decision will help you develop the discipline that is necessary to make adjustments and achieve your goals. Thus, using a decision model like the AIME model can be very useful for anyone faced with an important decision. Next time you need to make a decision, think about how you can use such a model to help you organize your approach to the decision.

Staff Ride Notebook:
Timely Decisions: AIME Decision Model

Q1. How are decisions made in your organization? Do leaders use a common model or do they each make decisions in their own way? If they use a decision model how does it compare to the AIME model? (Assess the situation, initiate a simple plan, make it happen, and evaluate results.)

Q2. Are decisions in your organization evaluated? Does it make sense to formally revisit key decisions to reaffirm or make changes?

Q3. How do you make your decisions? Do you use a decision model? If so, how does it compare with the AIME model (assess the situation, initiate a simple plan, make it happen, evaluate results)?

Q4. When you make decisions, do you consciously develop and compare possible courses of action to come up with your plan?

Q5. How conscious are you of the organizational consequences of either postponing or avoiding decisions? Do you realize how deferring decisions impacts your team's ability to perform their job?

EXERCISE: Think about a recent decision that you made for your organization or team, or perhaps one that someone else made. How did they go about the decision-making process? Was it deliberate or did it appear to be arbitrary? What factors were considered? What courses of action were considered? How was the decision communicated? How was it implemented? What were the outcomes? Was the decision ever evaluated?

EXERCISE: Think about a decision that you need to make in the future. Could you apply the AIME model to your decision? If so, how would you plan each of the steps? (Assess the situation, initiate a simple plan, make it happen, and evaluate results)

CHAPTER ELEVEN
OPERATING PRINCIPLES AND VALUES

SUCCESSFUL ORGANIZATIONS USE OPERATING
PRINCIPLES AND VALUES TO FRAME
THEIR CULTURE, GUIDE BEHAVIOR, AND
ALLOW FOR FREEDOM OF ACTION

All successful organizations and leaders conduct their day-to-day activities based on a set of organizational values and operating principles. They do this because it provides a framework for their conduct and meaning for their actions. Every organization has a personality or culture. This is the manifestation of their values and operating principles. In some organizations, the values and operating principles evolve over time. They may or may not be consistently aligned with their mission. Great organizations understand that when there is alignment they can use the power of their values and operating principles to achieve the desired results. The leaders of these organizations spend time cultivating an organizational culture that supports their mission. They do this by making sure that the values and operating principles are truly embraced by everyone in the organization.

Operating principles and values are more like guidelines rather than strict rules. Some organizations have a rule-based culture where they try to anticipate everything that can come up and prescribe a rule for it. These organizations craft a thick set of rules to hand out to the team so that everyone can be familiar with the rules for any given situation. They enforce the rules and don't expect people to think for themselves. Whereas every organization needs some rules, successful enterprises have fewer rules. They focus more on operating principles and values as guidelines. They trust their people to make good decisions based on these principles and values. These organizations set the tone for a culture based on trust and responsibility. Their general guidelines provide only guidance on how to act and behave. They have some built in flexibility for people to do "the right thing" depending upon the circumstances. They expect their people to act in ways that are consistent with their shared values. Which type of organization would you prefer to join: a rule-based or value-based organization? Most would prefer the latter rather than the former. Regardless of your preference, neither approach is right or wrong. In some cases, a rule-based approach may be more appropriate for the nature of the work. Thus every organization must decide how it will operate and frame its culture accordingly. One of the best ways to do this is for the leaders to make conscious decisions about the operating principles and values.

In addition to organizational operating priniciples and values, leaders themselves also have their own set of values and operating principles that are often manifested in their leadership philosophy. Hopefully these are consistent with those of the organization, otherwise there will be a vast disconnect between the leader, their followers, and the organization generally. If that is the case, a leader whose values are inconsistent with the values of the organization will not succeed. Just like organizations, all leaders have values, whether or not they have consciously thought about them. Seasoned leaders have deliberately thought about and practice their leadership philosophy. Their leadership philosophy statement reflects their personal values. It informs them about their relationships with their followers and the organization. It guides them in developing their own leadership brand. Their standards dictate how they will hold themselves and their followers accountable: Do they enforce their standards uniformly or simply overlook transgressions? Do they hold themselves to the same standards as others? Do they favor certain people while chastising others who fall short of whatever the standards might be? Effective leaders have consciously thought through their values and philosophies. Their behaviors and approach to leadership are consistent with these foundational concepts.

A leader's values and philosophy will also impact their personal leadership style. A style is different from values or philosophy. Style is more about the approach rather than underlying values. For example two different leaders, one with a more autocratic style and the other with a more democratic style, can both share a value of integrity. There is no one best leadership style, and sometimes the style may vary depending on the situation; however, the values should always remain consistent. The style or approach of any individual leader is only appropriate in relationship to the organization they are leading and the circumstances in which they find themselves. So sometimes a leader in an emergency will be more autocratic by necessity when their normal style is more democratic. Getting people through a crisis often requires quick decisions and action more than debate and consensus building. The difference in the style that is used in different circumstances does not mean that they have abandoned their underlying values.

Whether or not values or philosophy are affirmatively stated, a leader's actions will speak louder than their words. Since leaders tend to set the tone by their actions, all leaders should consider operating from a well thought out leadership philosophy. Their philosophy benefits them by making them leaders who will act more consistently. It also benefits their followers who can trust their leaders to act based on their known values. Leaders don't necessarily need to publish their philosophy statement; the exercise of thinking it through is more important. Regardless whether it is published or not, a leadership philosophy should describe an approach to leadership and what is valued most. It should describe a leader's relationship to followers, the team or the broader organization. The investment of time in developing a leadership philosophy will pay off as when a leader is able to move more quickly about day-to-day business. Whatever the approach to leadership, the philosophy will provide the leader with guideposts as he or she moves through challenges and makes decisions that impact people and the organization.

So consider an example of how this works as a practical matter. Look at the following leadership philosophy: "All people want to be successful. As a leader my role is to make sure that people have the right skills, information, and resources to be successful." With this philosophy, what would a leader do when confronted with a member of the team who is a substandard performer? Would he or she resort first to coaching or disciplinary action? Would the leader ignore the issue and hope that it will go away? The leader applying the philosophy in this example would likely first investigate the root cause of the problem. Is it a skill problem, lack of information, or lack of resources? Depending on the answer to the question, this leader would likely address the problem from that perspective rather than start with a disciplinary action. That doesn't mean that the leader wouldn't fire a nonperformer. It simply means that a leader with this philosophy wouldn't start there.

Ultimately, values and operating principles guide people in their behaviors. These behaviors are the outward manifestation of people's beliefs about themselves and their organization. Effective leaders model the behaviors that they expect their people and the organization to exhibit. If they say they value something but act inconsistently with the stated values, people will detect the inconsistency. In the most effective organizations, both leaders and followers consistently act in accordance with the organization's stated values. This is the foundation for a strong organizational culture. How they act in various circumstances will determine their impact on the people they interact with on a daily basis. It will also determine how well they collectively achieve their organizational mission.

Examples from Operation Overlord

What are some of the ways that operating principles and values were evident during the struggles of World War II in northern France? One good example is in the Allied approach to combat. The Allies were fortunate to have the resources of the U.S. industrial base to supply them with massive amounts of weapons, ammunition, and equipment. They used this advantage by employing overwhelming firepower to open the way for their ground forces and minimize casualties. Often this tactic did not have the intended effect because it was not effectively implemented, such as on Omaha Beach where the preassault bombardment did not work. However, the operating principle of using overwhelming firepower to minimize friendly casualties was a tactic that was frequently employed. Unfortunately, due to the destruction that resulted from employing massive firepower, there were also many civilian casualties and much private property destroyed. Yet the Allied soldiers knew that they could count on their commanders to use the full spectrum of their resources to minimize their own casualties. They knew that their leaders valued their lives and welfare.

Another operating principle favored mobile warfare over static defense. Clearly there were instances when the Allies were on the defense, such as in the Battle of Moritain; however, they employed the principle of mobile warfare to bypass resistance and maintain the initiative. Despite the Germans' reputation for blitzkrieg style warfare, the Allies actually had more mobility with their armored and mechanized infantry. Since they also had the advantage of air superiority over the battlefield, Allied units could maneuver without the threat of being exposed to an attack by the German Luftwaffe. This meant that they could operate with more freedom of action, circumvent strong points, and envelop enemy positions from the flanks or rear. Effectively using the operating principle of mobility was a key to the Allies' success in the Normandy campaign. Once the breakout was achieved by the Americans in the western zone of operations, the Allies employed their mobility to outflank the German army.

Operating principles and values also were part of the culture of individual units as well. For example, the elite units such as the Rangers and the airborne units had operating principles and values that were a part of their own culture. In both cases they valued bold, aggressive, and independent action. They expected to be given tough missions that were critical to the outcome of the overall campaign. This is what they were trained to do. They also knew that they would likely be outnumbered, isolated from the main force, and lacking some of their equipment. As anticipated, they were assigned some of the most important and difficult missions. Also as anticipated, they were outnumbered and isolated, often in small groups. Nevertheless, they had been indoctrinated into a culture guided by operating principles and values that supported bold, aggressive, and independent action. These soldiers took it upon themselves to act decisively rather than hunker down until more help arrived. In highlighting these specialized units, I do not mean to take away from the valor of other units who also acted with bold and determined aggressive action. I simply mean to demonstrate that values and operating principles apply at the small unit level as well as at the higher organizational levels.

What about leadership philosophy? General Marshall's leadership philosophy is a great example. Marshall's philosophy was to pick the best qualified person for the job and then delegate full responsibility and authority to him to get the job done. This was embodied in his guidance to General Eisenhower. After having nominated Eisenhower to fill the post of supreme commander, once he was confirmed, he held him accountable to execute the mission and make all decisions that impacted his command. Marshall only got involved as needed and requested by Eisenhower. He helped solve problems, such as obtaining additional resources or resolving issues with the British that needed additional support from the American senior leadership. Otherwise, Marshall advised Eisenhower to make decisions as he deemed necessary to carry out his mission and Marshall supported those decisions. In doing so, Marshall also set the example for Eisenhower and his subordinates on how they should operate with their own subordinates. Marshall modeled the behavior that reflected the values of trust and accountability. His strong leadership was felt throughout the U.S. Army everywhere during World War II but particularly in the European Theater of Operations because of his close relationship with General Eisenhower.

Examples from the Business Battlefield

How do other enterprises employ the principles of organizational values and operating principles? Let's take a look at the Marriott Corporation. Marriott celebrated its eightieth anniversary in 2007. From its beginning, Marriott Corporation has been guided by the values of the Marriott family. The company was founded in 1927 by J. Willard and Alice S. Marriott as a root beer stand in Washington, D.C. Over the years, the company expanded into a variety of food services businesses and in 1957 opened its first hotel. It now has over three thousand hotels in sixty-seven countries under a variety of well-known brand names. It operates resort properties, restaurants, and other businesses that provide high quality services to their customers worldwide. Underpinning all this remarkable growth and success has been a genuine commitment to their values and operating principles.

If you visit their corporate website, you will find a page devoted to their culture and values. If you have stayed in one of their hotels or visited one of their restaurants, you will identify with the values that you find on the page. Their brands have a reputation for quality service and products. One of their operating principles is a simple statement of "Do whatever it takes to take care of the customer." They accomplish this by empowering employees to do the right thing. Their employees take pride in the organization and pay attention to the details. These are more than just words on a page, they are the values that the organization imparts to their people and reinforces with rewards and recognition. Today, Marriott Corporation is widely recognized as one of the best run large companies anywhere and a great place to work.

Another commercial enterprise that uses the power of organizational values and operating principles is Federal Express. The company was founded by Fred Smith based on a concept he developed as an undergraduate student at Yale University. FedEx began its overnight package delivery services in 1973 with less than two hundred packages. It is now operating worldwide in over 220 countries and territories with multiple businesses. They no longer just ship packages, but provide innovative supply chain services to their customers, office and copy services at FedEx Kinkos, and ground freight delivery. The FedEx companies focus on three operating principles: compete collectively, operate independently, and manage collaboratively. These operating principles are reflected in their strategies that allow the FedEx businesses to work together while still operating independently.

Their reputation for reliable service is legendary as are some of the stories about their employees who have gone to great lengths to make sure that the packages are delivered on time for their customers. I distinctly remember reading many years ago an article in the *Wall Street Journal* about one of their planes that was experiencing some problems while flying over the Midwestern United States back to their Memphis hub. Although this was not an immediate emergency, many pilots would have landed immediately to have the plane looked at, but instead this FedEx pilot decided to fly through to Memphis so that the packages could be delivered on time. This may not seem like a big deal to many, but it does show the power of values and operating principles that inspire employees to accomplish their mission in the face of adversity.

On their website, FedEx features "everyday heroes." These are stories about FedEx employees who have gone above and beyond to serve their customers and their communities. Recently featured were several employees who had done some extraordinary things to help out in the immediate aftermath of hurricane Katrina. One of them made a local office of FedEx available to the Red Cross to allow them to use their facilities to coordinate recovery efforts. Another made 150 portable radios available to first responder and military officials so that they could communicate. Although these stories are noteworthy in themselves, what is more interesting is the way that FedEx publicizes these stories to their own employees and customers. In doing so, they reinforce their values, operating principles, and commitment to the customer. At FedEx and other great companies, the actions and behaviors support the stated values. The leaders and great employees model the expected behaviors. This is how they get all employees to act in accordance with the organizational values and operating principles. The stories become part of the culture and the behavioral norms of the organization.

A good example of a nonprofit organization based on values and principles is the International Red Cross/Red Crescent Movement. They have a clear statement of their principles that guide their affiliate organizations worldwide: humanity, impartiality, neutrality, independence, voluntary service, unity, and universality. Each of these values and principles has a detailed definition. In accordance with these principles, there is only one authorized affiliate in each country dedicated to the humanitarian work for which they are recognized worldwide: protection of prisoners, disaster relief, and prevention of human suffering. They remain neutral at all times, especially in times of conflict, and treat people regardless of race, religion, or nationality. Their adherence to these principles allows them to do their work worldwide with minimal interference. When governments or others attempt to force them to do something in conflict with these fundamental values and principles, the Red Cross will stand firm with the knowledge that their principles will generally prevail in the end. This strong brand is universally recognized worldwide, and their commitment to their values lets them do good work when other organizations sometimes are prevented from helping. The Red Cross/Red Crescent demonstrates how the power of organizational values and principles can be a very potent force in allowing any organization to fulfill its mission.

Your Personal Quest

Are these same principles useful in your personal quest in life? I believe that they not only can be useful but might even be essential for your success. If you have never taken time out to review your own personal values, you might find this to be a very useful exercise as suggested in the Staff Ride Notebook section for this chapter. The list of possibilities is long which might make it difficult for you to decide which values are more important to you. You should try to limit yourself to no more than five most important values. If you have more than five, it is difficult to remember which ones are most important and a longer list dilutes the importance of the individual values that you have chosen. If you complete the exercise, and embrace your values, then they can provide you with guideposts as you go through life's challenges.

Staff Ride Notebook: Operating Principles and Values

Q1. Does your organization have operating principles? If so, do you know what they are? Does the organization really use them to guide their day-to-day operations?

Q2. Does your organization have a set of values? Are they well known to everyone in the organization? Do people live the values in their daily work habits?

Q3. Effective leaders model the behaviors they expect others to use. Do leaders in your organization "walk the talk" by modeling appropriate behaviors? How would you change your behavior to be more consistent with the organizational expectations?

EXERCISE: Think about an organization that you belonged to in the past or another organization with which you are familiar. Did the organization have a well defined set of values? What were the values, or if there were none, what should they have been? Did they have any operating principles, or if not, what should they have been? How were the operating principles and values communicated? How were they practiced? Were they really part of the organizational culture? What could have been done to strengthen them? How were they communicated to you when you were new to the organization?

EXERCISE: Do you have a written leadership philosophy? How would you describe your philosophy? If you don't have one, write a few sentences that describe your ideal approach to leadership.

EXERCISE: What are your personal values? (For a list of values to choose from go to www.victoryprinciples.com) In what ways are you living your values? How do your values compare with the organizational values of your current organization? Are they complimentary or inconsistent?

CHAPTER TWELVE
RESILIENCE

SUCCESSFUL LEADERS ARE RESILIENT IN THE
FACE OF ADVERSITY. THEY REMAIN FLEXIBLE AND
ADAPT TO CHANGED CIRCUMSTANCES WHILE
VIGOROUSLY EXECUTING THEIR MISSION.

It is an old military adage often attributed to Fredrick the Great that no plan survives the first contact with the enemy. Thus, as the battle unfolds, events are often unpredictable despite your best planning efforts. This unpredictability results from a myriad of factors, not only the enemy's own reaction to your moves but also weather, terrain, battlefield losses, and sometimes just plain luck or lack thereof.

Regardless of the situation, one should expect the unexpected. Military actions are influenced by poor intelligence, faulty assumptions, changed conditions, and unplanned setbacks. It is the job of the leader to deal with these unexpected problems, make adjustments, and vigorously continue with the mission. This is often much easier said than done, especially in the unforgiving nature of combat where people are wounded or dying. It requires the ability to remain cool under fire, quickly think through the alternatives, and use the means available to secure the objective. This ability to effectively deal with setbacks, adversity, and change in general is key to success not only in the military but in all sorts of endeavors. What makes leaders effective is their resilience, "the ability to recover quickly from illness, change, or misfortune," as defined in the *American Heritage Dictionary*. They must be able to deal with the unexpected events in real time and recover quickly.

Resilience may require other skills and abilities. Certainly, it requires courage to move ahead in the face of adversity. When faced with a challenge some people become paralyzed and lose their ability to take action. They are overcome by the circumstances and lack the courage to forge ahead. The resilient leader will demonstrate personal courage by taking action and leading others to take action. The required action might not have been planned but is necessary to overcome the obstacles.

Resilient people must also have the virtue of perseverance. They never give up on themselves or others. Resilience also requires the ability to stay calm and think through the new situation. Regardless of how dire the circumstances, resilient leaders find within themselves the motivation to keep on pushing. They persevere. Additionally, resilience requires the ability to be flexible, make appropriate adjustments, and decide on an appropriate course of action. Thus resilient leaders are quick to analyze their predicament and make choices and decisions. This quick analysis may require learning agility. In fact, current research into leadership under extreme circumstances confirms that learning agility is the most important indicator of success. Under extreme conditions such as combat, people don't need to be motivated because the situation itself is motivating. What they need to succeed is the ability to quickly decide what is working and what is not working and apply the lessons. Resilience in this context embodies courage, perseverance, learning agility, and decision making all at the same time.

Examples from Operation Overlord

The story of Normandy offers numerous examples of resilient leaders and individuals. For example, consider the paratroopers who landed in unfamiliar territory without their weapons. Some chose to seek shelter until the morning light, but the vast majority struck out to find their units and improvised. They picked up weapons along the way or substituted what they had on hand to replace equipment that was lost or damaged in the jump. The Canadian paratroopers used mines when they lacked demolition charges to destroy the bridges assigned as their mission. Small unit actions were undertaken with under strength units to successfully attack major fortifications such as the Merville Battery, Point du Hoc or the concrete widerstandnests on Omaha Beach. Leaders such as LTC Terence Otway, Ranger First Sergeant Len Lomell, and Captain Joe Dawson demonstrated resilience by their courage to move ahead with their missions despite major obstacles, including not having most of their unit available.

Resilience was demonstrated on the assault beaches when the Fourth Division landed in the wrong place on Utah Beach. BG Teddy Roosevelt and COL James Van Fleet quickly sized up the situation and decided to move inland from where they had landed. Some might say that they really had no choice because it would have been almost impossible to reboard the assault craft. Yet they kept their cool, considered their options, and did not wait for further instructions. They remained flexible and made a decision to proceed rather than stick to their old plan. Then they vigorously moved ahead with their mission.

On Omaha Beach soldiers confronted adversity in the most extreme form when they stepped off the boats into the cross fire of pre-sited automatic weapons and artillery that covered almost the entire beach. Leaders such as BG Norman Cota and COL George Taylor demonstrated personal courage and resilience to move their men off the beach. Noncommissioned officers such as Sergeant Phillip Streczyk rallied men to persevere despite the fact that they were expecting the beach defenses to have been obliterated by the bombings in advance of their landing. Thousands of others demonstrated resilience up and down the beach as they moved to the shingle and recovered to use Bangalore torpedoes to blast their way through barbed wire entanglements. Offshore, the captains of the destroyers who risked their ships as they came in to provide direct fire on the beach showed resilience by defying orders in order to do what they knew needed to be done. Their courageous actions under fire perhaps saved the day on Omaha.

The Rangers also demonstrated resilience in the assault on Point du Hoc. It began when LTC James Earl Rudder took charge as he realized they were headed in the wrong direction and he directed their flotilla to move to the correct spot. Individual Rangers improvised when their equipment for scaling the cliffs did not worked as planned. When they got to the top of the point, they again demonstrated resilience by continuing their mission even when they found that there were no guns emplaced in the casements. Their perseverance paid off when they later found the guns and destroyed them by breaking the gun sites and placing thermite grenades on the traversing mechanisms. The Ranger force as a unit demonstrated resilience when they held their position for several days instead of being relieved on D-Day as originally planned.

In the days and weeks that followed, resilience was what carried the Allies through to victory. As they moved off the beaches and ran right smack into the hedgerows, they encountered stiff German defenses in terrain that they had not fully anticipated. They were repulsed time and again as they tried to make their way further inland to key objectives. In the American sector, the march to St. Lo and the capture of Cherbourg required successive assaults against determined resistance. Likewise, it was over thirty days before the British were able to capture Caen and even later until the Americans broke out into Brittany. In the process, they encountered setbacks from friendly fire and the lack of a deep water port to bring in more supplies and reinforcements. Despite the significant casualties and the physiological impact of weeks of constant combat, Allied soldiers demonstrated their resilience as they carried on with their mission to defeat the German Army in Normandy.

Examples from the Business Battlefield

The United States' National Aeronautics and Space Administration (NASA) is a great example of an organization that has demonstrated resilience in the face of adversity. Although NASA is a federal agency, it is in many ways a business in that its customers are the taxpayers and their elected representatives in Congress. If NASA doesn't serve its customers with a worthy program, it will not get the funding it needs to continue operations. This was recognized from the very beginning when NASA had a huge publicity campaign built around the original seven astronauts in the Mercury program. If you are old enough to remember, you will have memories of seeing these men on television during the 1960s and many well-publicized launch events. In the beginning, each launch was a major television event. The story of how NASA marketed them to America was later chronicled in the book and the movie *The Right Stuff*. In a very real way, NASA was competing for funding and limited resources, and it had to be run like a business.

When did NASA have to demonstrate its organizational resilience? Several examples come to mind: First is the example of the fire that destroyed Apollo 1 and tragically killed three astronauts. Next is the example of the Apollo 13 mission that was aborted in order to save the lives of the crew. Finally, there is the restart of the shuttle program following the tragedies of Challenger and Columbia that also resulted in the deaths of their crews. Each of these disasters would have been enough to totally derail many organizations and perhaps put them out of business. Yet NASA demonstrated the capacity to look inward, discover the root cause of the problems, and then resiliently recover with an action plan to continue its mission. NASA is an amazing organization and has achieved great results not only in manned spaceflight but also through its engineering innovations, which have contributed enormously to many of the devices that we now take for granted. One of the keys to NASA's success has been their resilience when faced with adversity.

One of the most inspiring visions for the United States and the world was the vision set forth by President Kennedy in 1961 to land a man on the moon and return him safely to Earth within the decade. There had been various technical problems along the way to deal with, including some public failures with early rocket launches and the loss of one of the Mercury space capsules, Liberty Bell 7, before it could be recovered from its splashdown in the Pacific Ocean. However discouraging these problems might have been, they did not involve any deaths. That tragically changed when a fire engulfed the Apollo 1 capsule on January 27, 1967. During a routine prelaunch systems test, a raging fire exploded within the sealed spacecraft while the three astronauts were strapped in their seats. The fire was accelerated due to the on-board oxygen-rich environment, and the men were quickly overcome by smoke exhaustion. They also sustained serious burns as their nylon spacesuits melted away. After dealing with the immediate loss of life, further missions were canceled until they could fix whatever problems had caused this to happen.

NASA officials appointed a review board of scientists and engineers to investigate the incident. They made a significant number of recommendations, which NASA embraced despite the almost two-year delay to the Apollo program. Although they never determined the exact cause of the fire, there were several obvious contributing factors to the loss of life: the super-oxygenated inside atmosphere, potential wiring problems, and inability of the astronauts to have a quick escape hatch. All of these and other problems were corrected, including newly designed space suits that were fire retardant. After resuming the Apollo program, the goal set by President Kennedy was finally achieved by the crew of Apollo 11 on July 20, 1969, when Neil Armstrong became the first man to step onto the surface of the moon.

NASA again demonstrated its resilience when tragedy struck on the Apollo 13 mission to the moon. The story has been made famous by the movie with the same name. Although the flight started out as a routine mission, on the way to the moon, it quickly became a crisis.

An oxygen tank ruptured during a routine procedure causing a hole in the side of their service module. Following this incident, the mission became one of saving the crew.

The team of NASA engineers quickly adapted to overcome a variety of problems to get the crew back to Earth safely. These included the ideas of using the gravitational pull of the moon to return the spacecraft to Earth, using the lunar excursion module (LEM) as a temporary life support system, and improvising solutions for scrubbing carbon dioxide from the air. The engineers also had to determine how to conserve the onboard electricity to power up the computer for reentry back to Earth. The flight director, Gene Kranz, famously coined the phrase "failure is not an option." As a leader who focused on solutions to problems, Gene Kranz demonstrated NASA's capacity for resilience in the face of adversity. The crew was ultimately returned safely to Earth through extraordinary efforts of the entire NASA team.

NASA was once again struck by tragedy in the loss of two of its shuttle spacecraft, Challenger and Columbia. The shuttle program had been largely successful until one morning in January 1986 as millions of viewers watched the Challenger shuttle explode on television shortly after takeoff. All seven astronauts on board were killed instantly. President Ronald Reagan made a heartfelt speech to the nation, and once again NASA convened an investigation to discover the cause of the problem. It was determined that a rubber o-ring was defective and the ultimate root cause of the explosion.

After another delay, this time over two years, flights were resumed. Then in 2003 tragedy struck once again. The Columbia space shuttle disintegrated as it returned to Earth. Another investigation revealed that when Columbia was launched, some foam insulation broke off from the fuel tanks and damaged the heat shield tiles on the wing of the spacecraft. Apparently this damage led to a catastrophic break up of the shuttle as it heated up upon reentry over Texas. After this tragedy, many people began to question the importance of continuing the entire space program; however, NASA proceeded to make the appropriate fixes, and with the launch of the Discovery shuttle in 2005, NASA continued its space flight missions, once again demonstrating its resilience.

Few organizations face such large-scale public failures as these and recover successfully. NASA's ability to persevere in the face of significant adversity is a tribute to the organization. Americans can be proud of its unwavering commitment to its mission as well as the entire team of brave astronauts and skilled technical experts that make this organization successful. We should all be grateful not only for NASA's contributions to scientific research, but also the many advances that we enjoy because they pioneered work in computers, electronics, and useful materials. None of this would be possible without the resilience that is a part of the DNA of NASA.

Your Personal Quest

Resiliency is one of the secrets to personal success. No matter how successful you have been in your life, I can guarantee that you didn't get to a high level of success without facing some adversity. Just growing up requires some level of resilience even though you did not consciously understand it. When you learned to walk and talk, your success depended almost entirely on your level of resiliency. No one starts walking or talking from the day they were born. Everyone goes through a personal challenge of trial and error to learn how to stand up on two legs and take a step forward. Likewise, everyone learns to talk by approximating the sounds made by adults even though you don't understand what they are saying. Only over an extended period of time do you finally grasp the meaning of words and does walking become a largely unconscious act. The stumbling and mumbling along the way require you to be resilient and try again until you get it right.

As we grow older, people become more conscious of their setbacks. If you have ever been cut from an athletic team in high school, you understand how devastating that can be to your ego. Likewise, if you were rejected by a college that you really wanted to attend or if you were fired from a job, you also know how these can also be difficult setbacks to deal with personally.

However, agonizing over what happened does not change the circumstances. You can only go forward, not backward. You can ask yourself what did I learn, or how could I have done something differently to get a different and more favorable result? If you take corrective action, you can reapply to a school or try out next year for the team. What you do in the interim makes all the difference. The sooner you recognize your reality and get on with a plan of action, the sooner you can start to achieve a different result for yourself. This is the essence of resilience. Paraphrasing Winston Churchill, you never, never give up if there is something important for you to achieve.

Will you always succeed? Of course not, but if you don't demonstrate resilience, it is a foregone conclusion that you will not succeed. You need to be resilient to take positive action in the direction of your goals. People who don't work at being resilient will generally be "paralyzed" for a period of time. They will be unable to take any meaningful action. They let their circumstances control them rather than trying to control their own circumstances.

All successful entrepreneurs, inventors, and athletes must have resilience to succeed in their chosen endeavor. Thomas Edison famously tried over a thousand ways to build a light bulb until it worked. Abraham Lincoln lost several elections before he became the president. Many of the world's most famous entrepreneurs failed multiple times at various business ventures before they landed on a successful model. None of them gave up. Each of them had the resilience to come back after a setback and try something different until they succeeded. Next time you are facing a setback, stop and think about what you just learned and what you can do differently in the future. Don't fret about what you didn't achieve. Make yourself resilient in the face of adversity.

It may be easier to think about this in the abstract than it is when something happens to you. For this reason, it sometimes is easier to think about a contingency plan if something goes wrong. Often professionals practice how to handle emergencies that are unplanned and often dangerous when things go wrong. Commercial airline pilots are famous for this. They are required to practice emergency procedures. Airlines require them to spend time in simulators where they can practice these procedures without endangering their aircraft or their passengers. You expect pilots to be resilient when something goes wrong; otherwise, most people would not be inclined to get on an airplane.

Police officers and firefighters also practice for emergencies. Having thought through what they will do when something bad happens makes all the difference. They know what to do and don't dwell on what just happened to them. They take immediate corrective action.

All professionals deal with adversity and how well they deal with it is what makes them a professional. Perhaps you can put this aspect of resiliency to work for you. Think about potential challenges that you might face and ask yourself, what should I do? Have a contingency plan in place. Be a professional. Be resilient!

Staff Ride Notebook: Resilience

Q1. How resilient is your organization? When your organization runs into problems, what is the typical reaction? How do the leaders handle themselves in times of adversity? What can be done to improve the organization's resiliency?

Q2. How do you rate yourself on resiliency? Do you quickly recover from adversity or do you "stew" on it over a long period before you can take constructive action to recover? Are there things that you could do differently to handle adversity?

EXERCISE: Remember a time when your organization or team suffered a setback. For example, your company may have needed to shut down a business, or perhaps they lost a key account. Write a summary of what happened. How did you and your organization deal with it? What was done to recover? How did the leaders deal with this? How did the people react? What could have been done differently for a better result? What lessons were learned from this event?

EXERCISE: Remember a time when you faced a personal setback either at work or in your personal life. For example, you were not hired for a job you really wanted, or perhaps were fired from one that you had. Write a summary of what happened to you. How did you feel about it at the time? What did you do to recover? What did you learn from this experience? How would you deal with a similar situation in the future?

CHAPTER THIRTEEN
YOUR TEAM AND TEAM BUILDING

LEADERS TAKE FULL RESPONSIBILITY FOR THEIR TEAM.

The final and perhaps most important pillar of victory is your team. The team is everything. Without an effective team, even the greatest leader cannot succeed. This is particularly true in the military. Among General Patton's numerous sayings is that an army "lives, sleeps, and fights like a team." The concept of team carries through in everything that is done in the military from the squad level to the division level to the army level. When the chips are down, it is the primary reason that soldiers fight. They may sign up for various reasons—patriotism, service to country, or perhaps educational benefits. However, numerous studies have shown that when they get into combat, soldiers fight for their team and comrades. Therefore, military teams try simulate combat in training so that when they get into tough situations, the team members know that they can depend on each other.

What makes a good team? There are a variety of components, but there is no secret recipe. Great teams start with great people who are led by great leaders. On great teams, each member of the team knows his or her role and what is expected. Everyone on the team depends on their teammates to do their job. They count on each other. They are well-trained and usually have bonded either through intensive training or an actual intensive shared experience. Typically, the more intense the experience is, the more the team bonds together. This is one reason why elite military units often have the most intensive training experiences. On great teams, the members share responsibility for getting the job done. In the military this means accomplishing the mission. They care about each other and the leader takes care of them. Although it is relatively easy to list the ingredients, a great team still depends on all of these things coming together in the right combination and under the right circumstances. So let's look at these components individually. We can use the acronym TEAM to help.

Examples from Operation Overlord
T Is for Training

There is an axiom in the military that a unit should "train as you fight." That means that units should conduct training that is as realistic as possible. There is no better way to build a team than to put them through an intensive training regimen. Tough, realistic training conditions require intense preparation and planning. Teams that go though such an experience usually forge a bond among the team members as they share the risks and are forced to depend on each other to succeed.

All elite units go through intense training. They deliberately stress their people and their collective abilities as a unit. They push teams to their limits so that they can have confidence to persevere even in worst case scenarios. For example, in advance of the Normandy invasion, the American Ranger units went through such training with the British Commandos. Likewise, the airborne units were trained intensively and practiced their drops with strapped on combat loads of equipment. In fact, the Rangers and airborne were all-volunteer units that were drawn from the other units. Draftees often volunteered for these units because they knew that they would get the best training and also be with other motivated volunteers whom they could depend upon.

Although the beach assault units were comprised mainly of draftees, they also underwent realistic training in advance of the invasion. The beach assault units all took their turns in mock assaults with live-fire exercises at the Assault Training Center at Slapton Sands on the southern coast of England. Senior Allied commanders recognized the importance of training under actual conditions. They rehearsed live-fire exercises that were planned on the prior experiences with landings in North Africa and Italy. They incorporated lessons learned from these earlier missions that did not go as planned. Eisenhower told Marshall, "Our people from the very highest to the very lowest have learned that this is not a child's game, and are eager to get down to the fundamental business of profiting by the lessons they have learned. I am going to make it a fixed rule that no unit from the time it reaches the theater until the war is won will ever stop training."[50]

Realistic training adds confidence to the team. The members gain confidence in themselves and in each other. Many veterans who are interviewed after a combat experience will state that, when the chips were down, their training kicked in and they did what had to be done. For this reason, training is not a luxury, but is an imperative to forging a successful team.

E Is for Everyone Knows Their Job

On any good team, it usually goes without saying that everyone knows their job. This is the second primary ingredient for a great team. On all really great teams, they often not only know their job, but someone else's job too. On great teams people are great at the fundamentals and their roles are clear. That means each person knows their job cold. There is no confusion about who is supposed to do what. He or she can do their job in their sleep. More often than not, they can anticipate where their teammates will be and what they will be doing because they also know someone else's job.

On great teams, members are cross-trained and can fill in for another job when needed to support the team. This is particularly true in the military, where soldiers need to be ready to step up and take over in the event of a casualty on the team. The same holds true for firefighters battling a major structural fire. On great teams, they are not only ready to do someone else's the job but also are ready to step up into a leadership role if necessary.

The story of D-Day is the story of men stepping up to do the job of their comrades or leaders who were wounded or killed while making the attack. In many of the assault units, particularly on the beaches, officers and sergeants were among the first casualties. On Omaha Beach, it was not uncommon in some of the first arriving units to have lost all of their key leaders within the first few minutes. This left the task of leadership to those who were ready to lead among the survivors, regardless of rank. Sergeants took over for lieutenants, and, in some cases, privates took over for both officers and noncommissioned officers.

A Is for Accountability

The third ingredient of great teams is accountability. On all great teams, people accept responsibility for their actions or failure to act. They are accountable to themselves and to the team for performing their role at a high level. When things go wrong, as they always will, they don't try to point the finger at someone else. They take responsibility and make necessary adjustments as quickly as possible. They don't make excuses. In the military there is a maxim for commanders: A commander is responsible for everything his unit does or fails to do. This sets the command climate for everyone to take responsibility for their role within the unit as well. Obviously, the commander cannot do everything by himself, so he or she delegates authority to subordinates. A commander can delegate authority but not responsibility. Great leaders are accountable for themselves and their teams.

A specific example of taking responsibility during Operation Over-lord was when Eisenhower drafted a press release for the possibility that the landings failed. He was prepared to accept full responsibility when he drafted the following message: "Our landings have failed....If any blame or fault attaches to the attempt, it is mine alone." He realized that the invasion was not a guaranteed success. If it failed, he was willing to take responsibility as the supreme commander. He knew that this was his responsibility as the leader.

He also shouldered this responsibility with the virtue of selfless service. In the event of failure, this was not only a command responsibility as he saw it but also a way to protect both Roosevelt and Churchill. He knew these men were critical to carrying on the war effort even if the landings failed. By taking any blame for failure upon himself, Eisenhower would make sure that they would still be able to carry on. Likewise, Eisenhower was prepared to hold his people accountable and did. He relieved several senior commanders and key staff officers for performance or other infractions of discipline. He also expected his senior subordinate commanders to do the same when necessary. Although some of these decisions are still controversial, Eisenhower and his key leaders did what they deemed necessary to hold subordinate leaders accountable for their own performance and the performance of their units.

M is for Morale

The final ingredient for great teams is morale. One way that leaders ensure high morale is to take care of their people. Some leadership experts might call this servant leadership, where the leader serves those they lead. Another famous leadership maxim states: people don't care about you as a leader until they know that you care about them. If you are a leader and take care of your people, they will reciprocate by taking care of you. This is not a technique to manipulate people, and if used in this way, it will not work. As a leader, you must genuinely care about those on your team.

As a senior leader, this means visiting frontline people for yourself where they work. Find out how they are doing and what they need to succeed. Great military leaders "lead from the front" by visiting troops where they are engaged. On June 7, 1944, Eisenhower crossed the Channel to see things for himself and to meet with his senior commanders. Throughout the European campaigns, Ike frequently visited the areas, not only to talk to commanders at all levels but also to talk with the soldiers. In part the goal was to see and be seen by the troops, but it was more than that—the supreme commander felt it necessary to be intimately familiar with the tactical situation in order to make sound operational decisions when required. He particularly needed to see the facts for himself when he received conflicting recommendations from his subordinate commanders.[51] All effective senior leaders followed this practice.

Examples from the Business Battlefield

A good example of a large company that practices teamwork is United Services Automobile Association (USAA). I have been a customer for over thirty years and the reason I stay with USAA is the excellent service that is delivered by a great team. USAA was founded in the 1920s by a group of military officers who needed to get automobile insurance. Originally started as a mutual insurance company exclusively for military officers, it has now grown into a large financial services firm. It is nationally ranked by Fortune Magazine as 176th in revenue, 90th in net worth, and 69th in assets on its most recent ratings of U.S. companies.[52] The firm now has diversified to a full line of insurance, banking, and investment products. It has also expanded its customer base to include noncommissioned officers as well as family members of existing members resulting in more than 5.6 million customers. They are consistently ranked at the highest rating by all the insurance rating agencies. They have been recognized with multiple awards for great service to their members over the years.

True to its roots, many of the senior USAA executives are retired military officers who had great careers in the military and almost all have earned advanced degrees. Having served in significant leadership positions before joining USAA, they are now using that expertise to run a great company. If you are a customer of USAA, you know what I mean when I say it provides great service to its members. Their reputation for providing great service is legendary.

So what are some of the hallmarks of this great company? USAA puts the VICTORY principles into practice. Like many other companies, they have a vision for the company: "We have what you need to make it simple, including insurance, free financial advice, banking, investing, member discounts, and shopping—all delivered according to our core values of honesty, integrity, loyalty, and service." However, the difference between USAA and many other companies is that they do a great job executing their vision. USAA hires great people, trains them well, and provides them with the resources they need to do a great job. They follow up with customers to make sure that they are getting the service that they desire. The bottom line for USAA is that it has developed a team of people who are clear about what they need to do. They work together to make it happen and are dedicated to the values and mission of the organization. This is all part of their corporate culture.

The employees at USAA strive together to achieve their common goals. They take responsibility for their actions and support one another to accomplish their mission. The senior leadership takes care of their people by providing the resources, rewards, and recognition as all good leaders do for their people. High employee morale and engagement translates to good customer service and financial results for the organization. The same principles involved in building any small team apply here, but only on a larger scale. Within the larger organization are a number of small teams of trained specialists in insurance, banking, and investments who share common values of the larger organization and the desire to serve their customer.

Another company that exceeds customer expectations with a great team is Disney. If you have young children and have visited one of the Disney theme parks you have most likely experienced their teamwork in action. Disney works very hard to make your visit "an experience" in the most positive sense. They select people with care to be part of their crew. Then they train their entire staff at the on-site campus of Disney University. This means everyone gets trained in the same principles, including the groundskeepers and custodians, as well as all the other employees. Disney management has identified all team members as important to their mission success. Research has shown that if a customer is lost or has a question, they may interact with a groundskeeper or custodian for help. Thus, their ability to support the overall mission of providing a positive customer experience, the "Disney magic," is just as critical as it is to the other members of their crew. They are all vital members of the team providing frontline service. In this way, Disney builds a great team of people, trains them all well, and holds them all accountable to achieve its mission.

Your Personal Quest

So how can you apply the principle of your TEAM? Despite the myth of the self-made man, all successful people have help along the way. Some people recognize those who have helped them, and others simply forget that they actually got some help to reach the top of the ladder. If you are a leader, perhaps you have a team of people who have helped you achieve success. It is not uncommon for leaders to bring along trusted subordinates when they take on a new opportunity. If you are a small business owner or an individual entrepreneur, you also likely have a team that you rely upon: an attorney, a banker, an accountant, and a great executive assistant or an assistant store manger, whatever the case. You may have an IT specialist or an outsourced functional expert in marketing, insurance, or other specialty. Stay-at-home moms or dads have a team of experts to rely on: a doctor, a babysitter, teachers, or a volunteer soccer team coach. My point is that everyone has a team of people that they must rely upon regardless of their role.

Think about your own situation, whatever role it might be, and ask yourself who is on your team. You might be surprised if you consciously thought about who you rely on to help you succeed in whatever you do. Once you have determined who is on your team, ask yourself if these are the best available people to help. In other words, are these the people who I would pick if I made a conscious choice to have a great team built around me? Remember, you are responsible for your team. Make sure that you have the right people with the right skills to assist you.

If you are in business, perhaps you might want to explore the concept of a mastermind team. A mastermind team is a group of experts whom you trust and can call upon to help you succeed in your endeavors. The concept of a mastermind team was presented by Napoleon Hill in his best-selling book, *Think and Grow Rich*. If you have not had the opportunity to read this book, I would recommend it.

The story of Napoleon Hill is very interesting. He was challenged by the famous industrialist, Andrew Carnegie, to write about the formula for success of super-achievers, such as Carnegie himself and many of his friends who made their mark at the beginning of the twentieth century: Henry Ford, Thomas Edison, John Wannamaker, John Rockefeller, and many others. One of the hallmarks of their success formula was the concept of the mastermind team. In fact, some of the supersuccessful individuals were masterminds to each other.

Now it is easier than ever to create your own version of a mastermind team. You can find experts in any field of expertise on the Internet. You can use tools such as social networking sites to make connections. You can easily have virtual meetings with people from across the globe using modern technology. These can be live meetings using voice over Internet, chat rooms, blogs, or discussion forums. These modern tools have made collaboration much easier than when Carnegie, Ford, and Edison were trying to do it. If you don't have a mastermind team, you should deliberately think about how you can develop one for yourself. No one can know all they need to know in order to be successful in whatever their chosen field. A mastermind team can help you fill in the gaps in what you might not know. Realize also that you can belong to more than one mastermind group.

Another role that we all have is family member. Unlike other teams, you don't get to choose your relatives. However, this is also true with some other teams as well. So, think about your family as a team and the relationships you have within your family. Are there ways that you can support one another? Can some of your family members be a part of your mastermind team? Perhaps they have some of the skills you need on your own journey to success, or perhaps you can help them succeed in their journey. If you are lucky you might find a family member can be a mentor to you, or you can mentor someone in your family.

So the concept of team can be a powerful principle for individual success. Think about who can help you and ask them to be on your team. Remember to look for ways to help them, too. All good teams will be mutually supportive. If you can connect with the right people and collaborate, you will then be on your way to personal VICTORY!

Staff Ride Notebook: Your TEAM

Q1. How do you rate teamwork in your organization? Do people have a strong feeling of teamwork? If so, why? If not, why not? What could be done to improve teamwork?

Q2. Does your organization value training for your team? If so, how effective is the training? If not, what training could be helpful to your team?

Q3. Are the roles on your team clear? How well do the people on your team know their job? Do they know the job of their teammates? Could they step up into a leadership role if necessary?

Q4. Do people on your team take responsibility? Do you as a leader take full responsibility for your team? Do you hold your people accountable? Do you take corrective action as necessary when they are not performing their job to expectations?

Q5. How is the morale in your organization? Do senior leaders really take care of people or simply give them lip service? As a leader do you take care of your people? Do you visit them at their worksite? In what ways do you show them that you care about them?

EXERCISE: Think about an experience that you had as member of a team that struggled or did not succeed. What were the reasons why the team did not succeed? What did the leader do that either contributed to the situation or did not improve the team's performance? What would you do differently?

EXERCISE: Think back on your experience as a member of a great team, whether it was business, sports, or any other endeavor. What were the elements that made your team successful? What did the leader do to make the team successful? Was there anything that you would have done differently to make it even more successful? What was different from your other experience with a less successful team?

PART THREE
THE STAFF RIDE:
TOURING THE BATTLEFIELDS

American Cemetery Overlooking Omaha Beach, 2005
Photo Author Collection

CHAPTER FOURTEEN
BATTLEFIELDS: YESTERDAY AND TODAY

With the passage of time since June 1944, Normandy has returned to the largely rural and bucolic area that it had been for hundreds of years before the Second World War. Yet, it is forever changed with the addition of monuments, markers, museums, and several large cemeteries as reminders of the horrific battles that once took place there. The primary invasion sites all have monuments placed in memory of the brave Allied soldiers who liberated France from Nazi occupation. Some of the field fortifications, casements, and defenses are still visible, although those that remain show signs of the violence with scars of destruction from bombs, artillery, and direct assaults.

Nearby museums tell the story of what happened. They feature discarded equipment and artifacts left behind by the opposing armies. The beaches are now cleared of mines and obstacles, and have been returned to their natural state with dunes and grass. People on holiday now enjoy the sand and surf where young men were once killed or wounded as they stepped onto the beach. Along the way you will find the cemeteries where those who made the supreme sacrifice were finally laid to eternal rest. Each of the combatant nations has honored their war dead on hallowed ground, and their grave markers bear witness to the terrible cost of war.

On a visit to Normandy today, anyone who has an interest in studying the events of 1944 will find it easy to do so because most of the key sites are designated as historical landmarks. The people who live there are friendly and gratefully remember their liberation despite the loss of life and physical destruction of their property that many of their families endured. Tourism related to the liberation sites has become an integral part of the economy. You can either find tour guides who will escort you to the sites or you can do it on your own. Self-guided tours are relatively easy if you have your own transportation and can read a map. Most of the actual sites are free to the public, and generally the admission fees to the museums are very modest.

Although some of the museums are quite good, you can get an excellent sense for what happened by simply reading the markers and monuments at the sites. It is also useful to get an inexpensive guide in the language of your choice at one of the ubiquitous souvenir shops. If you have read *VICTORY Principles* this far, you already have an understanding of the key events; however, the following details will update you on what you might expect to look for on a visit to Normandy today.

View of Omaha Beach looking down from the bluffs, 2008
Photo Author Collection.

Utah Beach

Utah Beach anchored the far-right flank of the invasion. It is the westernmost of the five invasion beaches. Today a museum sits just behind the beach where the U.S. Fourth Infantry Division landed. Some of the beach obstacles that were moved off the beach are now displayed on either side of the building. A monument in front of the museum is dedicated to the units that landed there. You can also find a Sherman tank and a German "88" flak gun on display. Also on display in front of the building is one of the "Higgins boats." These were the assault landing craft that ferried troops from the larger transports in the Channel to the beaches. There is also a restaurant next to the parking lot for cars that arrive there on the causeway road from St. Marie Dumont. The restaurant building has a souvenir shop and an Internet café. It has a communications theme because this site was where the first communications center was set up. From this site, the commanders of the troops ashore communicated with the fleet in the English Channel.

For those who conduct their own self-directed Staff Ride, you will want to visit Utah Beach at low tide. This will give you a better impression of what the beach would have looked like at the time the assault troops landed. If you are on the beach at low tide, you will see that the tidal flats extend for several hundred yards out into the Channel. As soldiers stepped off onto the flats, they would have had to cross this expanse to arrive at the point where the dunes begin. At low tide, the sand may still be somewhat wet, but reasonably firm. Scattered about you will be small ponds of seawater as you walk farther away from the beach toward the water's edge. When your feet leave an impression in the wet sand, you will also realize how difficult it would have been for soldiers to run to the relative safety of the dunes with their heavy loads of equipment. You will want to think about how much more difficult it was to cross the beach while under fire. You will then get a sense for what was accomplished here.

You may recall, however, that the German defenses on Utah were not nearly as robust as those on Omaha and that the preassault bombardment was more effective. As you look at the dunes from the beach-side, you will note that in most places the natural obstacles do not appear to be that formidable. The dunes would offer some defilade cover from direct fire weapons. This shelter would allow the soldiers to catch their breath for awhile until they moved out from behind the beach. The dunes rise gently and are only about ten to fifteen feet high in most places. This makes them much easier to climb than the bluffs on Omaha. After about fifty yards beyond the dunes, you are on firm ground where you will find the buildings mentioned earlier. A road runs parallel to the beach approximately 150 yards behind the dunes. A short drive to the west on this road will take you to the site where the Free French Armored Division landed under the leadership of General LecClerc later in August of 1944. There is also a Liberty Museum located just up the coast in the town of Quineville.

Leading off the beach road are the four beach exit causeways that extend into the towns and villages beyond. On either side of the causeways are pastures that now have cows and horses grazing, but in June of 1944 these fields were deliberately flooded. The Germans wanted to canalize the troops coming off the beach on these narrow roads. This would make them more susceptible to an artillery attack. The strategy did not work because of the effective work of the American airborne forces. Before the troops arrived from the beach, they were able to neutralize the German artillery positions.

They also eliminated the artillery observers who often located themselves in the village church steeples. As you drive toward Utah Beach, you will likely pass through the small town of St. Marie-du-Mont. In the middle of the town is a church that offers an example of the steeples that were used for this purpose. It extends about sixty-five meters in height and offers a panoramic view of the countryside to include the causeways and also Utah Beach itself. This steeple was destroyed by the 101st Airborne to prevent it from being used as an artillery observation post. It was later rebuilt to its original condition after the war in 1946. If you go inside the church today, you will find some photographs showing one of the first religious services conducted with the troops after they landed. There is also a note of apology from the Commanding General, 101st Airborne, Major General Maxwell Taylor for the unavoidable destruction of the steeple. If you are interested to learn more about what happened in St Marie-du-Mont, there is a small museum located just off the main road, which comes through the town and circles around the church before it turns off to the causeway toward the beach.

Farther inland behind Utah Beach are various sites where the American airborne units landed and fought significant battles. One of the key objectives for the 82nd Airborne Division was the town of Ste. Marie Eglise. When the paratroopers were landing on D-Day, a fire had broken out in the town. A bucket brigade of civilians and soldiers from the German garrison were attempting to put it out. Some of the paratroopers landed on the nearby buildings, including one on the church steeple in the middle of the town square. While many were wounded or shot as they were illuminated by the light from the fire, others who safely landed in the surrounding countryside were quickly assembled to capture the town. St. Marie Eglise was the first town that was liberated during the invasion of France. Consequently, today you will find that this town commemorates the achievement with visible reminders of the occasion. There is a monument on one end of the main town square. There are several shops along the square dedicated to selling souvenirs and artifacts recovered from the area, there is a replica of Pvt. James Steele hanging by his parachute from the church steeple, and there is an excellent museum dedicated to the airborne forces located just behind the parking lot next to the church. The airborne museum features a glider, a transport plane, and examples of the equipment used by the paratroopers. If you are there in June near the anniversary of the invasion, you might even find some reenactments, a band, and some vendors selling beer and brats as I found on one of my trips there.

Ste. Marie Eglise and the nearby town of Carentan were important because they were transportation hubs where road networks intersected. You can easily see these vital road junctions when you visit the towns. While the 82nd Division was defending the town of Ste. Marie Eglise from counterattacks, the 101st was preparing to capture nearby Carentan. They would secure the town five days later after some intense battles. When you visit there today, Carentan has reminders of the airborne visit. Carentan is larger than Ste. Marie Eglise and today is more focused on commercial activity rather than on the nostalgia of June 1944. Yet, you cannot help but notice flowers that were planted to depict the distinctive "screaming eagle" shoulder patch of the 101st Division near the train station and the Hotel de Ville, the town hall.

In the nearby village of Ste. Come-du-Mont is a museum dedicated to the airborne battles in the area. These were less well-known but nevertheless important airborne objectives that included key bridges or other facilities located at Pont du Chef and La Frerie. Although these locations have historical significance to avid history buffs, those who have more limited time will choose to visit simply Ste. Marie Eglise and Carentan, which are easier to find. Both the museum at Ste. Come-du-Mont, "Dead Man's Corner," and the airborne museum at Ste. Marie Eglise will provide a great overview of what took place throughout the area.

Much farther west from these immediate invasion sites of Utah Beach is the port city of Cherbourg with its deep water port. Securing the port was the primary objective of the U.S. VII Corps. The port was critical to growing supply needs of the Allied forces. Cherbourg was eventually captured by the VII Corps but not until after defeating the determined German garrison who destroyed the port facilities before they surrendered. Cherbourg is located at the extreme western end of the Contentin Peninsula and can be reached by driving highway N-13/E46. Cherbourg also is home to the "War and Liberation Museum" where you can learn about life during the Nazi occupation.

Typical historical marker for Normandy battle sites, 2008
Photo Author Collection

Point du Hoc and Omaha Beach

As you drive further east from Utah toward Omaha Beach you will encounter some important and interesting sights. Perhaps the most interesting are former German artillery batteries that made up the Atlantic Wall to defend the Normandy coast from invasion. The most famous of these is the position at Point du Hoc. You may recall that this is where the American Second Rangers assaulted a suspected 155-mm gun position that jutted out into the

English Channel between Utah and Omaha. These were the cliffs that the Rangers climbed with ropes and ladders while under fire from Germans defenders at the crest. When the Rangers arrived on D-Day, they were surprised not to find the guns. The Germans had removed them from their casements so that they would not be destroyed by the bombs. The Rangers later found them in a field farther behind the position and destroyed them with termite grenades. At the extreme end of the point, a monument was dedicated to the Rangers by President Ronald Regan in 1984 on the fortieth anniversary of D-Day.

The site is especially impressive because of the visual impact of bomb and naval gun craters, the reinforced concrete gun casements, and a view of the cliffs down to the water's edge. The enormous craters left from the fourteen-inch guns of the battleships and aerial bombardments by the army air corps are visible reminders of the violence that once shook this point. You can walk into craters that are easily twenty feet deep and just as wide across. If you do so, you will get the sense of the explosive impact required to make such a gigantic hole in the ground. Likewise, you can walk into the casements to get a sense of the surprise that the Rangers personally encountered when they discovered that they did not contain the guns. You can also peer over the cliff to get the same view as a German defender who saw the determined Rangers making their upward climb under fire. If you stand on top of the casements, some of which now have stairs that lead to observation platforms, you will also get terrific views of the English Channel. This will provide you with an appreciation for the danger that these guns would have posed to the fleet and the assault forces on the two beaches.

World Peace Statue at Grandcamp-Maisy, 2008
Photo Author Collection.

Not too far inland from Point du Hoc is the town of Grandcamp-Maisy. In this town you will find a Ranger museum that tells the story of the Rangers and their assault at Point du Hoc. Just off the main road on the way out of town is a turn for the "Maisy Battery." This site was recently rediscovered sixty years after the war and is now partially restored. Visitors can walk through the German trench system that lead to various bunker complexes. You will also find the firing positions for the 155-mm guns that were here on D-Day. These guns fired on the

American beaches for three days until the Fifth Rangers successfully assaulted this position following a five-hour battle on June 9, 1944.

As you travel the main highway between Caen and Cherbourg (N13/E46) you will pass by the town of La Cambe. This is where the German cemetery is located. It is open to the public, and there is an information center just off the parking area. The cemetery is the final resting place for more than twenty-one thousand German soldiers who died during the battles of Normandy. There are individual grave markers as well as a mass grave memorial in the center of the complex. Two statues represent mourning parents paying homage to all the German war dead buried here. There are also some Teutonic stone crosses in groupings of five scattered throughout the grounds to remind visitors of the casualties of war.

Typical Norman hedgerows in the bocage country, 2008
Photo Author Collection

A little farther east is the town of Vierville-sur-Mer. Below the town is the western end of Omaha Beach. It is here where the lead elements of the 29th Division along with the balance of the Second Rangers and Fifth Rangers came ashore. When they landed on D-Day, the tide was out. This meant that they had over three hundred yards of beach to cross to get to the seawall. So, the best time to visit is at low tide when you can walk out onto the beach. This will give you some appreciation of how far the assault troops needed to travel while under fire from gun positions on the bluffs above. At the seawall are the remnants of a German bunker above which is now placed a monument to the memory of the American National Guard troops. Farther up the bluffs you can still see a few of the concrete bunkers from which automatic weapons would have fired across the beach. At the top of the draw a road leads off the beach. Another monument dedicated to the 29th Division is located here. If you turn left at the top of the draw, the road will lead you to the town itself, where the Germans used the church steeple as an observation point. If you continue east along the road, you will be driving parallel to the beach behind the bluffs. Omaha beach extends about four miles along the coast.

The next road intersection will lead back to the beach. This is St. Laurent-sur-Mer and another draw. As you follow the draw back down to the beach, you will get a sense for how the assault troops had to fight their way up a steep hill crossing minefields and obstacles that were vigorously defended by German infantry. Off the draw road is a museum for Omaha Beach that features examples of the equipment used by the assault troops. At the base of the draw is the modern beach road and a large monument dedicated to the memory of the American First Infantry Division. A drive back up the draw and a left turn will take you east along the coast road again toward the town of Colleville-sur-Mer. Just before you get to the town is a traffic circle. Follow it around and signs will direct you to the entrance for the American Cemetery at Omaha Beach.

Youth Statue at the American Cemetery and Memorial, 2008
Photo Author Collection

The American Cemetery is not to be missed on a trip to Normandy. A visit to this cemetery is a very solemn experience. There are almost ten thousand grave markers that are set with precision on a beautiful and peaceful 170-acre setting overlooking Omaha Beach. It is one of the most popular sites in Normandy with visitors from many nations paying tribute to the fallen. This is particularly true for many visitors from the Allied nations whose soldiers were also part of the Allied forces that fought together with the Americans in Europe. Among the soldiers who are at rest here is BG Theodore Roosevelt. He was awarded the Medal of Honor for his actions on D-Day at Utah Beach. Roosevelt's brother, Quinten, who was killed in World War I, is the only soldier from the First World War who is buried here. He was laid to rest next to his brother at the request of the family. There are also several others here who were awarded the Medal of Honor, the nation's highest award for gallantry in action. If you walk the grounds, you will also note that there are a number of grave markers that simply note "Here rests in honored glory a COMRADE IN ARMS known but to God" for soldiers who simply could not be identified. There are also several statues, monuments with maps, and a wall with names of sailors and soliders men whose bodies could not be recovered and were most likely lost at sea. A chapel and a new visitor center are also located on the cemetery grounds.

There is a path at the top of the bluff from the cemetery down to the beach. If you take the walk, you will begin to get an appreciation for the tremendous physical effort required to assault dug-in fortifications from the beach. As noted before, if you visit at low tide, you will also understand the significant challenge faced by the assault troops who came ashore with a heavy load of equipment while facing automatic weapons and artillery fire as they moved across the beach through the obstacles. By climbing the stairs back up to the top, you will experience in a small way what they did to make their way up the bluffs that are several hundred feet to the top. Even just walking the footpath will require many visitors to stop and rest at one of the several benches along the way.

As you stand on Omaha Beach today, you will also be struck by the amazing serenity of a peaceful beach that is only occasionally interrupted by the crashing surf. One can only imagine the intense violence on June 6, 1944 with the noise and ferocity of the artillery, rockets, and automatic weapons that were devastating this same beach. It is a stark contrast from the peaceful surroundings of today.

Gold Beach

Gold Beach is the westernmost of the beaches in the British sector. It is situated about midway between the two extremes of the invasion force. The far end of the beach was not used because of the high cliffs that rise up from the water's edge. Gold Beach is where engineers built one of the two artificial harbors at Arromanches. (The other harbor was built off of Omaha.) Both of these artificial harbors were very important to sustain the beachhead with reinforcements and supplies. Unfortunately they were both destroyed in a severe storm that passed through the English Channel on June 19, 1944. The remnants of the artificial harbor at Arromanches are still visible today.

The British infantry that landed at Gold Beach pushed inland and headed west to link up with the Americans coming in from Omaha. Along the way they encountered the small fishing village of Port-en-Bessin. With its protected harbor, this is was where the Royal Marine Commandos fought a fierce battle with the German defenders who were holed up in a casino. Today the casino is gone, but you can still see the port and the cliffs on either side of the town. Boat tours are available to take you out into the Channel to view Omaha Beach from the sea. From that vantage point, you have the same view that the troops would have had as they approached on their Higgins boats.

A few kilometers inland from Port-en-Bessin is the Longues Battery. This was another artillery position that was built to defend the Normandy coast from a seaborne invasion. There are still four large concrete casements, some with guns still emplaced, to be viewed if you stop by to visit.

The British troops coming in on Gold Beach also had a mission to capture the city of Bayeau. Due to fierce German resistance, the city was not secured until D-Day+1. In the city you will find a British cemetery as well as an excellent D-Day museum nearby. It is not only one of the largest but also has one of the best displays of equipment, uniforms, and weapons among the many museums in the Normandy area.

Gold Beach at Arromanches near the site of the artificial harbor, 2008
Photo Author Collection

Juno Beach

Juno Beach, where the Canadians landed, is in the middle of the British zone. The beach has a gentle slope up to some sand dunes that are perhaps ten to twelve feet high and easily penetrated. Their landing was later in the morning than the landing on Omaha Beach. Consequently, it took place on a rising tide that submerged some of the beach obstacles. Although this allowed the troops to land closer to the dunes, the obstacles disabled or destroyed about thirty percent of the landing craft. After overcoming stiff resistance at Courseulles and Bernieres, by mid morning, the Canadians pushed about ten kilometers inland. There they were met with a German counterattack.

In the center of Juno Beach today at Courseulles is a fine museum dedicated to the Canadian forces. On display is a Sherman tank that was recovered twenty-seven years after the invasion. There is also a well-preserved German bunker. Outside the museum is a very unusual sculpture that depicts the Canadian soldiers coming in from the sea. Juno Beach is where Prime Minister Churchill landed on June 12 and later where General DeGaulle landed on June 14. King George VI also came ashore here on June 16. A large cross marks the spot where General DeGaulle landed near Gray-sur-Mer. Over two thousand Canadian soldiers are buried at their cemetery located at Beny-sur-Mer about five kilometers from Juno Centre.

Sword Beach

Sword Beach is the easternmost of the invasion beaches and the third beach in the British zone. About ten kilometers behind Sword Beach is the City of Caen, which was the D-Day objective for the British Third Infantry. Due to the fierce resistance by the German panzer units, it took over thirty days for the British to reach their objective. In the process, almost all of the City of Caen was reduced to rubble. It is rebuilt today, and there are very few signs of the massive destruction. The citizens of Caen have erected a Memorial and Museum for Peace so that visitors will not forget the lives and property lost which is the inevitable consequence of war. A special section of the museum is devoted to Nobel Peace Prize winners.

At the beginning of the invasion, the British Sixth Airborne secured some important objectives inland from the beach. First, a glider borne force led by Major John Howard secured the bridges over the Orne River and Caen Canal near the village of Benouville. When you visit there today, you will see this site but with a new Pegasus Bridge. The old bridge is now located behind a museum within walking distance from the original site. The new bridge was designed to look just like the original. There are monuments dedicated to Major Howard and his men. These mark the location where the gliders landed. On the west bank is a coffee shop that has information about the site as well as a guest registry.

British Major John Howard memorial near Pegusas Bridge, 2008
Photo Author collection.

On the east bank of the Orne estuary is the town of Merville. This was the site of another artillery battery, the Merville Batterie, which was another part of the Atlantic Wall. This gun emplacement was seized in the early morning hours of June 6, 1944. A battalion of British paratroopers led by LTC Terence Otway captured this position after an intense battle with the German defenders. The casements are well preserved today. When you visit the site, you will find a documentary film that tells the story inside one of the casements. Also on display at the site is a howitzer similar to the ones that might have been emplaced here. Also on display is a C-47 "Dakota" transport aircraft that was used by the paratroopers. It is painted with "invasion stripes" for visual recognition by the fleet. The layout of the site will show you where the Germans had their command post, ammunition magazines, and troop billets in addition to the four reinforced concrete gun casements. This perhaps is the best display to learn about the gun batteries built to defend against a seaborne invasion. By securing this objective, the British airborne troops saved many lives on Sword Beach later in the day.

Pegasus Bridge 2005, Site of British Airborne Assault
Photo Author Collection

Today, Sword Beach is a popular resort in the town of Ouistreahm. Several museums are located in Ouistreahm, one dedicated to the commandos and another to explain the Atlantic Wall. When you are down at the beach, you will note that it is very flat with almost no dunes behind it. The coast road that runs parallel to the beach is only meters behind it and lined with well-built beach homes overlooking the English Channel. There is a memorial at the beach to commemorate the British assault, but mostly people are too busy to notice it as they go about enjoying the sun and surf. When the invasion took place here, it was also on a rising tide. The beach narrowed as the tide came in which caused congestion with the armor and other vehicles as they landed on the narrow strip of beach. When you visit here, you can easily appreciate how the beach would have narrowed, but it is more difficult to understand why the British Army could not just move the vehicles quickly off the beach. Unlike the other beaches, there appears to be almost no natural obstacles that would impede the vehicles from driving off the beach. Once the German defenders were neutralized, it should have been possible to move inland quickly. If this had been accomplished, the British infantry would have had more firepower during the initial advance inland.

Finally, located south of Caen is the town of Falaise. At the end of August 1944, the Canadian Army fought to try to link up with the Patton's U.S. Third Army that was advancing from the south. If they had successfully linked up, the remaining German forces would have been surrounded and their path to retreat cut off. Anticipating that the two Allied forces might collide and shoot at one another, General Bradley ordered Patton to halt his advance at Argentan. Since the Canadians did not advance south from Falaise for several weeks, a gap between the Allied forces known as the "Falaise gap" allowed many of the Germans to retreat back toward their homeland, albeit without their equipment. The August 1944 Museum located in Falaise describes the actions in this vicinity and also has displays of the armored vehicles and uniforms.

EPILOGUE

Although the Battle for Normandy was the decisive campaign in Western Europe in World War II, the war in Europe continued for almost another year after D-Day. It was not until May 1944 that the Nazi war machine was utterly defeated and the formal surrender documents were signed. During those intervening months, many more casualties on both sides would be sustained. The Allied strategic bombing campaign would continue unabated, causing many civilian casualties. Many of the cities and towns along the route of advance would be in ruins by the war's end. The firebombing of Dresden in Germany alone would claim perhaps up to forty thousand civilian deaths. The actual number is difficult to determine.

In September the Allies launched a bold plan, Operation Market-Garden. This was General Montgomery's plan to drive his armored units through Holland and into the German industrial heartland for a quick end to the war. Allied airborne units dropped behind the German lines into occupied Holland to seize key bridges across rivers and canals while the British armored force attacked through from Belgium. However, their drive was stopped at the German-Dutch border where the Germans almost annihilated the British airborne in the Dutch town of Arnhem. When the Allied attack failed, Operation Market-Garden would be remembered as "the bridge too far."

In December 1944 on the German-Belgium frontier in the Ardennes Forest, the Allies and Germans would fight a desperate battle. We know it now as the Battle of the Bulge. This was Hitler's last-ditch effort to split the Allies and capture the Belgium port of Antwerp. A huge panzer force broke through a part of the American sector that was weakly defended and created a "bulge" in the line. Eisenhower rushed reinforcements forward including the 82nd and 101st Airborne Divisions. They were unprepared for winter warfare and lacked proper equipment and ammunition. The 101st was temporarily cut off and finally surrounded at the crossroads in the Belgium town of Bastogne. Just before Christmas, the American commander, General Anthony McAuliffe, famously refused the German offer for surrender with the simple one word reply, "Nuts!" The paratroopers tenaciously held out until an armored force from Patton's Third Army was able to break through with supplies of ammunition, medicine, and food.

After the Bulge, the German Army was no longer able to defend their homeland. While the Americans and British crossed the Rhine River from the west, the Red Army advanced from the east toward Berlin. The Russians would leave a trail of devastation in their wake as revenge for the earlier onslaught of Hitler's legions in the motherland. As the Russians crossed into Germany, Berlin would be utterly destroyed. Hitler would take his own life in the last days of the Red Army onslaught. By the war's end, overall loss of life and property in the east would be far greater than in the west. Additionally, many others also perished in the slugfest on the Italian peninsula. When the war in France assumed priority after D-Day, some referred to the Italian campaign as the "forgotten war," but for those who fought there, it was a bitter contest.

Despite the setbacks along the way, the final outcome of the war in Europe was largely determined on June 6, 1944. Once the Allies had breached the Atlantic Wall and put over 150,000 troops ashore on D-Day, they were in a position to reinforce their armies with many more men and seemingly endless supplies of equipment. The Germans in contrast could not replace their losses and they could not continue to fight on multiple fronts. While there were several times when the outcome was perhaps uncertain, specifically during Operation Market-Garden and the Battle of the Bulge, it is now clear that the Allied victory was never really in doubt. Throughout the campaign, Eisenhower still had to deal with the larger-than-life egos of his generals who wanted to have the priority of effort in their sector. These inter-Allied rivalries would require the supreme commander to assert his authority to pursue his "broad front" strategy advancing his armies simultaneously across the entire western front. Near the very end of the war, Eisenhower made the decision to stop the advance at the Elbe River. He wanted to avoid fratricide with the Russian allies and prevent additional American and British casualties. Due to the political consequences of the Cold War, his decision remains controversial to this day. Ultimately, it was a combination of the planning and execution of Operation Overlord and the men who landed in France on D-Day that made the final victory in Europe possible.

The victory did not come cheaply. Many of these soldiers, airmen, and sailors were wounded, and many others paid the ultimate price with their lives. Their determination and sacrifice should never be forgotten. We owe them all a great debt of gratitude for their sacrifices. Their contributions ensured that, after the war, Europe and the world would be able to rebuild and live in relative peace. While we honor them for their service, we should do so without romanticizing the war. Those who survived are justly proud of their heroic accomplishments, but they would be the first to tell you that they would never want to experience war again. Perhaps herein lies one of the most important lessons of all: Before the nation commits to war, it should be the only option left. The cost of war, including the human and economic costs, is simply too high not to otherwise pursue all other options short of war.

After World War II, Eisenhower was elected to be the President of the United States. In 1953 he gave a speech to the American Society of Newspaper Editors, which is now known as "The Chance for Peace" speech. In that speech, he said the following: "Every gun that is made, every warship launched, every rocket fired signifies, in the final sense, a theft from those who hunger and are not fed, those who are cold and are not clothed. This world in arms is not spending money alone. It is spending the sweat of its laborers, the genius of its scientist, the hopes of its children....This is not a way of life at in any true sense. Under the cloud of threatening war, it is humanity hanging from a cross of iron."[53]

As a soldier and statesman, Eisenhower had personally witnessed the terrible cost of modern war. He saw firsthand the destruction of cities, the suffering of refugees, and the thousands of civilian casualties. He also knew all too well the cost of victory in terms of his own soldiers who were killed or wounded. Those who have experienced war are often the most reluctant warriors. They are also the most ardent proponents for peaceful settlement of international disputes through diplomacy. Certainly the nation needs a strong defense establishment because there are times when use of force is necessary. It also strengthens our ability to exercise diplomacy and deter war. However, as Eisenhower suggests, our defense priorities must be set without precluding investments in education, health care, and infrastructure that are also necessary to a vibrant economy. We need to have these capabilities, too, if we are to remain a strong nation. We also need visionary national leaders who will use the full spectrum of national power, including economic, diplomatic, and moral standing, to accomplish our national objectives. Maybe this is his lasting lesson for our nation today and his wish for a legacy of peace and prosperity.

For the rest of us who are fortunate enough to be the beneficiaries of the sacrifices made so long ago, the question for us is "What will be our legacy?" Each of us has unique gifts that we can share with the world. What is your great work that you will contribute? What can you do to make the world a better place? As the final lesson in this Staff Ride journey, I hope you will give this some thought. I also hope you are inspired to take action and make your contribution of some great work to the country and the rest of the world. In this way, you can honor the sacrifices that were made on June 6, 1944 and during the final campaigns of World War II.

COMMAND STRUCTURE AND ORDER OF BATTLE

Allies: <u>Supreme Headquarters, Allied Expeditionary Force (SHAEF): General Dwight Eisenhower</u>

Allied Ground Forces and British 21st Army Group: General Bernard Montgomery

> British Second Army: Lt. General Miles Dempsey
>> British XXX Corps Lt. General G C Bucknell
>> British I Corps Lt. General J T Crocker
> US First Army: Lt. General Omar Bradley
>> US VII Corps: Major General J. Lawton Collins
>> US V Corps: Major General Leonard T. Gerow

Allied Expeditionary Air Force: Air Chief Marshall Trafford Leigh-Mallory

Allied Expeditionary Naval Force: Admiral Bertram Ramsey

Germans: <u>OB West: Field Marshall Gerd von Runstedt</u>

Army Group B: Field Marshall Erwin Rommel

> Armed Forces Netherlands:
> General of Fliers Friedrich Christansen
> 15th Army: Colonel General Hans von Salmuth
> Seventh Army: Colonel General Friedrich Dollmann

Army Group G: Colonel General Johannes Blaskowitz

> 19th Army: General of Infantry Georg von Sodenstern
> First Army General Kurt Von der Chevallerie

Panzer Group West: General of Panzer Troops Baron Leo Geyr von Schweppenburg

First Parachute Army: Luftwaffe Colonel General Kurt Student

MAPS OF NORMANDY, FRANCE, AND INVASION SITES

Maps from the U.S. Army Center of Military History

Overlord Area of Operations, Northern France (US Army CMH)

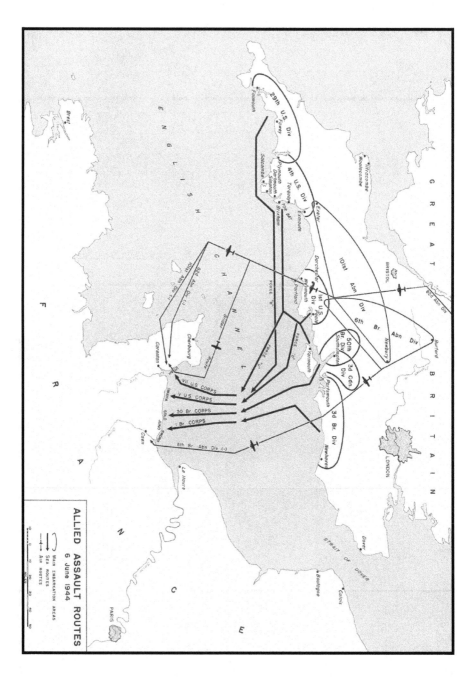

Allied Assault Routes (US Army CMH)

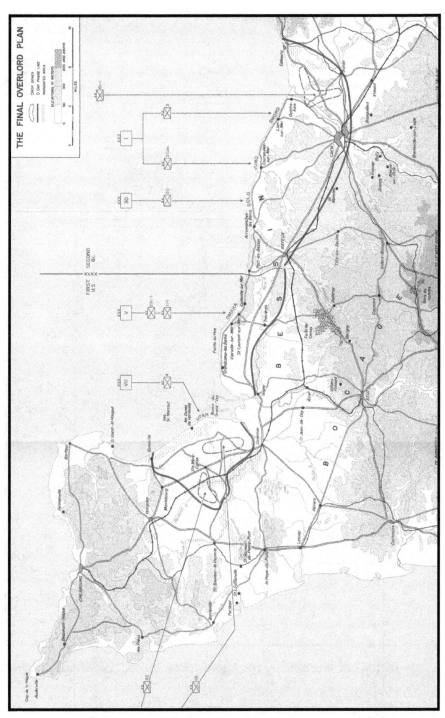

The Final Plan for Operation Overlord (US Army CMH)

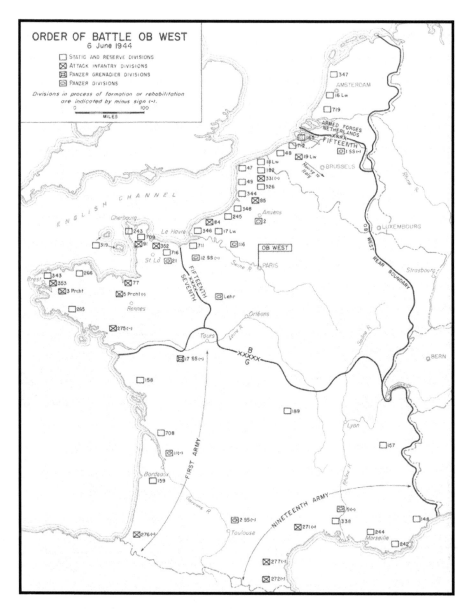

Disposition of German Forces on June 6, 1944, D-Day (US Army CMH)

ABOUT THE AUTHOR

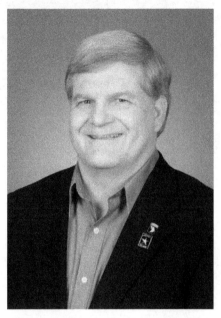

Col. Leonard Kloeber, Jr (Ret.)

Col. Leonard Kloeber, Jr. has hands-on practical experience as a leader in both military and business organizations. A 1971 graduate of the U.S. Military Academy and honor graduate of the U.S. Army General Staff Officer Course, Colonel Kloeber has over thirty years experience in command and staff positions in small and large military organizations. He has commanded units at the company, battalion, and brigade level and also held senior general staff positions.

His business experience includes leadership positions in a broad range of private and public organizations. He has led and managed start-up businesses and also held leadership positions with large public companies. His line and staff assignments include over twenty years of line management experience and nine years as a senior human resources executive for a large multinational company.

Len also has an MBA from Boston University and a JD from William Mitchell College of Law. He and his wife, Jevne, live in Prior Lake, Minnesota. He can be reached by email at staffride@gmail.com.

BIBLIOGRAPHY

Alexander, Bevin. *How Great Generals Win*. New York: Norton & Co., 1993.

Ambrose, Stephen E. *Band of Brothers*. New York: Simon & Shuster, 1992.

———. *D-Day June 6, 1944*. New York: Simon & Shuster, 1994.

———. *The Supreme Commander*, New York: Doubleday & Company, 1970.

———. *The Victors*. New York: Simon & Shuster, 1997.

Badsy, Stephen. *Normandy 1944*. New York: Barnes and Noble, 2000.

Badsy, Stephen, and Tim Bean. *Battle Zone Normandy, Omaha Beach*. Phoenix Mill, UK: Sutton Publishing, 2004.

Balkoski, Joseph. *Beyond the Beachhead, the 29th Infantry Division in Normandy*. Mechanicsburg, PA: Stackpole Books, 1989.

———. *Omaha Beach, June 6th 1944*. Mechanicsburg, PA: Stackpole Books, 2004.

———. *Utah Beach, June 6th 1944*. Mechanicsburg, PA: Stackpole Books, 2005.

Black, Robert. *The Battalion*. Mechanicsburg, PA: Stackpole Books, 2006.

———. *Rangers in World War II*. New York: Ballantine Books, 1992.

Bowen, Robert M. *Fighting with the Screaming Eagles*. Mechanicsburg, PA: Stackpole Books, 2001.

Brinkley, Douglas. *The Boys of Point du Hoc*. New York: Harper Collins, 2005.

———. *World War II: The Axis Assault, 1939–1942*. New York: Henry Holt & Co., 2003.

Burgett, Donald R. *Currahee, A Screaming Eagle at Normandy.* New York: Dell Publishing, 1967.

Chandler, David, and James Lawton Collins, Jr. *The D-Day Encyclopedia.* New York: Simon & Schuster, 1994.

Davies, Norman. *No Simple Victory: World War II in Europe.* New York: Penguin Press, 2006.

D'Este, Carlo. *Decision in Normandy.* New York: Konecky and Konecky, 1983.

Duggan, William. *Napoleon's Glance.* New York: Nation Books, 2002.

Dunphie, Christopher, and Garry Johnson. *Gold Beach.* South Yorkshire, UK: Pen and Sword Books, Ltd., 1999.

Eisenhower, Dwight D. *Crusade in Europe.* New York: Doubleday & Company, 1948.

Folly, Martin H. *The Palgrave Concise Historical Atlas of the Second World War.* New York: Palgrave McMillian, 2004.

Ford, Ken. *D-Day 1944, Gold and Juno Beaches.* Oxford: Osprey Publishing, 2004.

———. *D-Day 1944, Sword Beach and the British Airborne Landings.* Oxford: Osprey Publishing, 2004.

Fowler, Will. *D-Day, the First 24 Hours.* London: Amber Books, 2003.

Fraser, David. *Knight's Cross, A Life of Field Marshall Erwin Rommel.* New York: Harper Collins, 1993.

Goldstein, Donald, et al. *D-Day Normandy.* McLean, VA. Brassey's, 1994.

Griess, Thomas. *The Second World War Europe and the Mediterranean.* Wayne, NJ: Avery Publishing, 1984.

Hamilton, Nigel. *Montgomery, D-Day Commander.* Washington, DC: Potomac Books, 2007.

Harrison, Gordon. *Cross-Channel Attack*. Washington, DC: Center of Military History, US Army, 1951.

Hart, Russell, and Stephen Hart. *The Second World War (6), Northwest Europe 1944–1945*. Oxford: Osprey Publishing, 2002.

Hastings, Max. *Overlord*. London: Pan Books, 1999.

Hesketh, Roger. *Fortitude, The D-Day Deception Campaign*. New York, The Overlook Press, 2002.

Howarth, David. *Dawn of D-Day*. London: Greenhill Books, 1959.

Isby, David. *Fighting the Invasion, The German Army at D-Day*. London: Greenhill Books, 2000.

Keegan, John. *The Second World War*. New York: Penguin Books, 1989.

———. *Six Armies in Normandy*. New York: Penguin Books, 1982.

Kemp, Anthony. *D-Day and the Invasion of Normandy*. New York: Harry N. Abrams, 1994.

Kershaw, Alex. *The Bedford Boys*. Cambridge, MA: Da Capo Press, 2003.

Koskimaki, George. *D-Day with the Screaming Eagles*. New York: Presidio Press, 1970.

Lewis, Adrian. *Omaha Beach, A Flawed Victory*. Chapel Hill, NC: University of North Carolina Press, 2001.

Lewis, Jon E. *Eye-Witness D-Day*. New York: Carroll & Graf Publishers, 1994.

Miller, Donald L. *The Story of World War II*. New York: Simon & Schuster, 2001.

Mitcham, Samuel W., Jr. *The Desert Fox in Normandy*. Westport, CT: Praeger, 1997.

Moen, Marcia, and Margo Heinen. *Reflections on Courage on D-Day*. Elk River, MN: DeForest Press, 1999.

Morrison, Samuel Eliot. *The Invasion of France and Germany 1944–1945*. Edison, NJ: Castle Books, 1957.

Parry, Dan. *D-Day Reflections of Courage*. London: BBC Books, 2004.

Penrose, Jane. *The D-Day Companion*. Oxford: Osprey Publishing, 2004.

Perret, Jeffery. *There's a War to be Won*. New York: Ballantine Books, 1991.

Perry, Mark. *Partners in Command*. New York: Penguin Press, 2007.

Pogue, Forrest C. *George C. Marshall, Organizer of Victory*. New York: Viking Press, 1973.

Reynolds, Michael. *Eagles and Bulldogs in Normandy 1944*. Havertown, PA: Casemate, 2003.

Ruggero, Ed. *The First Men In*. New York, Harper Collins, 2006.

Smith, Thomas, W. *Decisive 20th Century American Battles*. Indianapolis, IN: Alpha Books, 2003.

Stoler, Mark. *George C. Marshall, Soldier-Statesman of the American Century*. New York: Simon & Shuster, 1989.

Stone, David. *War Summits*. Washington, DC: Potomac Books, 2005.

Van Der Vat, Dan. *D-Day, The Greatest Invasion*. Toronto: Madison Press, 2003.

Von Luck, Hans. *Panzer Commander*. New York: Dell Publishing, 1989.

Wallace, Brenton G. *Patton and His Third Army*. Mechanicsburg, PA: Stackpole Books, 2000.

Webster, David Kenyon. *Parachute Infantry*. New York: Random House, 1994.

Weinberg, Gerhard L. *A World at Arms*. Cambridge, UK: Cambridge University Press, 1994.

Whitlock, Flint. *The Fighting First*. Cambridge, MA: Westview Press, 2004.

Wilmot, Chester. *The Struggle for Europe*. Old Saybrook, CT: Konecky & Konecky, 1952.

Wilt, Alan F. *The Atlantic Wall*. New York: Enigma Books, 2004.

Young, Peter. *A Short History of WWII 1939–1945*. New York: Thomas Y. Crowell Company, 1966.

Zuehlke, Mark. *Juno Beach, Canada's D-Day Victory June 6th 1944*. Vancouver, BC: Douglas & McIntyre, 2004.

ENDNOTES

1   Henry Steele Commanger, *The Story of World War II,* ed. Donald L. Miller (New York: Simon and Shuster, 2001), 25.

2   Douglas Brinkly, *World War II The Axis Assault, 1939–1942* (New York: Times Books, Henry Holt and Co, 2003), 117.

3   Chester Wilmot, *The Struggle for Europe* (Old Saybrook, CT: Konecky & Konecky, 1952), 20.

4   Geoffrey Perret, *There's A War To Be Won* (New York: Random House, 1991), 23.

5   Mark Perry, *Partners in Command* (New York: Penguin Press, 2007), 62.

6   Henry Steele Commanger,, *The Story of World War II,* 64.

7   U.S. Army Center of Military History, "Sicily: U.S. Army Campaigns of World War II," U.S. Army Center of Military History. http://www.history.army.mil/brochures/72-16/72-16.htm

8   Rick Atkinson, *Day of Battle* (New York: Henry Holt, 2007), 86.

9   Ibid., 109.

10   Forest Pogue, *George C. Marshall, Organizer of Victory, 1943–1945* (New York:: The Viking Press, 1973), 321

11   Adrian R Lewis, *Omaha Beach: A Flawed Victory*, (Chapel Hill: University of North Carolina Press, 2001), 101.

12   Ibid., 06.

13   Ibid., 103.

14   Anthony Farrar-Hockley. "Airborne Forces," in *The D-Day Encyclopedia*, ed. Chandler and Collins (New York: Simon and Schuster, 1994), 11.

15   Stephen Ambrose, *D-Day June 6, 1944* (New York: Simon and Shuster, 1994), 319.

16   Ed Ruggero, *The First Men In* (New York: Harper Collins Publishers, 2006), 95.

17   Stephen Ambrose, *D-Day June 6, 1944,* p 198

18   Joseph Balkoski, *Utah Beach* (Mechanicsburg, PA: Stackpole Books, 2005), 251–52.

19   Stephen Ambrose, *Band of Brothers* (New York: Simon and Schuster Pocket Books, 1992), 95–102

20   Ed Ruggero, *The First Men In*, 26.

21   Ibid., 145.

22 Ken Ford, *D-Day 1944: Sword Beach and the British Airborne Landings* (Oxford: Osprey Publishing, 2004), 44.

23 Alan F. Wilt, *The Atlantic Wall* (New York: Enigma Books, 2004) photo caption 152–53.

24 Ken Ford, *D-Day 1944: Sword Beach and the British Airborne Landings*, 40–43.

25 Joseph Balkowski, *Utah Beach*, 91.

26 U.S. 29th Infantry Division, 116th Infantry, Company A, "After action report and interviews with survivors of D-Day," U.S. National Archives.

27 U.S. Army Center of Military History, "Normandy: U.S. Army Campaigns of World War II," U.S. Army Center of Military History, 30. http://www.history.army.mil/brochures/normandy/nor-pam.htm

28 Flint Whitlock, *The Fighting First* (Cambridge, MA: Westview Press, 2004), 148.

29 Robert W. Black, *The Battalion* (Mechanicsburg, PA: Stackpole Books, 2006), 60.

30 Ibid., 132

31 Robert Black, *Rangers in World War II* (New York: Ballantine Books, 1992), 226.

32 Bernard L. Montgomery, "Notes for My Address to Senior Officers Before Overlord," PRO (PREM 3-339/1) in Carlo D'Este, *Decision in Normandy* (New York: Konecky and Konecky, 1983, 1984), 210.

33 Carlo D'Este, *Decision in Normandy*, 112.

34 Christopher Dunphie and Garry Johnson, *Gold Beach* (South Yorkshire, UK: Pen Sword Books Ltd., 1999), 29.

35 Ken Ford, *D-Day 1944: Gold and Juno Beaches* (London: Osprey Publishing Limited, 2004), 25.

36 Carlo D'Este, *Decision in Normandy*, 112.

37 Samuel Mitcham, *The Desert Fox in Normandy* (Westport, CT: Praeger, 1997), 57.

38 Ibid., 22.

39 Bernard L Montgomery, *Normandy to the Baltic* (Boston: Houghton Mifflin, 1948), 28.

40 Samuel Mitcham, *The Desert Fox in Normandy*, 78.

41 Williamson Murray, "In the Air, on the Ground, and in the Factories," in *The D-Day Companion*, ed. Jane Penrose, (Oxford: Osprey Publishing, 2004), 120.

42 Ibid., 122.

43 Samuel Mitcham, *The Desert Fox in Normandy*, 65.

44 Alan F. Wilt, *The Atlantic Wall*, 128.

45 Max Hastings, *Overlord* (London: Pan Books, 1984), 369.

46 Erwin Rommel, *The Rommel Papers*, ed. H. B Liddell-Hart (New York: Harcourt, Brace, Jovanovich, 1953), 476–77.

47 Carlo D'Este, *Decision in Normandy*, 409.

48 Ibid., 517.

49 Carlo D'Este, *Eisenhower: A Soldier's Life* (New York: Henry Holt & Co., 2002), 386; in *Partners in Command*, Mark Perry.

50 Dwight David Eisenhower, vol. 2, 984; Mark Perry, *Partners in Command*, 178

51 Doulas Kinnard, *Eisenhower: Soldier-Statesman of the American Century* (Washington, DC: Brassy, 2002), 47–48.

52 www.usaa.com

53 Dwight David Eisenhower, "Chance for Peace Address," Dwight D. Eisenhower Presidential Library and Museum. http://www.eisenhower.archives.gov/speeches/Chance_For_Peace.html

BONUS OFFERS AND INFORMATION

Available free at www.victoryprinciples.com

➤ a summary at-a-g;lance of the VICTORY Priniciples

➤ an e-guide to conducting After Action Reviews

➤ a list of values.

Find out more about

➤ VICTORY Priniple webinars

➤ Leadership training and seminars

➤ Consulting and coaching

➤ Staff Rides

visit www.staffride.com or contact the author at
staffride@gmail.com

BUY A SHARE OF THE FUTURE IN YOUR COMMUNITY

These certificates make great holiday, graduation and birthday gifts that can be personalized with the recipient's name. The cost of one S.H.A.R.E. or one square foot is $54.17. The personalized certificate is suitable for framing and will state the number of shares purchased and the amount of each share, as well as the recipient's name. The home that you participate in "building" will last for many years and will continue to grow in value.

Here is a sample SHARE certificate:

YES, I WOULD LIKE TO HELP!

I support the work that Habitat for Humanity does and I want to be part of the excitement! As a donor, I will receive periodic updates on your construction activities but, more importantly, I know my gift will help a family in our community realize the dream of homeownership. ***I would like to SHARE in your efforts against substandard housing in my community!*** *(Please print below)*

PLEASE SEND ME _____ SHARES at $54.17 EACH = $ $_____

In Honor Of: _____

Occasion: (Circle One)   HOLIDAY   BIRTHDAY   ANNIVERSARY

        OTHER: _____

Address of Recipient: _____

Gift From: _____ *Donor Address:* _____

Donor Email: _____

I AM ENCLOSING A CHECK FOR $ $_____ PAYABLE TO HABITAT FOR HUMANITY OR PLEASE CHARGE MY VISA OR MASTERCARD *(CIRCLE ONE)*

Card Number _____ Expiration Date: _____

Name as it appears on Credit Card _____ Charge Amount $ _____

Signature _____

Billing Address _____

Telephone # Day _____ Eve _____

PLEASE NOTE: Your contribution is tax-deductible to the fullest extent allowed by law.
Habitat for Humanity • P.O. Box 1443 • Newport News, VA 23601 • 757-596-5553
www.HelpHabitatforHumanity.org

Printed in the USA
CPSIA information can be obtained
at www.ICGtesting.com
JSHW012014140824
68134JS00025B/2409